The Clinical Psychologist Collective:

Advice & Guidance for Aspiring Clinical Psychologists

by

Dr Marianne Trent

The Clinical Psychologist Collective: Advice & Guidance for Aspiring Clinical Psychologists

Created, Compiled, Indexed and Edited by Dr Marianne Trent; Proofread by Hannah Grady and Chrissie Fitch.

Cover Photographs: Damien Trent

Cover Design: Damien Trent

Author Photograph: Damien Trent

Photograph of Dr Stephen Wright: Kindly supplied by Mrs Charlotte Wright

About the Lead Author

Dr Marianne Trent is a Clinical Psychologist in Private Practice. She specialises in Trauma, Grief, Anxiety & Depression. She also helps support and guide people into developing their own passive income streams.

This is her second book, with her first being *The Grief Collective: Stories of Life, Loss & Learning to Heal.*

She created the 'Our Tricky Brain' Kit, a compassion-focused therapy resource kit for professionals working with trauma and depression.

She offers 1:1 therapy for trauma, anxiety, grief and depression as well as running free 5 day Feel Better Challenges and The Feel Better Academy, an online program for adults who want to learn to soothe and calm themselves compassionately.

Marianne is a regular blogger, writing about mental health related topics and concepts. She has been interviewed live on BBC News and written for The Guardian, Platinum Magazine, Huff Post, The Telegraph and more. You can catch her LIVE 5 days a week in her #4MinuteClinic on Facebook, YouTube & LinkedIn.

She is an ambassador for AtALoss.org and a clinical advisor for 'Our Time' a charity who support young adults who have experienced parental loss.

Website:	www.goodthinkingpsychology.co.uk
Instagram:	@GoodThinkingPsychological
Facebook:	Good Thinking Psychological Services
YouTube:	Good Thinking Psychological Services
LinkedIn:	Dr Marianne Trent
TikTok:	@drmariannetrent
Twitter:	GoodThinkingPs1

Dedication

This book is dedicated to the memory of Dr Stephen Wright, a wonderful clinical psychologist whom I'm sad I never got to meet. We often spoke via Facebook and his wit and professionalism were so admired by me and others within our network.

He was passionate about supporting children, young people, and their families with their mental health needs. At the time of his unexpected death from Vaccine Induced Thrombosis with Thrombocytopenia, (VITT) in January 2021, he was days away from starting a new role with Great Ormond Street Hospital and he also worked in private practice in his business Oaks Child & Adolescent Psychology.

He is survived by his wife Charlotte and their two young sons: Izaac and Elijah. Charlotte and Stephen met a few years before he started training and they had their first child in 2013 shortly before starting on the course in 2014. He qualified in 2017.

He is also much missed by his parents, Anne and Richard and his sister, Sarah, brother-in-law, Sam, and his nephew Fynley.

Dr Stephen Christopher Wright 1988 – 2021

Contents

Contents

Contents

Where to get support: A Quick Guide

The path to Clinical Training is not without its stresses and strains. Risk and mental health issues crop for all of us and for the clients we work with at various times. It didn't seem right to produce a book as a mental health professional which didn't at least give a brief overview of appropriate service to reach out for. This is not an exhaustive list but it's a good start.

Abuse & Violence

National Domestic Abuse Helpline - 0808 2000 247

National Centre for Domestic Violence - 0207 186 8270

Action on Elder Abuse - 0808 808 8141

Victim Support - 0808 168 9111

Children & Young People

Childline - 0800 1111

NSPCC - 0808 800 5000

The Mix (under 25s) 0808 808 4994

YoungMinds - 0808 802 5544

Bereavement:

Cruse Bereavement - 0800 808 1677

Winston's Wish - 08088 020 021 (For Bereaved Children)

At a Loss: www.ataloss.org

It's Time. (parent loss) https://www.itstimecharity.co.uk

The Good Grief Trust

Losing a Child

The Lullaby Trust – bereavement support after the loss of a baby or child

SANDS stillbirth and neonatal death charity

Oscar's Wish – www.oscarswishfoundation.co.uk

Child Bereavement UK

Mental Health

Samaritans - 116 123

Shout TEXT helpline - 85258

Mind - 0300 123 3393

RETHINK - 0300 5000 927

SANEline - 0300 304 7000

Respect – Men's Advice Line - 0808 801 0327

Campaign Against Living Miserably (CALM) (for men) - 0800 58 58 58

Papyrus HOPELINEUK, for under 35's feeling suicidal or anyone concerned about someone like this - 0800 068 4141

The Mix (Under 25s) – 0800 808 4994

About This Book

I often find that some of my best ideas come to me whilst out for a run, in the shower or asleep. This book was the product of a shower. I have always believed in the power of people and a collection of voices to tell stories, support and normalise. *The Grief Collective* demonstrated that this is an effective method for supporting and validating people with grief which is a time we can feel lost and alone. I was, however, acutely aware that at different stages of my journey into clinical psychology I had also experienced some of the same emotions. Therefore, the idea for this book had been rattling around my head for a while, although the self-critic and the critical observer kept piping up to keep the idea solely available on the bookshelf in my brain. But whilst taking a post-run shower on a Friday in mid-May 2021, I suddenly had clarity of thought and determination and drive, and I knew that today was the day I was going to start putting this project together. I decided I would aim for a publication date of 01/09/2021, the day the Clearing House Applications process was due to open. To some it may have seemed daunting or perhaps an impossible prospect to write and publish a whole book in under 3 ½ months. But I had form, I had somehow managed to produce the entirety of *The Grief Collective* in the month of September 2020 so 3 ½ months felt like a luxury in contrast![1] From that post-run shower onwards, I started crafting web pages and forms and emails. By the Monday I was ready to start recruiting case studies from Qualified Clinical Psychologists or Trainee Clinical Psychologists. I then spent the next few months talking to

---

[1] Although as I proofread this section again on 28/08/2021 it doesn't feel that luxurious and I could do with a little more time!

contributors, recruiting and giving supportive reminders about the deadline!

What I have learned in the process of my first book is that organisation is key but also that automated processes such as email sequences and web forms save time and stress for both the editing team and the contributor! Anyone who expressed an interest in writing their story for this book was sent a briefing document with more information about the project and a consent form. Then my wonderful VA Hannah took over the consent process - apart from the one day I tried and accidentally emailed the whole book to a contributor or two – oops, to err is human right?

The case studies, or 'stories' as they're referred to in this book, started to come in from July onwards. When I began to read them, I was so humbled and honoured that people had put them together because I asked them to and that they were so willing to share them with me, to share them with you! As health professionals, depending on our therapeutic orientations and personal choice we can often feel uncomfortable about sharing details of our lives publicly. However, what unites us in *this* Collective is the memory of our own voyage into clinical training and our desire to support and nurture others in their own journey. I believe it is that memory which has empowered the authors to put pen to paper and to share their wisdom, compassion and true selves with you. All contributors have been rewarded for their time only with a free paperback copy of this book. Please read all stories with kindness in your heart and take the advice which resonates with you forward into your own career. All of the people within these pages really, really, really care about others. They are all very special people with unique skills and talents. Honestly, it makes my eyes and my heart mist up when I reflect upon the level of expertise, passion, dedication and years we have within these pages. Do please take time to leave reviews on Amazon and Good Reads to allow this talent to reach a wider audience and support more people to tap into this wealth of incredible advice on offer within these pages. I decided after I had put the consent form together that I totally should have asked how many years of experience people had as it would make a great fact for the book. I tasked Hannah with rounding it up but because it was pretty last minute, we didn't get the full set of figures back. However, of those who did reply, the average number of years of Psychology experience including education and relevant work was 15.76 years. The total number of years' worth of relevant experience and education disclosed by all contributors is a whopping 615 years! Wow! That figure is mind blowing to me and the wealth of their wisdom and guidance is now at your fingertips in this very book.

Each story is wonderful and they're all their own. We edited them, changed some of the order and flow, and tidied up the odd typo here or there and asked for clarification in some areas. But I hope you will find that you can hear each person's individual voice and writing style. In *The Grief Collective,* I knew a big chunk of contributors before starting the book project. It meant that I could hear them talking their story to me from the pages. With a big address book of Clinical Psychologists at my disposal I had assumed that this book may be similar. I have actually, however, only been in the same physical room with just three of the contributors in this book. The vast majority of contributors I had never spoken with at all until this project came about. I believe this really demonstrates how determined people are to offer their guidance and support to the next generation of clinical psychologists, to you - and I'm so proud of all of the contributors and the wonderful, humble, compassionate way they have told their stories. I feel like Vivien in *Pretty Woman* when I say: "In case I forget to tell you later, thanks, I had a really good time!"

The stories vary in length and style. I purposefully haven't grouped them in terms of span or features. I think there is so much to learn and to gain by reading about another's life without necessarily knowing in advance which 'genre' it falls into. That said, if you did want to read about particular topic then there's an index at the back of this book which will give you a helping hand for where to start.

Why write this book?

I still remember the first time I got wind of an actual qualified clinical psychologist. Her name kept cropping up in my team when I was working for Milton Keynes Council physical rehabilitation team. She was working in a team a few miles away and each time I heard her name it was like an electric current was in the air. I needed to get some facetime with her in the days where that meant actually being in the room with someone! I only knew her name but that was enough – she was locked in my sights! But what if you never get that hot lead in your professional life? What if you aren't currently working in a setting where you might cross paths with a clinical psychologist or a trainee? What do you do then? The journey into clinical training can be so daunting and it really can be helpful to talk to others who are already travelling that road or who have already traversed it! That's why this book has been created. It's my way of putting you in the room with 25+ others who get it and can help support you to optimise your chances of success and consider blind spots and areas of strength you might otherwise not have seen.

Why write this book at 21:49pm on 31/08/2021?[2]

Frankly at this time I'm wondering why I started this project at all. I've been working super long days and nights. I'm tired, my wrists ache. I want to go to bed, but I know I won't rest until I've got this sorted! Currently the page numbers won't behave and it's like exquisite torture to be this close and yet so annoyed! I also realised ½ an hour ago that our 'working titles' idea to call each chapter number '7' was still in place until about 30 minutes ago! One pesky chapter's formatting won't behave itself either. Any mistakes are my own, if you find any glaring ones, please give me a shout and I'll get them fixed. A book entirely full of chapter 7's, it was a close call.

---

[2] 26 hours later I was here again finalising and uploading the pretty significant changes and new chapters required due to the HEE announcement on 01/09/2021!

Why me? Why now?

In terms of the why me? I would say why not me? Why not you? In the last 18 months I have really given myself permission to go forth and create, to put myself out there and run with the ideas I think up. It has been so empowering, and I have learned so much about product design, book editing, course creation and more. We can often stand in our own way with reasons why we shouldn't or can't do something and come up with a variety of obstacles to hold us back from even attempting to get out there! I'm a big fan of the incredible, Denise-Duffield Thomas a money mindset guru. I enjoy her books: 'Lucky Bitch', 'Get Rich Lucky Bitch', and 'Chillpreneur', and her podcast series, 'Chill & Prosper'. Initially in 2015 she had approached publishers with her idea for 'Lucky Bitch', but no one had wanted to run with the idea. The closed doors didn't stop her believing in her idea and backing herself though.....she did it anyway! She self-published her book......and she did really pretty well, to the extent that she sold over 20k copies![3] She did so well in fact, that in 2018, a publisher she had originally spoken to 3 years earlier took notice and offered her a 3-book deal including republishing 'Lucky Bitch!' The thing is, if she had let her doubts about putting herself out there stand in her way, she would be yet to sell a single book! We have to get out there and communicate our message to the world. If you have a dream, why not give yourself permission to at least try to achieve it! Imagine it happening. As Denise would say, 'manifest that dream!' If you're interested in learning how to self-publish your own 'book baby' then do

---

[3] Thanks to Denise for providing these figures for me and for being so kind and gracious when I contacted her to ask about including them here.

check out the 'From Words to Books' information at the back of this book.

I have never been more energised professionally than I am right now. I adore what I do and to quote myself and my friend Kara from circa 2009, *'I feel pretty* smitten' to be here! When people in business networks ask me what my *'why'* is, my reply is *'to ease distress in others.'* I'm confident my husband would point out that if I was serious about easing distress in others that I would keep the porch tidier and develop a little more order to the pile of books on 'my side' of our room, but that's an aside. Everything I do in my business - whether it is 1:1 therapy; delivering content for my course; teaching people how to create their own self-published books; supporting them in their grief with *The Grief Collective*; coaching people on how to create passive income streams for themselves or guiding and assisting *your* journey into clinical psychology - is *on topic* for my desire to ease distress in others. With a little sprinkle of compassion and content from the work I do I really hope that it helps people. It helps them feel like they have a clearer sense of direction, that they feel less isolation and increased normalisation and validation. This in turn benefits everyone.

When I introduced the prospect of this book to a Facebook group for prospective clinical psychologists the response was almost universally positive. Apart from one person who commented that it was totally unjust to charge people for this book and that it should be free. In an ideal world of course, this would be great, but putting resources together takes time and money. Without even considering a cost for my time, in virtual assistant hours alone this book has cost me about £600 to put together. Buying and sending contributor copies will be another £300. Paying for virtual assistant hours to help me spread the word will easily be another £1500 in the next year alone. Book sales, unless you end up as a 'best seller' is not a way to get rich quick. It will take me well over 1000 book sales to even break even on my staff costs without even paying myself a wage so, with respect, and all the best will in the world, whilst I would love to be able to create this as a free resource for people, I'm sorry to say that it's not possible.

Richard, (whom you'll meet in chapter 17 on page 150), and I are both early risers it seems. One Sunday morning at the end of this project we found ourselves LinkedIn messaging at an early hour. We were discussing his story edit and I also asked for his cumulative years' experience figure[4]. I sent him this section to ask his opinion about whether it came across as brash and defensive or interesting. He said it was interesting but also kind of sad that I'd been put in a position where I felt I had to justify or defend myself. He said:

'I think the person who complained is likely annoyed they didn't think of the idea first and anyway, you're in sole private practice and have bills to pay, you're not a charity and already do loads of useful free stuff for people like the webinars.[5] This is Clinical Psychology we are talking about! You will probably get some hate but also some acclaim too and it'll be useful for years to come for loads of people."

---

[4]If you're interested, it's 9 years and counting and he didn't study psychology at A Level.

[5]In the 2020 application season I did a series of completely free Live Q+A sessions to support applications which you can catch on my YouTube channel. I plan on doing the same for the 2021 season and if you sign up to my mailing list you'll be kept in the loop about when they are happening.

I do hope you're on 'Team Richard' and that you hope you find this book to be a good use of your money and that it helps you strive for your goals of furthering your career in psychology. If you find it helpful, please do mention it to others and leave us reviews in all the great places where people will see them.

Who is the book for?

This book is for anyone who would one day like to become a Clinical Psychologist. It is for people of all ages and at all stages of their career. It is also for qualified clinical psychologists who might like a look inside the lives of other Clinical Psychologists to consider new clinical areas to venture into with their training and experience. In that way it's a bit like 'through the keyhole' or 'Cribs!' It's also for people who love you and want to seek to understand why exactly this *golden ticket* is so worth having! I hope this book will help offer context for your loved ones about just why the journey to clinical psychology can be so relentless and all-consuming at times. I hope it offers some validation and normalisation for the process which in turn helps them know how to optimally support and encourage you in your quest too.

Where did the idea for individual stories come from?

In my work and personal life I love a story. I love knowing about people and how their lives have been. It helps me think about people for work and in my personal life to have a rich tapestry of human examples to draw upon. I really love the work of Irvin Yalom who writes case studies about his therapeutic work with patients. I also seem to recall from my training days there is also a book by Patrick Casement which does the same using clinical examples. Growing up, when I was in sixth form, I also read a book called 'Women on Top' which was case studies written by women about their sexual fantasies. It was such an interesting style of book and my decision to write this book and *The Grief Collective* in this style has been inspired by this style of writing. Readers of *The Grief Collective* told me that they really liked the informal emails which were included at the end of some stories and so they are back again in this book but this time for every story.

So, what is Clinical Psychology anyway?

I t's possible that you've stumbled across this book, and you don't know what Clinical psychology is. Perhaps it's on a bookcase in a holiday let and it's pouring with rain, and you have nothing else to read or do. Thanks for picking it up. Sorry about the weather. To add context to what people will talk to you about in this book I will explain briefly what a 'Clinical Psychologist' is and what the U.K. access routes into the profession are. For those of you who already know this, you might like to skip over this section. But imagine how exciting it would be if someone who wasn't already in 'psychology world' read this book and then thought it sounded so fantastic, they wanted to get into it too!

According to the NHS[6]:

"Clinical psychologists work with people of all ages on a wide range of psychological difficulties in mental and physical health.

This can include anxiety, depression, psychosis, 'personality disorder', eating disorders, addictions, learning disabilities and family or relationship issues.

Yes, I'm pretty content with that explanation. In fact, it's relieved me greatly from the cringe I've been carrying since August 2020 when Noel McDermott asked me what it was during our LIVE

---

[6]https://www.healthcareers.nhs.uk/explore-roles/psychological-therapies/roles/clinical-psychologist

stream for episode 68 of his 'well-being show.' At the time I felt like I had fudged a truly awful answer but actually seeing this I don't think it was that bad at all! Well done me, and the NHS content writer, you did good too.

Prerequisites for training

There are various mandatory and desirable criteria to become a trainee clinical psychologist:

Many people study A Levels or equivalent often including but not essential – psychology, philosophy, sociology, biology, maths.

You need to have done an undergraduate degree, usually but not always, Psychology or as a joint honours, with Psychology and another subject.

Your undergraduate degree must offer Graduate Basis for Chartership (GBC) (formerly GBR) with the British Psychological Society (BPS). This attests that the knowledge imparted to you by your undergraduate university is appropriate for those going on to a career in psychology. If your undergraduate degree did not give you GBC you can undertake a GBC conversion course with a number of different universities.

Some candidates choose to strengthen their research and clinical experience by doing a Master's (MSc) or Postgraduate Certificate (PgCert) or some other kind of postgraduate education. Some candidates choose to strengthen their skills and experience by doing a PhD.

All successful applicants will usually have had at least a number of years of 'relevant experience.' This relevant experience could be working as an Assistant Psychologist, researcher, support worker, research assistant, PWP, High intensity IAPT, Low Intensity IAPT, teaching, social work, nurse etc.

It can be very useful indeed to have been supervised by a clinical psychologist and / or have one as one of your referees.

Accessing Training

Access to the majority of training places is currently via application to the Clearing House scheme.

At the time of writing, Trainee Clinical Psychologists are employed by local **NHS** trusts at the agenda for change band 6. Currently this is around £32,000 a year[7]. That is not a small amount of money and with other access routes into the psychology profession usually being self-funded, this is why Clinical can feel a bit like the holy grail and 'winning the golden ticket' if and when you 'get on'. That's not to say it's the right salary for the role and of course the pay freezes across the **NHS** have affected bandings, although that's a whole different book! Nonetheless, the average full-time salary for the U.K. is £31,461, (The Office for National Statistics (ONS)2020), so it's certainly higher than average. The current band 7 starting salary for qualified Clinical Psychologists is in the region of £40,000 but dependent upon experience, people can sometimes start at band 8a, which currently starts at around £47,000. I know of Clinical Psychologists currently working at band 9 (£93,735) and it still amuses me that one of them once asked me to borrow a fiver when he had forgotten his wallet. Thanks for paying it back so promptly Dr L, I was happy to help!

---

[7] All Agenda for Change banding figures in this section were taken from:
https://www.nhsemployers.org/articles/annual-pay-scales-202122

Funded Places

The current list of universities offering funded places is:

Bangor University - North Wales	University of Liverpool
University of Bath	University of Manchester
University of Birmingham	Newcastle University
Coventry and Warwick	North Thames - University College London
University of East Anglia	Oxford
University of East London	University of Plymouth
University of Edinburgh - NHS Scotland	Royal Holloway - University of London
University of Essex	Salomons - Canterbury Christ Church University
University of Exeter	University of Sheffield
University of Glasgow - NHS Scotland	University of Southampton
University of Hertfordshire	South Wales
Institute of Psychiatry, Psychology and Neuroscience - King's College London	Staffordshire University
Lancaster University	University of Surrey
University of Leeds	Teesside University
University of Leicester	Trent - Universities of Lincoln and Nottingham

Self-Funding Places

At the time of publication, it was possible to apply for self-funded places at 3 universities: University of Essex, University of Hertfordshire and Salomons: Canterbury Christ Church University. Salomons only accept self-funded applications directly to the University, Essex only accepts via The Clearing House whereas Hertfordshire accepts both methods. If you choose to apply for self-funded places, you must be able to provide your own funding either by getting a scholarship or organising sponsorship of some kind. In 2021, self-funding fees are in the region of £24,000 a year with some courses having slightly lower rates for students with home fees status and the higher rates applying to overseas students. Additional Placement fees of between £1750 & £1900 are also quoted. Given that this is 3 full years of academic teaching, usually twice a week, and 3 days a week of placement, you'll also need to bear in mind that you'll need money to cover your living expenses such as rent, food and bills too. I feel so incredibly grateful to the NHS that I was funded to train in the job I adore.

The information in this section is intended for reference only. Before applying or making life decisions please research the options further.

Additional Access Criteria for England Courses

On the 01/09/2021, just as we went to press, it was announced that changes had been brought in for any applicant who has already received funding from Health Education England (HEE) within the last 2 years.

On the 02/09/2021 it was announced that implementing this decision might be delayed.

On 03/09/2021 it was announced that this decision will be delayed until the 2022/23 application cycle.

On the 9/09/2021 it was announced that implementation of this decision would be delayed until after the 2024 intake.

At the time of going to press the plan was to offer NHS funding to all entering any of the psychological professions training listed below who receive offers from clinical psychology training programmes in 2023 or 2024. This means that there will now be no 'retrospective' application of changes to those who have started or are about to start one of these trainings.

If this information changes again[8] I will endeavour to update this book.

In a nutshell, the initial announcement told us that from September 2022, people who have completed a funded course would now only be eligible to apply for training as a Clinical Psychologist after they had completed 2 years in their qualified

---

[8] Fingers crossed it won't change again HEE.......!

role. The 2-year period was due to start from the date of their qualifying exam board. Prior to that time, they would have been ineligible for funding for their fees and salary for the duration of training as a Clinical Psychologist. In the previous section you will have seen that the cost to self-fund is high.

As of 01/09/2021 the announced list of affected roles was:

Adult Psychotherapy
Child and Adolescent Psychotherapy
Children's Wellbeing Practitioner
Clinical Associate in Psychology
Cognitive Behavioural Therapy
Core counselling training
Counselling psychology
Education Mental Health Practitioner
Family and Systemic Psychotherapy (qualifying level)
Forensic Psychology
Health Psychology
Psychological Wellbeing Practitioner (PWP)

This may be updated periodically, and we will endeavour to keep this book as up to date as possible. However, please do investigate this further if you think that this might affect you for the 2024 training cohorts onwards.

Reactions to the proposed changes

It appears that at least one English university already had this guidance in place and other access routes already had minimum service requirements.

However, with this seemingly coming without warning it caused some ripples and some tears too of course. I had the author's consent to share the below with you:

> Anyone else had a little cry about the new PWP criteria? I signed my contract last week and uprooted my entire life to work in the service thinking it would help me get onto the ClinPsyD. I rejected an AP interview for it. It's taken a lot of money, time and mental anguish, and hearing this has really been a slap in the face... We do intense training and gain a qualification, straight into the deep zone of assessments AND treatment, how is this not good enough?
>
> 😢 Sad   💬 Comment

This absolutely paints a raw and vivid picture, and I too would have felt exactly this way had this affected me at the time. My heart goes out to anyone who is hurting as they read this. People do often undertake PWP roles as valid experience for the clinical psychology doctorate. They put their lives on hold sometimes travelling vast distances for commutes and even living away from their family and friends mid-week. They might well have thought this was a manageable plan for a year and hoped they might get onto Clinical Training thereafter. Suddenly realising that this is a longer-term plan and without their informed consent is likely to feel a bit difficult. However, others were less surprised and were in fact shocked it had taken this long for this decision to be made. They based this opinion on the reportedly high staff turnover in roles such as PWPs. They saw that imposing this rule would allow for better stability in mental health services which in turn would be better for staff and service users. It's a difficult call and of course staff are people too.

This decision will affect the flavour and variety of the upcoming 2023 and 2024 cohorts too. People who might once have become some of your closest friends and allies will now not be in your year and you may never meet. It affects life choices of people wanting to start families, get married or any other important stages. It's kind of a big deal and it's likely that there will be a reaction of shock and maybe even trauma too. People might well feel that they had a clear sense of direction and now feel trapped and a bit despondent.

For more reactions to the proposed changes do check out Ercan and Emily's stories on pages 237 & 243 of this book.

Frequently asked wonderings

People were understandably reeling from the initial and subsequent announcements. Commonly asked questions were:

1) "What if I want to change jobs to a non-HEE funded role, such as an Assistant Psychologist, from the job I had the HEE funding for?"

It would seem that it is *likely* to be a paper exercise of matching up dates from the date on your HEE funded course certificate to the date of your Clinical Psychology training course. Two years or more must have elapsed between these dates. It's unlikely that the HEE would be able to trace whether you had been working as your funded role or in a different capacity and of course you'd still be using the skills you have from your qualified role in a different mental health role. For example, Assistant Psychologists would absolutely use the skills acquired during PWP training even if no longer working as a PWP. However, this point may be clarified by further announcements from HEE and I will endeavour to update this section if it is.

2) "Can I change roles to a different HICBT role?

There's no indication that you have to spend your 2-year post-qualifying period in the same role or NHS trust. It would seem feasible to move jobs within this time period especially if moving to a job with the same job title.

3) "What about sick leave or parental leave? Will that count within the 2-year period?"

It would seem potentially discriminatory to exclude the time spent on either parental leave or on sick leave. I do wonder whether the stress caused by this announcement could actually lead to a rise in sick leave too but that remains to be seen. Updates will be made as and when the position is clarified by the HEE. As with many things, time will tell.

Number of Applications

I remember when I was applying for training that I was told that courses *'like to see perseverance... if they offer you feedback on an application that they like to see it has been acted upon and that you continue to show up.'* I've no real idea whether that's true but it certainly stayed with me, and it propelled me to make sure that I acted upon my year 1 application feedback of:

'Academic experience needs strengthening'.

By starting a Masters. And I responded to my year 2 feedback along the lines of:

'More varied clinical experience required.'

By moving away from forensic adults to forensic young people. I was offered a place on training from my 3rd application.

I believe that I got on training when I was ready and that I was aware that I probably applied 2 years early for 'experience and to chance my arm just in case I got lucky!'

When reviewing the stats for number of applications and the associated 'success rates' on the next page it is definitely worth considering that there are likely to be more like me in the mix, who are applying for practice and with a dash of hope and optimism!

Given that the HEE announcement only affects English courses, might this lead to more people applying for the Welsh, Northern Irish and Scottish courses? Although, given that not everyone can be so flexible as to pack their lives up and relocate for 3 years, this will not be an option for all. For your information, and because I always think it is super interesting here's how the success rates and application numbers[9] have fared for the last few years:

Table 1: Number of applicants, places, and success rates for funded DClinPsy courses from 2015 - 2021

Year	Applicants	Places	Success Rate
2021	4,544	979	22%
2020	4,225	770	18%
2019	4,054	614	15%
2018	3,866	593	15%
2017	3,932	594	15%
2016	3,730	595	15%
2015	3,698	591	15%

[9] Clearing House for Postgraduate Courses in Clinical Psychology (2020, Oct). Numbers. Clearing House for Postgraduate Courses in Clinical Psychology. Retrieved 2nd September 2021 from https://www.leeds.ac.uk/chpccp/numbers.html

Support for Disadvantaged Students

These changes might well have disadvantaged some applicants and the official HEE official statement on this matter was as follows:

"Steps will be taken to mitigate any potential short-term unintended impact of this change on inclusion of financially disadvantaged entrants to clinical psychology training by extending the funding of paid experience programmes for disadvantaged aspiring clinical psychologists in 2021-22. Queries from individual applicants should be directed to their prospective Higher Education Institutions."

Currently 'unaffected' routes into DClinpsy

These changes might well have put the proverbial cat among the pigeons and made people feel *even more anxious* in Autumn than they normally might at this time of the year. However, there are of course many routes which do not currently attract any HEE funding and these routes will be 'unaffected by this decision.' I say unaffected with my ironic inverted commas because for anyone who has ever seen a job alert for an Assistant Psychologist post drop into your inbox whilst you're at work, think to yourself "Right, tonight that's my plans on hold because I am applying for that job....!" only to finish your shift, get home and realise the application has already closed due to a high volume of applications, you'll know that it's hard enough to even get an AP interview anyway let alone a job. You have my sympathy. Trust me. I've been there and I still remember the feelings of frustration and disappointment. Especially because I had already googled the area, worked out my commute and imagined how great I was going to be at that job! AP posts aren't the only route into DClinPsy and beyond. Other common ones also include research assistants and academia. I can only assume that applications for non-affected routes into Psychology might well become even more popular.

Approximate Application Timeline

There are various different stages and processes involved in applying for a trainee clinical psychologist post. Here is an approximate timeline which seems to occur most years:

Process	Date
Applications Open	September
Submit early to save £10 on application fee	Usually, mid-October
Application Closing Date	Usually, mid-November
References Submission Deadline	Usually, 1st of December
Applications are released to courses	Usually by the end of January
Some universities offer shortlisting tests	Between December and March
Confirmation of Interview Dates	Usually in the early part of March
Interviews	Courses vary from March to May
Interview Decisions	Courses must respond in very early June
Candidate Response Deadline	Usually, first part of June
Reserve List Places Offered	After stage above
Courses start	Usually between September and October

So, you can very easily see how the process can be pretty involved because a full cycle takes 10 months; it can indeed feel a bit like a perpetual cycle of striving and hoping, waiting and wishing.

Section References:

ONS, (2020) 'Employee earnings in the U.K.: 2020. Measures of employee earnings using data from the Annual Survey for Hours and Earnings (ASHE).' Accessed at: https://www.ons.gov.uk/employmentandlabourmarket/peoplei nwork/earningsandworkinghours/bulletins/annualsurveyofhour sandearnings/2020 On 20/08/2021 at 10:24am

The Clearing House for postgraduate courses in Clinical psychology: https://www.leeds.ac.uk/chpccp/

The Health Education England Announcement: https://www.hee.nhs.uk/our-work/mental-health/psychological-professions/funding-psychological-professions-training-programmes accessed at 16:08pm on 03/09/2021[10]

---

[10] Thanks HEE, it's been a pretty busy few days, can we take a break from daily announcements and daily book edits and re-submissions for a while now please...... (14/09/2021, no, it seems not!)

A Note on 2021

The beauty of books is that they can live on indefinitely. Therefore, I can't know what year it is you'll be reading this in. This book was created in 2021 and I'd like to briefly mention that 2020 and 2021 have been challenging years for, well, pretty much the whole world really. This is the time when COVID-19 first became a worldwide concern. It also brought with it a higher-than-normal death rate and obstructed just about every area of our lives. It impacted upon people being able to access jobs and education and also meant that interviews for clinical training have been carried out remotely too! This time has shown us all that the things we thought 'couldn't be done' differently, could in fact be done entirely differently! The world quickly moved online and the health service advanced by about 15 years in the space of just a few months. It remains to be seen how remote working will play out for society but with any luck I think it certainly continues to stand a good chance of making psychological therapy more accessible and inclusive both for clinicians and clients in future. The start of the pandemic also led to many, many more eyes on the news. During this time, a man called George Floyd was murdered and the public shock, terror and outrage of this led to the 'Black Lives Matter' movement, developed by 3 Black women in 2013, to be rejuvenated. This has also advanced the health system and the equality, diversity and inclusion of workforces all over the globe too. Many clinical courses have been offering additional support, guidance and access programmes to attempt to level the access for people from a wide range of backgrounds which are often under-represented in psychology. This book also features diversity as well as adversity, and in the 'story recruitment' phase a number of attempts were made to specifically engage clinicians with a broad variety of experiences. I hope that whatever your background that you will most definitely find something and someone to relate to within these pages.

About the Cover Image

On the 27/08/2021 I casually mentioned to my husband and chief creative right hand man, that we needed to make a book cover this weekend. He reminded me that a little more notice might have been nice, but duly cracked on with the task the following afternoon. I am thrilled with the results. To make it involved a very large dictionary, some snazzy lights and a post-it note. I hope you like the cover – it's also worth saying that it was a truly massive dictionary and didn't seem to have a 'main entry' for Psychologist but of course did for 'Psychopath' it seems! The man (my husband not the unspecified psychopath) is a creative genius, and I did mean to pay him with takeaway tonight, but I've only just remembered that and he's already paid half so........

Anonymity

Some contributors have asked for their names to be changed. This has been done. Others were happy for their full names and contact details to be listed whilst the rest of the contributors preferred just their first name or a pseudonym. All contributors have consented for their story to appear within this book.

What to Do Now You're 'In the Collective?'

Who doesn't love being in a club right? One of my earliest memories of being in one was when I was at primary school. I'd stolen my Mum's self-adhesive Kay's catalogue stamps and taken them into school with me to use at the top of the membership forms for whatever club it was we were forming that day! I hope that you'll find being part of *The Clinical Psychologist Collective* helpful.

Do please take photos of you enjoying the book or it on your desk or sofa and tag us on social media. We also have a hashtag #ClinPsychCollective

I'd love to know what you think of this book and whether it has been as useful as I hoped it would be when I first dreamed it up! Whilst I can't promise you a place on a doctorate course, or even a toaster, or a kettle like I may have falsely promised my primary school friends with their stamps, I can promise you warmth, validation and tonnes of actionable advice within these pages.

Speaking of pages, do come and give us a wave over on the Good Thinking Psychological Services Facebook page and if you love this book leave us a great Amazon review and pass this book on to the next generation once you're done with it! Unless you love it too much of course – then you could just buy an extra one as a gift for prospective clinical psychologists and keep your own copy for nostalgia! ☺

The
Stories

The Stories

1

Dan's Story:

The Underdog

My name is Dan and I have a dirty little secret. I got a 2.2 in my undergraduate degree. To most people in the realm of clinical psychology, this means that I am incompetent. My academic ability is questionable, and I would struggle with the level of academic work required to get through the Doctorate programme (DClinPsy). I may as well give up as, even for people who get a 2.1, the process is just SO competitive. I will never be a clinical psychologist.

I am a 37-year-old, white British, heterosexual male who was born in the U.K. As far as western society goes, I am pretty much the definition of average. Since I was young, I have always been seen as someone who was very capable but often lacked motivation. The headmaster of my grammar school noted on my university application form that I was "bone idle". Despite this glowing recommendation, however, I was able to secure a place at the University of East Anglia on a course which, at the

35

time, was framed as a revolutionary approach to psychology and sociology. A BSc in Psycho-social Sciences! I chose this course as I had an ongoing fascination with people and human behaviour.

 In the early noughties, tuition fees were pretty much a bargain by today's standards. Going to university based on a vague interest in something which you were unable to definitively utilise to start a career was, therefore, a viable option. Even though it was "cheap", university was still tough. But, looking back on it, not in any extreme way. No one close to me died. I did not suffer a mental breakdown. I was stressed, but not overly so. I had a part time job at Pizza Hut which, coupled with a decent student loan, provided me with more than enough money to see me through university, so, financially, I was not under immense pressure. What I did struggle with, however, was finding the courage to apply myself. I was so afraid of failing that I ended up not even trying. If I did not try, I always had a viable excuse for not doing well. This pattern of behaviour had served me well up until this point. I was very aware that I was not achieving but, at the same time, I also was not failing either which meant everything was okay. I also put a lot of emphasis on my social relationships. On many occasions, my friends, and their needs, took priority over studying. There were also several romantic relationships which all, in some way, took their toll emotionally on me. All these things combined meant that I maintained my average status. I continued to not excel, but I also did not fail, and I felt relatively comfortable with the social status I had forged. It was also thanks to this approach that, during my second year while working at Pizza Hut, I met the woman who later became my wife.

After three years of not really applying myself, spending too much time with my friends and managing to not sabotage an emerging long-term relationship with my girlfriend, I graduated with a 2.2 in Psycho-social Sciences from the University of East Anglia. During my final year, my interest in psychology had begun to grow. I was hoping to try my luck at applying for an

Assistant Psychologist post when I graduated. This plan, however, soon had to be revised. Upon completion of my degree, the course leaders had been unsuccessful in gaining accreditation for the degree to grant graduate basis for chartership (GBC) by the British Psychological Society (BPS). For those of you not aware, this is a key factor in many graduate psychology jobs, as it identifies your degree as "relevant" to the field of psychology. Now, not only did I just have a 2.2 but my degree was not "recognised" by the BPS. I was pretty much fucked.

With my lame degree in tow, I tried applying for several care worker positions, thinking that, if I were unable to evidence my academic ability, the least I could do is gain some relevant experience. I landed a job as an "opportunities worker" for a charitable organisation, based in Norwich, providing support and accommodation for people with learning disabilities in the community. My role was to help provide opportunities for people to get engaged with their local communities and develop their interests and hobbies. I was assigned two supported living projects and had two people under my care. Both had severe learning disabilities, did not communicate verbally, and lived with other people who also had severe learning disabilities and/or autism. I stayed in this job for a couple of years. It was brilliant in many ways, but also very hard. I would often get assaulted multiple times in one day as the people I worked with struggled to get their needs met and would become distressed. I had to work long hours and, though a lot of what I did was active and fun, it could often be physically exhausting. After a couple of years working with this organisation, there was an advert for an assistant manager at one of the projects where I was already working. I figured I could handle some more responsibility (and more money) so I applied and was successful. Even though I was still making less money than I was making at Pizza Hut before I left (never underestimate the value of tips), the job was rewarding and interesting. As I was earning slightly more money, this meant it was now possible for me to do further education and, perhaps, get my degree accredited with the BPS? I started doing some digging.

It turns out that there are plenty of opportunities for people to transform their non-psychological degrees into BPS accredited degrees. Thankfully, the BPS are quite aware that people may want to switch careers after graduating and they have devised several routes to build upon existing qualifications, rather than start from scratch. I found a postgraduate diploma in psychology, available through the Open University, which acted as a conversion course and would allow me to take additional modules in psychology to put on top of my "psychology based" undergraduate modules and enable me to get GBC with the BPS. Two thousand pounds of tuition fees later, as well as lots of stress with maintaining a job while completing a diploma, I achieved a Merit and GBC in the postgraduate diploma in psychology. "Finally!", I thought, "I can start applying for Assistant Psychologist posts!" Turns out I was wrong.

Every single advert for an Assistant Psychologist has the essential criteria: "a 2.1 (or above) in an undergraduate degree in psychology (or other relevant subject)". Even after all that time, money, and effort, I was still no closer to getting my foot in the door. I was seriously considering doing another undergraduate degree when I happened upon an advert for a "psychological assistant" at one of the local prisons. The essential criterion was phrased as "must have a relevant undergraduate degree". Seeing this was SO refreshing and filled me with hope. I had never considered working in the prison service before, but I figured it would allow me to get just as good, if not more relevant, experience than being an assistant manager for a charity. The change, however, would mean taking an annual pay cut of nearly £8,000. At the time, the starting salary for a psychological assistant was little over £13,000 per annum (full time). After much deliberation and some intense discussion with my, now slowly-becoming-quite-serious girlfriend, I decided that I should go for it!

Working in the prison service was, and still is, one of the best jobs I have ever had. As a psychological assistant I was working in the programmes department which had the aim of rehabilitating prisoners via psychological intervention. There were several different "programmes", each focusing on specific problems related to offending (such as drugs and alcohol) or a type of offending behaviour (such as violent offences or sexual offences). I was line managed by one of the trainee forensic psychologists and started off facilitating a group for people who had committed violent offences while drunk. After a couple of groups, I was sent to train as a facilitator for the Sex Offender Treatment Programme (SOTP). At the time there were different types of programme designed for different risks of offenders. I was trained to deliver the Core SOTP (for medium-high risk offenders) and the Better Lives Booster Programme (BLB – relapse prevention programme for medium – high risk offenders). A few years later I was also trained as a facilitator for the Extended SOTP (for very high-risk offenders). This suite of programmes has since been heavily revised and now only two variants exist titled Horizon and Kaizen.

My training with the prison service introduced me to cognitive behavioural therapy (CBT) and schema therapy. More importantly, the constant process of supervision and training meant that I really started looking at myself and how I operated. I started thinking about my own schemas, about how I was so afraid of failure and I wanted everyone to like me. I realised that I had been my own worst enemy for the better part of my late teens and early adult life. I will always remember my first performance review with my line manager when she sat me down and shared how brilliant I was doing; how I had a good attitude and was clearly a very intelligent person. She ended this ream of praise with "but, I know you can do better!" At first, I was very upset. But after thinking about it for a bit it was very clear. She was absolutely right.

I started trying even harder. The many hours my colleagues and I had spent chatting and inventing amusing parlour games in the office were not the best use of my time. I became more interested in forensic psychology and considered applying for a trainee forensic psychologist position. At the time, the forensic psychology route consisted of 2 stages, stage 1 was the working equivalent of a Master's in Forensic Psychology, stage 2 was working towards evidence-based competencies under supervision of a qualified forensic psychologist. Before I applied, however, this was changed and to be considered for a trainee position, you had to have completed a taught Master's in forensic psychology (or equivalent), therefore only stage 2 focused on paid employment with the prison service. Another degree meant more money (which I did not have). After much deliberation I figured that, if I were going to do a Master's, I may as well do a Master's that would help me become a clinical psychologist as, apparently, this would widen the opportunities of employment available to me. I have no idea if this notion is true, I just read several blogs which said that being a clinical psychologist and working in forensic psychology was far easier to achieve than being a forensic psychologist and working in clinical psychology. With my mind set firmly on clinical psychology, I decided to quit the prison service and, with over four years of forensic experience in hand, try to get one of those illusive Assistant Psychologist posts and gain some clinical experience.

I made lots of applications. Too many to count. Essential criteria be damned! I wore my 2.2 honestly and hoped that my experience would just overshadow the fact that many other candidates were probably better qualified than me. I managed to secure two interviews, one for a post in Newcastle and another working for a newly established private hospital for people with learning disabilities in Norfolk. I was informed for both interviews that I performed well and was one of the top candidates. The Newcastle job, however, went with someone who had a 2.1. The Norfolk based hospital offered me a job, however the proposed start date coincided in the first week of a planned eight-week trip to New Zealand with my, now REALLY serious, girlfriend. We tried to negotiate a different start date, but in the end, they went with another candidate who was more available (and who had a 2.1). The lead psychologist, however, suggested I keep in touch and they gave me their contact details in case any further vacancies came up in the future. I emailed them and rang them regularly (at least once a month). Part of me hated doing this, but they had told me to do it, so I continued even if it was just to say hello and ask how the hospital was developing.

A few months later, after returning from New Zealand, I received a phone call from the hospital saying they were expanding the department and looking to hire another Assistant Psychologist. It appeared my persistence had paid off. I was invited to another interview, and it went REALLY well. Unfortunately, I did not get the job. When I received the call, the lead psychologist told me that the department were focused on supporting people to gain experience to apply for a clinical doctorate and, despite my good interview, having a 2.2 meant that I was unlikely to be successful. They, therefore, went with a candidate who had a better undergraduate degree. I was fuming. To have the carrot dangled in front of you, only to have it whipped away, is far worse than not being shown the carrot at all. Really, I was just devastated. It is worth noting, for all you aspiring psychologists out there, at the time I was completely oblivious to the variety of different career options one has when interested in working within a psychologically based field. IAPT (Improving Access to Psychological Therapies) was in its infancy back then and there was no such thing as a Psychological Wellbeing Practitioner (PWP). There were, and still are, many options for a psychology-based career which do not involve getting on the clinical doctorate. Many of these could, one day, lead to a place on the clinical doctorate, or not. They are still viable and worthy options. But I digress. I chose to commit to clinical psychology. I continued applying for Assistant Psychologist roles and continued to get the odd interview here and there but none of them came to fruition. Then, a couple of months later, when I was out walking with my FIANCÉE (yes, after many years fearing commitment, I finally plucked up the courage to pop the question) I received a phone call from the private hospital informing me that the other person had backed out and they wanted to offer me the position of an Assistant Psychologist. This was the opportunity of a lifetime. Particularly for someone like me with "only a 2.2". I just said yes. I did not even bother to negotiate a starting salary. Fuck it, I would have worked for free.

The Assistant Psychologist post was working for a private locked rehabilitation hospital for people with learning disabilities in Norfolk. It was hard, but it was brilliant. I was one of two Assistant Psychologists in the "therapies department" (we also had occupational therapy, speech and language therapy, art therapy and social work in our department as well as nurses and psychiatrists as part of our multi-disciplinary team). My supervisor was adamant that I should be able to get on to the clinical doctorate, despite my 2.2, I just had to demonstrate that I was academically capable and that I could do research. From the moment I got the job, they encouraged me to do research and get published. Initially, I hated this idea. I struggled with research in my undergrad, and in my diploma. This was a bad idea. My supervisor said that was nonsense and offered me regular "research supervision" with half a day each week dedicated solely to completing research. The only caveat was that I had to produce something tangible. So, I did. I met with my supervisor regularly, identified a topic area I was interested in, read A LOT and started writing. My supervisor also gave my colleague and I an opportunity to work part time (remotely) as a research assistant for a London university. In an attempt to challenge my underlying fear of failure, I accepted this opportunity. My fiancé had recently become my pregnant wife and I was open to exploring any opportunities that would allow me to earn more money AND gain more research knowledge and experience. After a couple of years of hard work, I managed to write a research paper and submit it for peer review to an actual journal. I was in shock! Surely only people with PhD's or many, many years of experience are able to do this kind of thing? Apparently, not. Apparently, anyone (even someone with a 2.2) can submit a research paper for publication in a peer reviewed research journal.[11]

It took many more months of amendments and correspondence but, in the end, I was able to get my paper published. With my publication in tow, I felt that I finally had evidence to supersede my 2.2 degree and prove that I was capable of applying for the DClinPsy. I made my first application and did not get shortlisted for any tests. My wife had recently given birth to our first son. I was now a father with diminishing career prospects. I was adamant that my lack of success in my DClinPsy application was because of my 2.2 undergrad degree, but my supervisor ALWAYS disagreed. They continued to tell me that I was worth more, that this part of my life did not define me, that I was a good clinician despite being unable to evidence my academic ability so early on in my life. To this day, this supervisor was the only person who gave me this message. Every other professional in the world of psychology whom I spoke to about applying for the DClinPsy told me it was a pointless endeavour, that the chances of success were minimal at best. Despite these messages, I continued applying to the DClinPsy and I continued trying to do better. I was fortunate to have someone who believed in me.

After several years working as an Assistant Psychologist (and several failed DClinPsy applications) I was promoted to the position of senior Assistant Psychologist. With this title came more opportunities for mentoring and responsibility which, after an initial period of denial, I embraced. I decided that I needed more evidence of academic ability to boost my chances of getting past the paper stage of the DClinPsy application, so I applied to do a Master of Research (MRes) degree with the University of East Anglia. This degree HAD to be part time as I was working as a senior Assistant Psychologist, had a part time

---

[11] Editorial note: Thank you for sharing this Dan, I'm so happy you did it! I did this too despite my 2.2. It's so sad to see people shy away from opportunity because they think their grades aren't good enough! Here's to erasing that negative culture!

job as a research assistant and was half of a parenting team to a new-born child who (thankfully) was quite good at sleeping. I was relieved to find that part time degrees were an option with the University of East Anglia (this is not always the case).

My MRes was split over 2 years. It was INTENSE. I had to negotiate flexible working time with my supervisor to accommodate my attendance at lectures and balance the pressures of academic assignments, part time commitments and parenthood with my job as a senior Assistant Psychologist. It was tough. Prior to graduation, however, I applied to the DClinPsy on the off chance that the prospect of me gaining an MRes would increase my chances of an interview. It did not, but for the first time since I started my applications, I was invited to take tests for one university. This was a sign. A sign of hope. It was an indication that, with the addition of my MRes, I may have a chance of becoming a clinical psychologist. Unfortunately, I did not get invited to interview. The hope, however, remained and I worked my ass off to obtain a distinction in my MRes. I also managed to get my dissertation published in a peer reviewed research journal. Though my DClinPsy application was unsuccessful this time, I now had two publications, many years of clinical and research experience AND a Master's degree. I had hope that my dream was possible. Really, this was all I could ask for.

The next year, I made my application to the DClinPsy confident that I would, at least, get the opportunity to take some tests again. Then, I received my first rejection email. It was from the university whom I had taken the test during the previous year. I sent them an email asking why I had not been invited to the test considering I was now a better candidate with more experience AND an MRes distinction. The university replied stating that my invitation to take a test last year had been in error and that I should never have been invited because I did not meet the shortlisting criteria. My world imploded. All my hope had been based on an error. I now had a second child on the way, and I was facing a dead end to my career. All my hard work had been for nothing. All hope was lost, and I would never be a clinical psychologist.

During supervision the week of my "rejection", my supervisor pointed out to me that this was one university and there were still three more universities who were left to communicate their decision regarding my suitability. I was defeated and pessimistic. My supervisor said I was being ridiculous. They were right. That year I received two invitations to take tests at other universities. Each of these tests led to invitations to an interview. Each of those interviews led to an offer from one university and second place on the reserve list at another university. The day I received my offer from Exeter University for a place on their DClinPsy I cried. Finally, despite my below average start in academia, I was going to live my dream of becoming a clinical psychologist.

Some of you may be wondering, why am I telling you this story? Well, my overall aim is to show you that it is important never to give up. While I ascribe to most demographics which define clinical psychology in this modern world (white, heterosexual, relatively well-off etc) there are some key aspects which I was lacking. I do not have a 2.1 (or above) in my undergraduate degree, I am a man, I am in my thirties, I am a parent of two children. While I appreciate that I still have many privileges that give me an advantage in society (particularly being a white, heterosexual male) there were key aspects of my character that put me at a disadvantage when pursuing a career in clinical psychology. I am, however, just over a year from becoming a qualified clinical psychologist.

Whatever your background, whatever your disadvantage, if you want to become a clinical psychologist, keep trying. It is possible, regardless of what everyone has said. You are capable and you can do it!

Dan is on track to qualify in the summer of 2021 and hopes to gain his first qualified post to guide, nurture and support the next generation of clinical psychologists in the unfaltering way he experienced.

Dan's Story:

Email from: Dr Marianne Trent

To: Dan

Hi Dan,

Yay! You're a swearer! I love it! Do you mean to say my hours of developing strategy and rules for office chair Olympics in my old Assistant post was not the best use of my time? You may be right, but I bet you'd have been on my team! When I got to the stage where you were offered your first doctorate place, I swear I choked up a bit! YOU are the epitome of perseverance and I'm so pleased you had supportive and encouraging mentors along the way who believed in you!

Well done to you and I'm excited to find out where your first qualified post will be! Do let me know!

Take care,

Marianne

P.S. Hats off to you for doing your training with 2 kids, that's the real deal, mine moan every time they see my laptop!

2

Melody's Story:

Shine

Between the ages of 7 and 11, I was a Winterbourne Girl. To me, that meant the world! Truth is, apart from being the last remaining single-sex state funded school in the country, Winterbourne Junior Girl's School was a run-of-the-mill school in a cosmopolitan area on the outskirts of London. But our school motto: "Vincam"- "together we conquer" was our mantra, our lifestyle, and it oozed from staff and pupils alike. Importantly, I was fortunate to feel safe and encouraged to develop my core values. Notably, I developed:

- Skilfulness- commitment to practicing and improving my skills and applying myself wholeheartedly.
- Contribution- satisfaction in helping, contributing to or orchestrating a positive difference.
- Honesty- upholding truthfulness, integrity and sincerity.
- Persistence- willingness to continue with faith and resolve, despite problems and difficulties.

These values[12] provided a robust foundation on which my journey to becoming a clinical psychologist has been built.

I grew up in environments where talking about mental health difficulties was very taboo. I'd heard of "mental breakdowns" and there were local characters, who, looking back, likely had mental health difficulties. But I had no framework to understand my own mental health, much less others'! So how did I get to hear about psychology to consider clinical psychology as a career?

I was fortunate to be exposed to the social sciences (the sciences of society and social relationships) relatively early on. In Year 9, at the tender age of 14, I had (what felt like) the epic responsibility of choosing my "Options" (i.e., the subjects I would be studying at GCSE Level). Some options were easy-Music over Art. French over Spanish. But for weeks, I agonised over my Humanities subject. Even back then, I was disconcerted with the colonisation of the History curriculum, so History wasn't an option. The best thing about Geography was our eccentric teacher, who liked to eat chalk. "High in calcium" he said, while munching on a chip of chalk off of the cliffs of Cuckmere Valley. Geography wasn't for me either. I felt stuck. In the eleventh hour, a new humanities subject was added to the catalogue: Sociology. "I'll take what's behind door number three," I thought. I found Sociology challenging because it illuminated and dismantled social structures that I'd taken for granted. Contrarily, Sociology contained and empowered me with frameworks to organise thinking and a forum to debate and process ideas. Unlike any other subject I'd studied before; it was liberating.

---

[12]Harris, R. (2019). ACT made simple: An easy-to-read primer on acceptance and commitment therapy. New Harbinger Publications.

I distinctly remember descending into a heap of happy tears when I opened my Year 11 GCSE results. I achieved 6As, 4Bs and a C. "I can't believe I got an A in English" I said to my English teacher. "Of course you did! I taught you!" she replied in jest. I'd built genuine, supportive relationships that had facilitated my learning which would act as a blueprint for supervisory relationships later in my journey.

I was sad to leave secondary school but reframed the transition as an opportunity to have a completely new experience. I opted to attend a "big college" across London, over a local Sixth Form. Things were very different and frankly, I didn't love it. Commuting was tiring, stressful and gobbled up the majority of my £30 weekly Education Maintenance Allowance (not complaining- such initiatives for low-income families no longer exist). For the first time in my education, I was expected to figure things out completely for myself. Or know when I didn't know something and proactively seek support. If I didn't, there was nobody to hold me to account. There were so many distractions, prioritising my studies was a constant uphill struggle and it showed in my AS Level grades. College was hard. In second year, I came up with a study plan to improve my grades. The self-discipline, grit, and willingness to defer gratification I harnessed in order to execute the plan would come in handy on my journey to becoming a clinical psychologist.

I achieved an AS Level in Government and Politics (grade C) and A Levels in Mathematics (grade C), Sociology (grade A) and Psychology (grade C). I was disappointed with my psychology grade because... well, how can I enjoy a subject so much and work so hard to grasp the concepts yet struggle to achieve a high grade? This line of thinking had me considering changing my plans to study psychology at university. Besides, I didn't get the 3 Bs I needed to study psychology at my first or second choice university. Deflated, I insensibly navigated the Clearing process. After calling several universities and being turned away, I managed to secure a place at university with my grades. I'm not going to lie- I felt like a failure. I was fortunate to be able to reflect on my feelings with my aunt. She said "when you talk about psychology, you light up. Do what makes your light shine".

I studied a BSc in Psychology (with professional development) at Brunel University- a 4-year BPS accredited course, which incorporated two 6-month work placements. I opted for two research placements and learned how co-dependent and intertwined research and clinical practice are. I developed an ease with the research process that many practitioner psychologists are devoid of. In addition to gaining relevant knowledge and skills, I benefitted from periodic conversations with the university careers service, which compelled me to consider how I would translate my degree into a career. I'd liked the sound of clinical psychology since college, but what a lecturer said during our first week of university haunted me: "You will all want to be clinical psychologists. But the reality is, most of you won't make it. It's very competitive". Recurrent conversations about my career led me to reflect that such "statistics" apply to a sample- within each sample there are individuals who cannot be predicted in the same way. It's competitive, not impossible!

Clinical psychology isn't one of those careers people stumble into. It takes deliberate intention, time and effort to gain relevant knowledge and skills. From final year until getting a place on the doctorate, I was on a persistent pursuit to gain relevant knowledge and experience. Instead of participating in clubs and societies at university, I volunteered. I was turned away from some voluntary roles (due to lack of experience), but eventually started my first voluntary role at Saneline. The shifts were intense, and I was drained by the end. But the support from my supervisor (a clinical psychologist) was like nothing I'd experienced before- she was incredibly skilled, and I was inspired. And importantly, a glimmer of hope from a caller was enough to keep my light shining.

I graduated with a First and some good experience. I lined up an NHS honorary Assistant Psychologist role through a BPS initiative to improve BAME representation in clinical psychology. There, I co-facilitated a cognitive stimulation therapy group and had some excellent supervision. But it took five long months of unrelenting applying before I landed my first proper, paid job interview. My supervisor gave me the gift of a mock interview and I had my first bitter-sweet taste of constructive feedback from a clinical psychologist.

I got the job! A research role supporting clinical trials in dementia- my university placements had prepared me well. I gained some excellent experience and even completed a MSc while working there. But sadly, the role was not supervised by a clinical psychologist. Without guidance, feedback and supervision from a clinical psychologist, it felt impossible to know how to progress my career. I applied for approximately one million (exaggeration) Assistant Psychologist roles and had a handful of interviews. The only thing more exhausting than investing my all in preparing for an interview was hearing, every time:

"Unfortunately, we won't be offering you the position on this occasion. You interviewed very well but there was another applicant that had just that bit more experience than you".

New strategy: I sent emails, attaching my CV, to as many clinical psychologists as I could find, offering my time in exchange for relevant clinical experience. I negotiated flexitime with my manager to free up time to:

- Observe a trainee clinical psychologist conduct a neuropsychological assessment.

- Attend multi-disciplinary team meetings at a psychosis service.

- Conduct mood assessments as part of a clinical trial of transdiagnostic Cognitive Behavioural Therapy (supervised by a clinical psychologist).

51

Under 20% of applicants get a place on the clinical psychology doctoratei. Despite feeling it was a long shot, I applied for the doctorate three consecutive years. The first time I applied, I was invited to one interview. I was ecstatic to be invited but, honestly, I was not ready. Let's just say the interview went badly (I tell this story in more detail in a YouTube video). The second year I applied I didn't get any interviews. I was distraught that year. By the third year I was feeling fatigued by the whole process. It was such a roller coaster of emotions and I was tired of putting my personal life on hold. I considered building a career in clinical trials research, so sidestepped into a clinical trials coordinator role. I didn't love it (understatement) and once again, despite the fatigue, I returned to pursuing clinical psychology, this time more determined than ever before.

I immersed myself into the "world" of clinical psychology. I read articles, manuals, lecture notes, guidelines, NHS service information- whatever! I networked at pre-qualification talks, engaged on forums and discussed work with aspiring, trainee and qualified psychologists with open curiosity. Putting myself out there wasn't easy but that year, I developed vicarious experience that helped me see I'd been gaining relevant knowledge and experience all along- I just needed support to reflect on and articulate it.

The third time I applied I was invited to one interview. My mantra: "you only need one interview, one place". During the interview I felt edgy but prepared. When I left, I felt satisfied that I'd done my best. Fast forward a few days, I was sat in my quiet work office. The email read:

> Email from: Doctorate Team
>
> To: Melody Smith
>
> "Re: PsychD Clinical Psychology.
>
> *Dear Applicant,*
>
> *Thank you for coming to the university and participating in the interviews.*
>
> *I am pleased to be able to offer you a place on the PsychD Clinical Psychology Programme......"*

It was such a moment. This was a life-changing email! My heart was racing, eyes were blurry, I was feeling hot and clammy and the butterflies in my stomach were wild! I walked out of the office, as inconspicuously as I could bear, to a nearby gardens, and then... I jumped, stomped my feet and gave thanks to God with every fibre of my being. Finally!

If applying for training was like a roller coaster, the clinical psychology doctorate was like riding my first vertical drop. Somehow, I talked myself into this ride. The anticipation as I approached was thrilling yet daunting. Once at the front of the line, being invited in, there was no sense in backing out. Plus, others had taken the plunge and they seemed fine.

Firmly on board, the ride began. It started off fine but with every ascended foot, I felt less grounded. Slowly, the realisation that I wasn't completely sure of what I was in for sunk in. Cue anxiety and imposter syndrome. By the time I was dangling eighty feet in the air, I was convinced I was out of my depth and desperately wanted to wave the white flag. The rest of the ride was a blur. I descended into existential crisis. At times I had feelings so intense I couldn't make a sound! I'm almost certain I passed out for a few seconds! But by the end of the ride, you better believe I was kicking and screaming about the gruelling process.

I was ecstatic to hop off that ride. But it wasn't all bad. In the five years it took me to complete the doctorate (longer than usual) I became enlightened as to who I am and the power in my unique experience. More than just a ride, the clinical psychology doctorate equipped me with boundless skills to support others and a proverbial passport into an illimitable, meaningful career.

Dr Melody Smith is a clinical psychologist, university teaching fellow and career coach. Dr Melody Smith passionately supports aspiring psychologists to reflect on psychological concepts and get onto the clinical psychology doctorate. You can find Dr Melody Smith on Instagram @doctormelodysmith or YouTube: "Dr Melody Smith".

Email from: Dr Marianne Trent

To: Dr Melody Smith

Oh Melody!

Thanks for writing your story for this Collective and also for your incredible support and enthusiasm for this project. As you know, behind the scenes here it's taken me a fair few reminder emails and sequences to support and encourage people's creative flair and submissions. I was so humbled and encouraged that you replied to every single one with positivity and excitement for the project. It was just wonderful. Usually when sending replies, no matter how witty or interesting the content people will read (if you're lucky) and take action but it is so rare for someone to hit reply. I just wanted to say a massive thank you for that especially because it was so appreciated and really helped spur me on. I'm almost a bit sad to have taken you out of the email sequence. I may start a Melody only email sequence, so you email me more often! People are super lucky for having you in their world and thanks so much for coming into my world via this project!

Keep being Melody and shining your light bright and far for all to see!

Stay in touch, thanks again and take care,

Marianne

Melody's Story:

Email from: Dr Melody Smith

To: Dr Marianne Trent

Oh Marianne!

What a lovely message at the end of my chapter. So so lovely! So happy to have you in my world too!! I'm so inspired by your work rate!! But also, your warmth! Looking forward to staying in touch.

P.S. We went on an impromptu visit to the coast last weekend too. It was lovely. Hope you had a lovely week away!

Best wishes, Melody

Email from: Dr Marianne Trent

To: Dr Melody Smith

You are beyond lovely – Can I add this email in too?
So pleased you got to have some 'vitamin sea' as my VA Hannah calls it! Honestly, how you manage to be so fabulous with children even younger than mine I'm not sure, but you're ace! Marianne

Email from: Dr Melody Smith

To: Dr Marianne Trent

Hi! Oh Marianne, the mutual appreciation we have is so pure it warms my heart! Yes, sure you can share that email (without the typos, though!)
Love the 'Vitamin Sea!' Was so needed.

Best wishes, Melody

3

Jayshree's Journey

I wish I could give you a few simple and logical steps to get onto clinical training. You're reading this, so already, I believe that you are going above and beyond; doing everything in your power to further your understanding of clinical psychology and trying your very best to get the 'right' experience. It's not an easy career to choose and there are no guarantees, yet many of us continue to embark on this long and unpredictable voyage in the hope of becoming a clinical psychologist. I have shared a summary of my journey along with some 'top tips' in the hope that it will give you some ideas about different avenues to pursue and to reassure you that you are amazing. Yes, you are amazing! I want you to hold onto that thought as you read this and as you continue along this path and beyond.

I attended The University of Hull as it was and still is (now in conjunction with the University of York) the only University to accept undergraduate Psychology Students onto the Doctorate course. If you haven't applied for university yet, then I would recommend having a look at Hull and York as possible University options, as it could potentially save you from having to gain further experience following your undergraduate degree. I was interviewed in my second year and narrowly missed out on a place. This was really disheartening and my first experience of not gaining a place. Inevitably, this set off a chain of events to try and get onto the clinical psychology course. I spent my summer holidays trying to increase my experience of working with different clients in different sectors because this was what I thought I needed to do to improve my chances of success.

I gained experienced during my undergraduate degree by doing the following:

- I got a job as an agency worker in multiple care homes with older residents who had an array of mental and physical health problems.
- I volunteered as a Youth Worker in a secondary school providing young teenage girls with psycho-education on various topics, informal support and a private space where they could feel able to discuss more sensitive topics.
- I worked on research looking at the attachment styles of males in prison as part of a study that was being conducted by the University.
- I was also a member of various University clubs which included Nightline (a student support service), a psychology group and a BAME forum.

Although this feels like a lot, I think it would be a good idea to either attend a university that offers a placement year to gain experience and/or think about working within a relevant field when you able to.

After I graduated, I wanted to continue building my CV up and felt that the only way possible would be to either get an Assistant post or to further my studies. I moved back home and spent the best part of a year applying for different jobs all over the country! I was prepared to move anywhere just to get my foot in the door (which I appreciate is not possible for everyone to do). This was a very difficult time because I continued to work voluntarily despite not having any assurance that I would actually get an

Assistant post one day and that it may or may not help me to get onto the course.

It takes a lot of resilience to pursue a career in clinical psychology. There is so much uncertainty, but those pursuing clinical psychology tend to have particular qualities, that help to drive us and keep on going despite the odds. Most of the feedback I received from initial interviews was that I had *just* missed out and that the chosen candidate had a bit more experience. It felt like Catch-22. I needed a job to get experience, but they were asking me to gain more experience in order to be offered a job. In the end, after endless applications I got my first post in London and off I went to live in the big smoke.

Ironically, during my first post, I felt like I didn't have enough experience of clinical psychology and therefore chose not to apply for the doctorate. My advice now would be that it really isn't about the quantity and so much more about the quality. You need to make the most of your experiences within your current role and be able to sell your skills. You are amazing and you have to believe this in order to convince others! When in post think about making the most of the opportunities that are available to you.

- Network with different team members and think about how this is beneficial and sometimes challenging.
- Work on understanding your client group, what has led to them presenting to your service and how are you able to work with them in order to help them and the system around them. These are all valuable reflections that can be taken to supervision.
- Talk to Psychologists who have trained at universities that you may be interested in applying to. Although training across different courses are similar, you will find that there may be differences in the ethos, types of placements available and the 'feel' of the course that you

may be more drawn to. I found reading *The Alternative Handbook: Postgraduate Training Courses in Clinical Psychology* a useful (and regularly updated) resource in providing trainees perspectives of the course rather than just reading about factual information available on university websites.

- Link in with an assistant's group. This could be with other assistants in the department, or it could be a regional group. However, be mindful of the purpose. I remember that during application time, everyone would feel quite stressed which would be difficult to be around due to picking up on and experiencing that anxiety myself or because of the need of wanting to fix the distress of those around us. It can be helpful to take a step back or even have a break during this time in order to help you stay focused on your own application.

- There are now opportunities being developed to help those who are under-represented in clinical psychology to get onto training. As part of our profession's commitment to equality, diversity and inclusivity I am a part of a mentoring initiative designed to help mentees from minority backgrounds to develop their confidence and experience and provide them with insight/guidance of different stages of the application process. It may be worth researching if there are similar mentoring schemes available in your area.

I found that after I had my first assistant job, I was able to find other assistant jobs more easily because I had built up experience and I had networked so was more aware of other posts in the area that were available. I applied for the course twice during this time. The first time I managed to get an interview and the second time I managed to get an interview (and on the waiting list for a place) as well as on the waiting list to be interviewed for two of the other courses! However, I did not manage to get onto the course. I remember feeling really upset and internalising the experience, thinking that there was something wrong with me, which really isn't the case at all. It was helpful to have supervisors to look at my application, practice interview questions and to liaise with different professionals. I remember sending my form to supervisors and having discussions with those who also stated that they didn't understand why I had not got on with the level of experience and knowledge that I had. Although this helped with not feeling that there was something missing it also felt frustrating not knowing what I could do next.

Following my third Assistant post, I started to panic about whether I would ever get onto the course even though I was more determined and committed than ever. I decided that I needed to have a different option available to me that would not only further develop my skill base but could also be an alternative career. With so many options being available in terms of courses to study and research to pursue I decided to do a MSc in Cognitive Behavioural Psychotherapy. I felt that this course was the right fit for me due to the modules covered, the practical element which involved being on placement and receiving supervision. Yet again, I engaged in a juggling act which involved 1 day at University (as I studied part time to be able to afford it!) 1 day on placement (in a GP practice), 2 days working as an Assistant Psychologist, 1 evening and a Saturday morning working as an English and Maths Tutor and 1 day 'free' to complete all of my University work. It was a lot to juggle and during the course I did take a break from the application process as I had so much going on. It's important to remember that as you embark on this journey, life continues to move forward! Sometimes it can be helpful to have some time out from the process to give you a break and feel re-energised (although for others this break can be stressful, so you have to think about what's right for you).

I really enjoyed the course and I think what was most helpful was that it increased my confidence in a number of areas; returning back to studying after a break, having to do regular presentations, video recording my client material, critiquing it and discussing it in supervision, completing 'observed structured clinical examinations' (OSCEs) and of course having to write my thesis and experiencing a postgraduate viva! I decided to apply for clinical psychology again when I was in my final year of completing the course and amazingly got interviews for all 4 of my options! It was a surreal feeling, but I felt that I had reached a point where I was as ready as I could ever be. With hindsight, I think I was offered interviews because of my confidence in my abilities to become a trainee and being able to communicate this on my application form and then through my interviews. It is important to take your time researching different clinical psychology courses and thinking about the 'right' fit.

As I said before, there really is no quick fix. Everyone's journey is so different, and we all bring unique qualities and experiences. If there is one thing that I would like you to work on, that would be your confidence. Practice speaking in front of different people; whether it's delivering training, doing a poster presentation, contributing to client meetings or even social events. I know it's easy to get carried away by the process of ticking as many different boxes as you can but ultimately, it's about you. How do you come across? What makes you, you? What is your passion and why? What drives you? What's your story? Take time to reflect on yourself, your role and how you function with and within different systems.

You have to believe in yourself and find a way to let your brilliance shine through. You can do this; I believe in you! I really hope that you manage to get onto training and then feel able to help others to get onto the ladder too. As a profession it is important that we find ways to grow and develop further and be representative of the community that we live in. I'd like to thank you for reading my journey and hope that it will inspire you with your own.

Good luck!

Email from: Dr Marianne Trent

To: Dr Jayshree Avasthy

Hi Jay,

Thanks so much for your submission to The Collective.

I would most definitely have wanted you on my team rooting for me to progress my own career in Psychology.

Thanks also for the care and attention you put into your story and to being totally onboard with this process and getting what an important project it is.

Wishing you the best of luck in all you do in future,

Thanks again,

Marianne

4

Teresa's Story:

It's who I am

Shortly after completing the DClin, one of my fellow Trainees said to me 'How do I know if this is the right job for me?' My response,

'I can't answer that question for you, but for me, it's not what I do, but who I am, it's who I have always been, I am a psychologist'.

What I knew in that moment is that being a Clinical Psychologist is important to me, it's entwined with my values, and my journey to qualification (and beyond) has led me to the most wonderful friendships.

I'm now five years post qualification. To get here, I have had to jump through hoops, and leap over (at times walk through or crawl under) hurdles. I'm not sure that will ever stop, striving

64

seems to be part of the profession. I remember sitting in the teaching room on my first day of clinical training and thinking that the next three years (turned into four) would be hard work, but that I could stop striving for a while and enjoy the moment. Not so!

Graduating and officially becoming 'Doctor' was one of the proudest moments of my, and my parents' lives. In reality, I very rarely use my title, but I do still enjoy seeing letters addressed to 'Doctor...' and can't quite believe they're for me. I'm from a working-class family, the first to go to university, and I have multiple disabilities. Qualifying as a Clinical Psychologist was a big deal.

It wasn't where I had expected life to take me. I attended secondary school in the 1980s, where psychology wasn't offered. I enjoyed school and decided on a career in teaching. I didn't enjoy it.

Soon after I began teaching, I spent three weeks in intensive care, and developed PTSD as a result. Psychological services were even more limited 22 years ago, and I was left to find my own way through. This took the form of starting a part time psychology degree with the Open University. A chance remark by my first tutor, made me aware that Clinical Psychology was a thing, and ten years later I secured a place on the DClin.

My physical and mental health, in addition to raising a family, limited me in what I was able to do by way of gaining relevant experience. Having finally been referred for psychological support for my PTSD, I asked them, and was given one of the best pieces of advice I've had with regards to being successful in applying for clinical training. I was told that that it's not what experience I have, but how I reflect on it, what I learned from it, and how it might be relevant to the role of a Clinical Psychologist. How was my experience applicable to direct and indirect clinical work, research, service evaluation and audit, teaching and training, and leadership?

Over the next few years, I took on various volunteer roles. I became a Trustee at a local crèche and learned about staff management and developing education and social support plans for young people from 0-23 years. From there, I became involved in writing and presenting a bid to secure funding for our local SureStart programme. As a partnership board member, I learned to work with commissioners, delivered workshops to community groups and was instrumental in organising and presenting at a national conference.

Alongside this, I became a patient representative for critical care in my local NHS Trust. I provided the service user voice, and took part in audits and business planning, before being asked to join the NICE guideline development group for critical care rehabilitation. This led to working with the Intensive Care Society to improve patient outcome and experience, and then becoming a Trustee of ICUSteps charity. We were regularly asked to participate in research, and I became the Research Manager for the organisation and a co-applicant on a number of national projects, in addition to commenting on research applications made to NIHR. All the time, remembering to make a note of what I was learning and how it was relevant to being a Clinical Psychologist.

On completion of my psychology degree, I completed an MSc in Clinical Applications of Psychology at Newman University College. This was such a great course and opened my eyes to exactly what I was working towards. I know that people who consider applying to the DClin question whether they need an MSc to secure a place on training. Having shortlisted recently, I know that this is not the case. For me, it was the right decision, as it enabled me to continue to feel like I was moving forward, until I felt ready for work.

My first interview was for an Assistant Psychologist (AP) post in Child and Adolescent Mental Health Services (CAMHS). I had no experience of working in psychology and it was clear that due to my health and family commitments, I could only work part time. I didn't get the job, but I found a Mentor, and someone who opened the door for me. The let-down came with an interesting offer. It was recognised that I brought value and experience that may not be traditional, and that I had a lot to offer. It was also made clear that I would struggle to find an Assistant post that wasn't full time. I was offered the opportunity to become an honorary Assistant Psychologist for two days a week. This was the first time this had been offered within the Trust and was before it really became much of a thing. I know there is a lot of debate around people working for free, and the potential impact this might have on a number of things. However, I was in the fortunate position that I could undertake voluntary work, and it felt like a gift. I will be forever grateful to the person who saw something in me and took a chance. I am still in touch with them, and they still have my back.

I spent a year developing outcome measures in a paediatric psychology service, alongside doing a little therapy work (I'll let you in to a little secret, I had only worked with three people therapeutically when I secured a place on training), and most importantly learning from those who were doing the job. When the person who had been successful at my interview left, I was encouraged to apply. I was delighted to receive the call offering me my first and only AP post, and even more so when they were willing for me to work part time

As my child was now in secondary school, I felt able to consider applying for training. Although I knew I wasn't quite ready, I had heard that for most it takes more than one application. I figured going through the process would help for future applications. I interviewed for two courses that year and wasn't successful at either. The questions at both courses were almost the same, as were my responses. My feedback from one course was positive, and said whilst I wasn't quite there, they would like to see an application from me the following year. From the other, I was told that I didn't understand what it meant to be a Clinical Psychologist. The learning I took from this has stayed with me through many rejections following interviews for qualified posts. I may not be everybody's cup of tea, but that's okay. If the people interviewing me don't feel like I am a good fit, then it's not the right place for me to be at that time.

The following year, I was offered a place on the course who hadn't liked what they saw the previous year. I didn't believe it and rang back twice just to check. My Mentor was as pleased as I was but did offer me some words of caution. They reflected that I 'had been around the block' compared to most other Trainees and that I had experience in areas that some may find challenging. I was advised to keep my 'head down and play the game'.

Unfortunately, that wasn't possible. There isn't space, and it isn't appropriate, to go into details, but early in training, I felt stigma in relation to my PTSD. I felt disabled by my mental health condition for the first time, because of the reaction of Clinical Psychologists. The emotional impact of navigating this in the first few months of training led to my questioning whether I wanted to be part of the profession and resulted at times in a difficult training experience (not helped by experiencing a number of family crises). However, facing these challenges led to me developing a very clear picture of my values, boundaries (and how to hold them), the importance of 'good enough', and the type of Clinical Psychologist I wanted to be.

There's no escaping it, clinical training was one of the hardest things I've done, and if I wasn't the type of person who has to finish reading a book even if they're not enjoying it, I may have walked away. Why didn't I? Being honest: 1. I wanted to be the first in my family to be a 'Doctor'. 2. I wanted to be a good role model to my child. 3. I love the job. 4. My fellow Trainees, all 17 of them. Being a part of that cohort was special and I feel privileged to have trained with them. For all the challenges of training, I found something beautiful and meaningful in learning with and from others, thinking with others, and forming bonds that have carried me through the life challenges I have experienced since. I know that not all year groups are like this, but I was lucky.

I needed to take a few months off for health reasons, so finished a year behind everyone else. At the time that felt huge, and I worried I would be viewed differently as a result. I needn't have as this is quite common, and it hasn't affected my career progression. If anything, I learned to do things when I was ready. I waited to complete Supervision training, and I sat in a Band 7 post for longer than most, because that was the right path for me.

My first qualified post was back where I started as an Assistant. A chance maternity leave cover in adult neuropsychology led to my learning that my strength lies in assessment, formulation, staff consultation and training, more that it does in therapy. Being honest, therapy is bottom of the list for me (maybe I shouldn't admit that, but it's true).

In the past year, I have learned that I am neurodivergent (not a massive surprise), and whilst this has helped to make sense of why I have a preference for certain type of work, I have again experienced some stigma. I've chosen to take steps to challenge this more widely and have begun to speak more openly about my conditions. I have also returned to the Open University to teach psychology.

From enrolling on my degree to graduating with my Doctorate took 14 years. It was worth it.

So, what do I now say to others who are thinking about starting this journey:

- Being a Clinical Psychologist is great, but I could have been happy doing something else (NHS management, charity work, third sector community work, policy development, academia/research).

- Do you want to be a therapist, or are you interested in everything else a Clinical Psychologist does? Training as a therapist may be an alternative way forward.

- Learn to hold your boundaries and prioritise self-care as early as possible.

Teresa's Story:

- You don't have to fit the 'mould', and you don't have to follow the traditional route into the profession, diversity and lived experience add value.

- Remember to reflect on what you have learned from your experiences and how it is relevant to being a Clinical Psychologist.

Email from: Dr Marianne Trent

To: Dr Teresa

Hi Teresa,

Thanks so much for your submission to The Collective. I really like how you have been able to ask for what you want and hold your ground and get what you want even if not immediately. The fact that lived experience was looked down upon within CP is pivotal. It is important to point out that people's personalities come into play even though they may be clinicians too and I think sometimes we can feel that our colleagues won't judge because of their line of work but it seems that's not always the case and I'm sorry you experienced that.

There is most definitely a lot to be said for learning to become happy with who we are and holding our heads up high.

Well done to you for all you have achieved and continue to strive for despite some adversity along the way.

Thanks again,

Marianne

5

Clarabella's Story:

So, you want to be a psychologist?

It is 2005 and I am in my early twenties. Since leaving school and home as quick as I could at 17, I have worked my way up in retail and I am doing well in my job as a shop manageress. I seem to have developed a healthy confidence and ambition despite a complicated childhood. A little belief and encouragement from those around me goes a long way. Together, this informs the mantra I choose to live by at the time: "Whatever the mind can conceive, it can achieve". This newfound sense of safety and optimism allows me to take leaps of faith. I enrol on an Access to Psychology course at a local university[13]. I do not have the conscious intention to study for anything other than interest – I was certainly a "Why?" child as it felt there was a lot to question in the environment I grew up in – so psychology naturally appealed to me and the option to

---

[13] Access courses are designed to prepare people without traditional qualifications for degree study.

pursue things further if I wanted seemed a win-win situation. Not long into the course I am sitting in the library and come across the British Psychological Society career booklet "So you want to be a psychologist?" This lists the core psychologist professions and routes into them. Most seem appealing, but there is soon no doubt, I definitely want to be a clinical psychologist and I will not stop until I get there...

The journey itself actually took 13 years. It involved many highs, lows, twists and turns. This story is an account of some of that. Even though the original fantasy has not quite matched the reality in becoming a clinical psychologist (and that is no bad thing by the way), I look back to who I was in my twenties and thank that young woman for her tenacity and self-determination. Surely a meaningful life has got to involve following your dreams? As for now, I again take a leap of faith in writing this – Is anyone really interested? Can I live with it being an imperfect account? Will I upset anyone with anything I say? You see, for all the countless positive things clinical psychology has given me, it (along with age) has also made me far more tentative. I seem to struggle to speak my truth at times, which can feel very stifling. So, this is my attempt at daring greatly in sharing my story –

" When we deny the story it defines us, when we own the story, we can write a brave new ending" Brene Brown

I started my psychology degree in 2008 after finding a course that would allow me to work and pay my mortgage alongside my studies. In the first year of my degree, I was made redundant from my job and scoured the internet to find something that would allow me to survive financially and continue my studies. Eventually, I was offered a part-time job as a research administrator at a large university and, needless to say, this was a huge relief. I was still desperate to get some clinical experience and persuaded the psychologist associated with the research project to let me shadow him in his dental anxiety clinic. In the second year, I opted to take a work experience module, but this involved finding my own placement. I marvel at the boldness of it, but I contacted every psychology-related department I could and eventually one offered me a placement. I spent half a day a week working on an eating disorders research project and managed to fit this in with my paid job and studying - it is certainly easier to write those words than it was to coordinate those things! As far as I can tell, the majority of people pursuing clinical psychology put an enormous amount of effort into gaining experience and qualifications; I think this is even more impressive for those facing or having faced additional personal challenges, life adversity, and discrimination. Despite leaving school with virtually no qualifications, I finished with a First-Class Honours Psychology BSc and this remains one of my proudest achievements.

I enjoyed academic life as it gave me much a much-needed sense of achievement, so it made sense to continue studying. During my BSc I applied for a competitive Master's degree and was ecstatic to be offered a place. However, despite my enthusiasm, I had a pretty rough experience. This was a lot due to factors in my personal life impacting my mental health. Additionally, I felt a bit like a fish out of water at the university due to my perception of class and education difference from others. Together, this left me feeling uncertain and uncomfortable, particularly interpersonally. The youthful confidence that propelled me into studying psychology seemed to have disappeared and I felt withered and weary. I coped the only way I knew how – by continuing to push myself to succeed. In what felt like a herculean effort, I managed to achieve a Distinction for my Master's and so my perfectionism was appeased for the time being.

Clarabella's Story:

During my Master's I also managed to get my first paid clinical job working for a child protection charity. This involved supporting men who had been arrested for downloading indecent images of children. Subsequently, I worked in forensic services for a year while completing a Postgraduate Diploma in Criminological Psychology (feeling hugely out of my depth most of the time). I was privileged to work with some inspiring people, but I am now much more mindful of the potential impact of dealing with traumatic subject matter and the necessity of a safe and structured supervisory relationship. At the time, I think I found it hard to even acknowledge, let alone raise any concerns, as I wanted to appear competent and found evaluation threatening. On reflection, this is still a bit of a work in progress for me professionally. However, I am a great believer you can always learn and grow from even the toughest experiences; it provides a pleasant sense of purpose that I went on to complete my Doctorate in Clinical Psychology (DClinPsy) research on secondary trauma and burnout in specialist police staff.

Rightly or wrongly, it is not uncommon that aspiring clinical psychologists are willing to move around a lot to secure a post anywhere that provides the golden opportunity of more clinical experience. I spent the two years before getting onto training in Oxfordshire. My first role involved driving long distances to different care homes (we took the plunge to buy a new car to allow this, adding further to the debt accruement involved in career progression). I discovered the company of audiobooks and downloaded *The Compassionate Mind* by Paul Gilbert. I played it on repeat and slowly benefited from the wisdom and healing it offers. It was exactly what I needed at the time as an antidote to my constant striving and self-criticism and I still apply it in my personal life and professional work.

Around this time, I experienced my second unsuccessful attempt a securing even an interview for the DClinPsy. Given my nature, I dealt with what felt like crushing rejection and existential crisis by (you guessed it) pushing myself to get more clinical experience. I secured a Trainee Psychological Wellbeing Practitioner role in IAPT. The mood, anxiety and relational difficulties that had been playing out in recent years seemed to come to a head and decided for me that I needed some external help. I ended up having psychodynamic psychotherapy in the NHS (while being an NHS employee). While this felt excruciating at times, it supported me to approach certain things in my life differently. My upbringing had resulted in me being a hugely independent person and I have thrived in many ways because of the self-determination this involves. However, I had to accept this was not always entirely healthy or proving conducive to getting on the DClinPsy and, ultimately, the reality of effectively working in mental health care. I have come to learn those things involve the sharing of minds, mutual support, and collaboration. I started to run the local Assistant Psychologist group and it was important for me to try and instil a sense of compassion and safety as an antidote to the competitiveness that can exist in peer settings of this nature. I like to think I achieved that by sharing my own hopes and fears and valuing the experiences of others.

Importantly, it was during this tricky pre-qualification time of uncertainty that I really did become clearer on what psychological models I felt most aligned to, my values, and my professional strengths and weaknesses. I used this as my compass to decide which clinical courses might best suit me and enable a positive training experience. The Alternative Handbook was really useful with this, particularly reading trainee experiences of how well courses attended to their welfare.

75

Clarabella's Story:

I was sitting in a Tunisian hotel dining area when I was offered a place on the North Wales DClinPsy (my third application). That moment was very surreal and incredibly special. It was quite rightly celebrated with a bottle of fizz despite it being not long after breakfast. A few months later I had rearranged my life yet again to move to a new house and embark on training. This involved my partner and I deciding to live separately for three years so we could both focus on giving work our all. I do not think it is easy to support an aspiring psychologist and I am grateful he provided hope when needed and strapped himself in for the ride. During training I lived in a house with my beloved cat overlooking the Irish Sea and with a nature reserve as my back garden. Despite the inherently stressful environment of the DClinPsy, I had an amazing three years and felt psychologically well due to engaging in mindfulness practice, regular runs along the North Wales coastline, and trekking the Snowdonia National Park (I am also not ashamed to say I also drank a lot of Pinot Grigio). I mention this not just for the nostalgia, but to highlight the crucial need for self-care and hobbies to balance the demands of work. Up until training I had not really had that in my life due to the constant need to juggle paid work and striving constantly to progress.

In attachment terms, training provided me with a secure base in my development as a clinical psychologist. A large part of this was the support provided by my training coordinator, the course team, and some brilliant supervisors. I had indeed picked the right course for me. Despite the impatience I felt in the years preceding training, the experience I gained along the way resulted in a far smoother and more enjoyable time. There is no doubt the evaluation involved in passing placements was a constant assault on the ego, but this enabled me to see in writing the positive impact of my work in client's lives. It is a genuine privilege to work clinically.

So, that is a version of my story - imperfect, both in execution and telling, but that is okay. I sometimes wonder what my younger self would have answered to the question: "So you want to be a psychologist?" if she really knew the reality of things to come...I hope I would be able to reassure her...as it really was through the journey that I learnt, grew, and changed in ways I could not have imagined (and of course I am still on my journey). As a clinical psychologist, I feel this has allowed me to better understand and support the people I work with using collaboration, empathy, and compassion.

"The lotus is the most beautiful flower, whose petals open one by one. But it will only grow in the mud.

In order to grow and gain wisdom, first you must have the mud - the obstacles of life and its suffering" Goldie Hawn

Dr Clarabella Gray is a chartered and registered clinical psychologist working in the NHS and private practice. Email: clarabella.gray@gmail.com

Clarabella's Story:

Email from: Dr Marianne Trent

To: Dr Clarabella Gray

Hi Clarabella,

Oh, I love it, thank you and well done! I can't wait for others to read it; I think it's really inspiring. Also, so pleased you discovered compassion along the way because it certainly sounds like you were your own harshest critic!

I love and am slightly envious of your coastal runs during training – the underpasses of Coventry don't really compare!

Thanks for including the photo of that pivotal "So, you want to be a psychologist?" magazine cover, I'm gutted but the way the book is printed, sadly I don't think we will be able to include it. I really like that it's still important to you (and I) to have key significant life and journey trinkets too though!

Do stay in touch and stay kind to you,

Marianne

Email from: Dr Clarabella Gray

To: Dr Marianne Trent

Hi Marianne,

I'm so pleased you like it; I think the book is a great idea! I recently bought The Grief Collective for a friend who sadly lost her father, so it is wonderful to be involved in something related. Huge congratulations to you for both books - very inspiring and important work :)

Oh, training in North Wales really was so special in terms of the landscape. The convenience and opportunities of living "down South" again now is great, but I do so miss the mountains and sea.

The formatting looks fine to me and absolutely no worries at all about not including the picture. I mainly pasted it in there as a bit of an inspiration to myself in writing and then didn't remove it before submitting.

Best wishes,

Clarabella

6

Linnie's Story:

Self-Compassion would have made for fewer bumps in the road!

My route into clinical psychology is somewhat typical; however, I did have to work hard to make it happen and whilst I love my job and everything it offers, I do sometimes query the need for the sacrifices I made and whether there were more compassionate ways I could have got here... 'here' being my dream job as a Lead Clinical Psychologist in a Child and Adolescent Mental Health Service, alongside being an Associate with a small private practice. More recently I have been invited to provide clinical opinion on specialist subjects in mainstream media e.g. The Telegraph and Metro. I have also been trying to develop my presence on social media, including developing a Podcast called 'We Need to Talk: Candid Conversations on Mental Health' and slowly working on the development of Twitter and Instagram accounts.

Needless to say, my current career opportunities are far more diverse than I could have imagined, over and above the already eclectic job role of a Clinical Psychologist. Anyway, I digress.

For me, my journey to becoming a Clinical Psychologist began at the age of 12 or 13, following reading a book about a young lady who developed and recovered from anorexia nervosa. From the moment I finished the book I knew I wanted to work with people with eating disorders. At that stage I didn't know what a clinical psychologist was, or how I would fulfil my ambition, but I was adamant that helping people with eating disorders would be my career choice. Little did I know that my dream would lead to a twelve-year stint at university, followed by another two years not long after qualifying!

The specifics of my ambition to work with people with eating disorders somewhat baffled careers advisors and I progressed to my A Levels not really knowing what path I should take to reach my goal. Against my parents' wishes I picked AS Psychology, a topic they viewed as 'trendy 'rather than a subject with which I could pursue a career in. However, being stubborn, I continued anyway. Ironically, I didn't do particularly well in this subject and achieved a 'D 'and didn't go on to complete the full A Level.

However, when the time arrived to apply for University, I selected Psychology. I recall searching for the 'best 'universities, with prestige being an organising factor. However, my predicted grades were somewhat hampered by glandular fever, ruling out the university seeking the highest grades. My predicted grades, however, still gave me a good choice of universities and I concentrated on the courses that inspired me the most. I eventually chose Swansea University due to its core module in the third year that focused on eating disorders, which I was desperate to complete. At this stage I was not much the wiser as to what a clinical psychologist did, however, I instinctively knew the degree was the correct path for me and I felt completely hyped for its course content.

My time at university was not particularly easy, I struggled with my mental health and almost failed my first year. Feeling the fear of failure and desperate to proceed with my dream I regrouped and thought about my career options and what I needed to do to get there. During my first year I had heard of the British Psychological Society (BPS). I registered as a student member, and I began to investigate opportunities associated with the professional body which led me to become a BPS student representative. I also sought out the position of editor for PSYCH-TALK, a BPS student publication.

As I became increasingly aware that I had to develop my CV, I took on roles such as Nightline Co-Ordinator and student journalist, writing articles on mental health issues for the University newspaper. To showcase breadth of skills and interests I also began working towards completing my gold Duke of Edinburgh award. I even approached the Award strategically, using my extra-curricular psychology activities to 'tick 'boxes for the Award. I also, recall entering a competition for the U.K. Student of The Year award for these extra activities, in the hope it would enhance my CV. In this instance it didn't, and I didn't get any further than being shortlisted, but I took it in my stride with the attitude of 'if you don't try, you won't get.'

As I began to understand the clinical psychology pathway better, I realised I needed to build a CV of 'experience. Therefore, in the summer between my 2nd and 3rd year I set about securing relevant placements. I contacted a number of services that inspired and interested me. This led to opportunities to work voluntarily as an Assistant Psychologist (AP) under the supervision of a Clinical Psychologist in an adulthood eating disorders team. The post still holds some of my happiest memories of work to date and was great and supportive in introducing me to clinical work, helping me to make theory to practice links from the outset. At this time, I also, secured a support role in a local consortium helping adults with mental health needs and undertook some voluntary work for a local eating disorders charity. I worked these voluntary roles alongside paid work in an older adult's residential home. It was a busy summer, which offered a lot of personal growth as well as professional development. Importantly, it added to my CV, creating a strong foundation for the next steps. During this time, I kept an anonymised clinical log with learning points, to act as a reminder of activity to help me navigate future job applications and interviews.

The following year I finished my degree achieving a 2:1. I looked for AP roles and realised that they were few and far between and that my solid 'foundation' did not mean that the next steps would be easy. After much consideration, I decided to stay on at Swansea University to complete a Master's in Abnormal and Clinical Psychology, again swayed by the eating disorders modules on offer. I achieved a grant to support with funding and, got a position as a Residence Tutor meaning that I had free accommodation and breakfast for the year in exchange for supporting first year students in halls of residence.

I realised that large gaps in my experience also remained and with few NHS opportunities for AP posts locally, I decided to advertise my 'want' for a position as an AP in the BPS magazine. By chance, a Clinical Psychologist in Private Practice saw my request and following an interview, I was offered a position as an honorary AP within her new neuropsychology practice. It was a remarkable opportunity, which saw me embark on a three hour commute every week! I didn't care though; it was a gift, and I loved the role. Under close supervision I had opportunities to observe administration of psychometric tests, support with clinical note taking, contribute towards the development of psycho-educational packs and even undertake 1:1 work. This opportunity in itself led to further opportunities with my supervisor making me aware of a voluntary AP role closer to my home, again in adult eating disorders, but exciting none the less. This too eventually led to a paid role, but this time as an NHS member of staff. It felt like my hard work had finally begun to pay off.

Linnie's Story:

As part of the Master's degree, I completed a thesis on Pro-Anorexia. My supervisor at the time encouraged and inspired me to undertake a PhD in this area. I had no idea what I was taking on or how I would pay for it, however, again was convinced that this was essential for the 'dream career 'and took on the pressure of funding further studies. I probably should have consulted with Clinical Psychologists at the time as to the necessity of this path, as I later found that only a few people do this! That being said it enabled me to embrace opportunities to teach on the Master's course that I had just completed, as well as mark undergraduate essays and supervise dissertations. I also presented at several conferences; some went better than others... I recall one as being a particular disaster ... but a learning point nonetheless!

Following the first year of my PhD I ended up returning home to live with my parents and continued my studies long distance. I was able to continue with essay marking, supervising thesis projects and teaching. To further support myself financially, I achieved a position as a healthcare assistant on an adult inpatient psychiatric ward, whilst this lacked the magic AP 'title', it was a massive learning curve. It really started to build my understanding of power and difference, hear stories of lived experience of mental health whilst also developing my communication skills.

During my third year of my five-year PhD, I applied for my clinical doctorate, for lots of reasons I wasn't ready; knowing how hard it is to get onto the courses I wanted to have a trial application year. I was successful in terms of invitations for interviews but the experience of interview itself highlighted to me gaps in my experience as an AP and I felt inadequately prepared for the questions. Remarkably, however, I was short listed as 1st reserve for one course and by luck achieved a place, which of course was not the plan, but I could not turn down the opportunity as I was scared it would not come again. I arrived feeling like a fluke and with a great sense of imposter syndrome. Although, I was relieved to be reassured by peers that this was the case for many regardless of experience or whether or not you had been a reserve.

The course itself was quite a journey and for me, not linear, perhaps best evidenced by me taking some time out. Whilst this had been unplanned and not what I had wanted or envisaged, it helped me gain greater perspective about the course. It remained, very much, what I wanted, but no longer did it sit on a pedestal. During my time out, I invested in my health and self-care. A part time job as a home carer helped me gain better perspective of clinical training. The time out enabled me to revisit my passion for working with people, concepts of dignity, authenticity, compassion, and power and difference. I became less driven by the 'glory' of training and instead propelled forward by my values and ethics.

Needless to say, my training trajectory was not as I expected or hoped, but placements and remarkable and inspirational clinical supervisors made the long journey worthwhile. It was the experience in the field which helped me connect with and act upon my values to work out how to become the psychologist I wanted to be rather than the one I thought I had to be, or I thought the course wanted me to be.

Despite the bumps in the road, I did qualify. With hindsight, by the time I got to clinical training I had become lost to 'the dream.' This is perhaps best evidenced by how when selecting courses, I did not think about how course ethos aligned with my values and interests, instead I was organised by location and the type of interview. I was willing to attend any course near me rather than one that I was particularly drawn to or inspired by. Whilst of course geography was an important factor, my advice for my younger self would be to consider broader variables when picking a Doctorate; it can feel like the course picks you, but it's important to remember you also pick the course. Ultimately, I would not change my career path, but I think I would encourage my younger self to engage in self compassion and finding balance and life away from my career goals, attending to relationships, travel, hobbies and interests; ensuring that I did not sacrifice personal happiness and other opportunities for fulfilment along the way.

Dr Elina Telford is a clinical psychologist working for the NHS and in private practice. To listen to Linnie's podcast search for we need to talk, candid conversations about mental health.

Email from: Dr Marianne Trent

To: Dr Elina Telford

Dear Linnie,

Thank you for your wonderful submission to The Collective. I am just in awe of the tenacity and drive you showed from a young age to head towards your very specific goal. The people you work with are very fortunate to have someone so passionate about the areas in which you work.

Wishing every success with your podcast – let me know if you need a guest! And the very best of luck with your podcast,

Marianne

7

Hannah B's Story:

One Wedding, Two Babies and A Doctorate

My journey onto the doctorate was pretty straightforward however completing the doctorate was not so much!

I have always been a naturally curious person since being a child. For this reason, I think I was always supposed to find my way into Psychology. Like everyone growing up I had my share of difficulties – my parents divorced when I was 8, and then we moved from the South to the North of England. This meant starting over in a new school in the North of England hundreds of miles away from my dad. Having a "posh" southern accent meant I didn't fit in too well.

Being naturally curious and experiencing some of my own difficulties in life meant that when I discovered Psychology at A Level everything started to make sense. I started getting the answers to lots of the questions I had long held. I felt like I found where I belong – corny I know!

Hannah B's Story:

From here it became my life quest to become a Clinical Psychologist. I didn't even consider doing any other subject or career and that's not changed to this day.

My road to the holy grail aka the doctorate looks a bit like this....

- Joint honours degree in Psychology and Sociology

I was constantly told to get relevant work experience and encouraged to take up volunteer work however I never listened as I was too busy enjoying being a student. In hindsight, I should of probably listened and I often wonder if this would have changed anything?

- MSc Health Psychology

- Support Worker/Employment Coach - While completing my Master's I worked as a support worker in a mental health charity for 2 years. This also included 6 months as a part time employment coach.

- 1ˢᵗ NHS Assistant Psychologist (AP) post (1 year) was a split post across a Tertiary Psychodynamic service and Tertiary CBT service. I was the only AP in this service at the time. This was a VERY steep learning curve and a bit of a shock to the system as a first AP post. That aside I gained some incredible experience that has impacted on the type of psychologist I am today.

- 2ⁿᵈ NHS Assistant Psychologist post (2 years) was a split post in a Health Psychology department in an acute hospital. I was predominantly based within the Burns & Plastics team and did a small amount of work into a generic health psychology team. I got a wide range of experience in this post and was amongst many other APs and trainees which I found hugely beneficial. I absolutely adored this job and its where my passion for health psychology first began.

- I applied to the doctorate for the first time in the first year of this post. I applied to 4 universities and didn't get one interview offer. I was devastated. My second year in this post I applied again and received 4 interview offers. I still to this day don't really understand what happened seeing as the 1st and 2nd applications were pretty much identical as I was still the same post and hadn't done anything extra/different. The only thing I really remember really changing is the section where you have to write about yourself and instead of writing what I thought they wanted to hear (I read psy journals in my spare time), I wrote that I enjoy hanging out with friends and drinking wine. Surely the wine drinking didn't bag me my place! Seriously though I think being honest and giving a real sense of who you are and how you de-stress (even if that is a glass of wine), is much more authentic and appealing then saying what we think they want to hear. Who really reads psy journals every weekend!?

- Doctorate, yey!

Up to this point things had been pretty straight forward, however, life happened at exactly the same time I got on the doctorate, typical!

I got married 2 days before starting the course so had the most whirlwind start to the doctorate. Getting my head round my new role as a psychologist, researcher, academic, reflective practitioner, student and now wife was quite a lot to juggle. To make things even harder we decided to start a family and I became pregnant in my first year. I am a firm believer (& proof) that you don't have to put your life on hold to do the doctorate and become a Clinical Psychologist. I took a year of maternity leave and returned to the course in the cohort below. Leaving one cohort and joining another was both challenging and exciting. It meant I got to meet and learn from a whole new bunch of like-minded aspiring psychologists.

I returned to the doctorate as a first-time mummy and went straight into my CAMHS placement which took a whole new outlook being a mum. I found this placement particularly difficult being a mum and would regularly go home in tears about what I had heard and seen. I think this was mostly driven by my own anxiety about being a 'good enough' mum. When I started the doctorate, I thought my CAMHS placement was going to be my favourite, but it actually turned out to be the most difficult. Similarly, I was most fearing my older adult placement as this felt out my depth, but I actually really enjoyed this placement. I soon learnt that you shouldn't rule things out because you think you might not like them as you may be surprised!

Towards the end of my second year on the course we decided to start trying for another baby. Overall, I had a really pleasant and well supported experience of having a baby on the course (much to my surprise to what I had previously heard). Sadly, we experienced a miscarriage, but I then fell pregnant quite quickly and took another year of maternity leave. This once again meant I returned to a cohort below. I experienced three very different cohorts while on the doctorate and I think this made my experience all the richer. After dragging the doctorate out over 5 years (due to two periods of maternity) finishing the doctorate in Sept 2019 couldn't have come quick enough. I was so ready to be done! I was so proud when I graduated especially because I had experienced a lot of judgment about choosing to have two children during the course. I was regularly asked if I was mad and told I wouldn't manage it. Well, I did.

I now work part time in the NHS in a health psychology department as Psychology Lead for a Chronic Pain service and part time independently for my own business and as an

Associate for Trust Psychology/Trust Pain Management. I love being a clinical psychologist and feel extremely lucky to have been able to train to do this job. It is a really hard slog but is worth it, I promise!

Dr Hannah Barraclough is an Independent Clinical Psychologist. Find out more at www.drhannahbarraclough.com.

Email from: Dr Marianne Trent

To: Dr Hannah Barraclough

Oh Hannah!

I think you are my hero! Getting married 2 days before you started the doctorate! Wow! Did you ever get a honeymoon? I do hope so! I thought I was hardcore getting back from travelling in India 2 days before my doctorate, but you've pipped me to the post there!

I am also in awe of you being pregnant and raising babes and small people whilst in training too. Having now done this in qualified life it certainly isn't easy so more admiration coming your way too! I think that having 3 cohorts must have given you such great experiences of fostering new relationships and maintaining old ones which I am sure has paid you rich dividends at all stages of your life and career since too.

Marianne

Hannah B's Story:

Email from: Dr Hannah Barraclough

To: Dr Marianne Trent

Thanks very much for your kind words, Marianne :-) We did get a 3-week honeymoon travelling around America in the Nov/Dec. The course honoured my leave as the wedding and honeymoon were booked well in advance of even applying for the course (and I may have kept quiet about it at interview!)

I had a really pleasant experience of having babies on the course although I'm aware that not everyone finds the same. I was congratulated at the end of the course on my stoicism which I think was code for "thanks for not making a fuss and just getting on with it". Good luck with the book. Can't wait to see the final version!

Hannah

8

Hannah J's Story:

The journey never stops!

"Are you sure you want to go into a caring profession?"

My sister looked puzzled. Actually, my whole family did. Working as a psychologist, in the NHS, just wasn't part of our family narrative. I come from a family of businessmen and women. I was expected to follow the trend and get a proper job! Not this naval-gazing psychology malarkey, what even was it anyway? What did a psychologist even do? I had done 'proper jobs'. I had tried. But it just didn't feel right, and I never got the buzz from it that my parents did, I wasn't a natural business brain. I wasn't a convincing salesperson, and I couldn't understand a balance sheet. I remember flicking through the university prospectus and eyeballing the courses ... Law? No. English? No. Marketing? No. Psychology....... Hmmm, now that sounds interesting!

That was a long time ago now, almost 18 years, and back then I wouldn't have thought I would have gone on to be a clinical psychologist, no chance! I had a few personal struggles at university, it was a very challenging period, and I had some very dark times. I am sure this was part of the reason I ended up on this career path, and doing what I do, I'm comfortable with people's struggles and pain, been there done that, I guess. For a long time, I didn't really know much about what a clinical psychologist was or did. I remember watching psychologists in films and on TV programmes and they always seemed really together and like nothing ever unsettled them. I remember thinking 'I want to be like that!'. Of course, 9 years post training, I am still working on being like one of them.

I was accepted onto the Clinical Psychology Doctorate without the reams and reams of 'relevant' experience that has become the expectation nowadays. I point this out not to gloat but to highlight that -

1) It is possible to be accepted onto training without having worked in every Assistant Psychologist (AP)/research assistant (RA)/honorary/dogsbody post going

2) experience is about quality not quantity to a degree

3) the application process is, in my opinion, a bit of a lottery

I will outline my experience before training as I know it can feel helpful to some, but each person's journey should be unique to them rather than a tick box experience. After my bachelor's degree I undertook a Master's in Health Psychology. I went on to be a research assistant and then an Assistant Psychologist. Alongside this I did some voluntary work on a crisis line and a few things when I was at university, volunteering as a research interviewer and on a hospice reception. A few hours a week volunteering was enough to gain some good experience whilst allowing time for other non-psychology related things and having a life. Although it wasn't a huge amount of experience, I felt like I had taken a lot from each different role.

Remember you can draw experience from pretty much anywhere as every situation can teach you something about yourself/others/ the world. Having now been on the other side of the application process as a qualified psychologist, this is what I think stands out on people's application forms and on interview day:

Has this person genuinely taken something from their experiences?

Of course, you are going to need some experience that relates directly to this profession, but you are likely to have had a long life before getting to this stage:

What reflections have you made about things you have gone through?

What went well and not what so well? What has happened that has helped develop your resilience?

We work with people, have you ever worked with people before (of course you have!) What was that like? What people skills have you got?

The jobs I had before I started on the clinical psychology hamster wheel taught me so much and really 'built character' (as my northern mother would tell me when I begrudgingly took on a job at a sauce factory cleaning spillages). I have never learnt as many skills in conflict resolution, de-escalation techniques, safety and boundaries as when I was a bartender in a particular dodgy club in run down area of Manchester. Life experience really does help so much in this sort of job and we all have that.

I enjoyed training but I think I am in the minority. I tried to keep in mind that at the end of everything, it is just a job. It is not life and death; much bigger things will happen. Becoming a clinical psychologist can quickly become an obsession, especially as it tends to attract quite driven people who expect a lot from themselves. Be aware that it can be an anti-climax when you finally get to training if you have sacrificed a lot for it. Hold onto the idea of training with a loose grip and have a backup plan in my mind. What would we say to our clients if they were sacrificing so much for a job and putting all their eggs in one basket? Consider what it is about this role that aligns with your values and if there is another career path that would allow you to live to these. I know this is not what people want to hear but the more you can keep a healthy perspective on your journey the better.

I have been a qualified psychologist for 9 years now. I have worked in both mental health and physical health. I enjoy my work very much. There are parts of it that are frustrating, but this is a job like no other and no day is the same which I love. Sometimes I do wish I had done something that allowed me to 'switch off' a bit more, as this can be a very stressful job at times, especially when you have your own 'stuff' going on. But the benefits outweigh the costs for me. My favourite part of the role is that within the right service you can use so many different skills and the job can be really varied. We also get to meet some incredible people who survive so much, I am often so humbled by my clients and their journeys. They demonstrate to me how resilient human beings are and I find that inspiring. Last year, my little family were thrown a curve ball and it shook us deeply. One thing that helped me keep going was remembering the people who sit across from me and how they have come through some of the most traumatic situations still in one piece. It was my comforting thought during such a difficult time and helped me to muddle through.

For anyone about to embark on this career path, or if you are already in the middle of it, my advice would be: be kind to yourself, enjoy the journey as it never stops, keep it in perspective and hang out with people who have nothing to do with psychology to help keep it real!

Good luck!

Dr Hannah Jackson is a Clinical Psychologist; email her on hjackson85@outlook.com.

Hannah J's Story:

9

Sanjeet's Story:

"But what is your formulation?"

What I wish I had told myself at the start of my journey to becoming a clinical psychologist, is to relax. The end goal is not getting on the course. In fact, your skills are constantly developing, your role is constantly changing, and you may choose to do further training and specialise in an area after the Clinical Psychology Doctorate. As I did. Let me tell you a little about me...

I was fortunate to have the opportunity to be on an undergraduate course at Aston University, where I had the option of doing a sandwich year. Through this I was offered a post as an honorary Assistant Psychologist within a Child Psychology team. This in turn supported my applications for Assistant Psychologist posts after graduating. Gosh, graduation itself turned out to be stressful. Prior to my final year exams, nationally, university lecturers were on a strike. This affected exams being written, dates for exams and marking. Consequently, our results day kept getting delayed and no one knew when we would find out our results. I continued applying for Assistant Psychologist posts but had no grade to put down.

It was no surprise that I didn't receive any interview offers during that time. We eventually got a date for results day... 28th June. How do I remember this date so many years on? The day before was my mum's birthday. I was popping out to pick up a takeaway. Just as I left the house, one of my best friends called... "Sanj... you have a 2:1!" Huh? How?! We were not supposed to find out until the next day! The results had already been posted online! Mum's dinner got a little bit delayed that evening and ended up being a double celebration!

I applied for the DClin for three consecutive years, with applications for assistant posts in between. Three years of hearing "you have everything we are looking for, but we gave the job to someone with more experience in this area". One day I told myself, "Relax, the interviews are just conversations, they just want to get to know me, and if I don't get offered the post/place, maybe it is not the best place for me". A switch flipped. Anxiety levels decreased and my interview performance changed. Maybe it was just a coincidence that I was offered a place on the Shropshire & Staffordshire course that year.

One of the things that stands out for me when I think back to preparing for interviews, was not feeling confident in knowing what a formulation was. I asked colleagues "what is formulation?" and I was signposted to literature that I went away and read. And then it happened. In an interview, we were given a vignette, an Overhead Projector Sheet (who remembers those??), and time to prepare a formulation. I thought I did pretty well, drawing out the 5Ps, and discussing it in front of the panel... and then the question came "But what is your formulation?" What had I been discussing all this time?? What I would have benefited from as an assistant was sitting down with someone and formulating with them, to help to enhance my understanding.

The actual DClin training went as expected... placements, teaching, assignments, thesis, and trying to balance it all while living life. There were a few losses and traumatic events that occurred during my training, which continued to remind me of the importance of playing hard as well as working hard.

Thesis time proved to be tricky for me, and in fact I wrote all about it for the Clinical Psychology Forum (check out the January 2014 publication). Not enough participants, a broken thumb, laptop died and nearly lost everything. And the viva. I waited for over an hour before my viva and I could see the external marker through the window waving her arms around. What was she saying? I passed with minor modifications, which amazingly only took me a couple of hours to amend one afternoon, to later be told casually by one of the lecturers, "you were very close to failing". Mind-boggling! How could I be so close to failing, but then pass with such minor modifications that were resolved in such a short amount of time? The responses that I gave to questions asked in my viva must have been pretty comprehensive to turn that result around. Whatever, I passed! Celebration time!

I had been applying for jobs from April of my final year. I was beginning to lose hope (especially with all the palaver around thesis time), and then I was offered a job in a Child and Adolescent Mental Health Service (CAMHS). There were a few of us that started at the same time, all having completed training that year. It was nice having this peer support and learning our new roles together.

I love working with children and families, supporting them alongside schools, and other professionals and agencies. I am passionate about being creative with the children I work with. Just to give a few examples of my therapeutic work:

- using a 12-year-old girl's love of rollercoasters to design a rollercoaster that represents her life

- using a 10-year-old boy's amazing drawing skills to create comic strips in PTSD work

- using a 17-year-old's experience of multiple personalities to help them understand how they were experiencing emotions...

There are many, many more. I have moved on from my first post after qualifying, and although I work with individuals across the life span, I still mainly work with children and young people (CYP) in a CBT pathway. However, I now have the opportunity to apply my creative skills to online therapies (I started this role pre-Covid-19).

A year after completing the DClin, I started training again. That was just the start - I had caught the learning bug! It was actually nice going back to formal learning. Since finishing Clinical Psychology training, I have completed a Postgraduate Diploma in Evidence-Based Treatments for children and young people (CYP) (Cognitive Behavioural Therapy (CBT)) and a Postgraduate Certificate in Supervision. I have been awarded accreditation from the British Association for Behavioural and Cognitive Psychotherapies (BABCP) as a CBT psychotherapist and supervisor. I have also completed all three parts of Eye Movement Desensitisation and Reprocessing (EMDR) training. Alongside my clinical work, I have been a tutor and supervisor on Children and Young People's Improving Access to Psychological Therapies (CYP IAPT) and IAPT training and have contributed to teaching on Clinical Psychology Doctoral courses. One experience that I found particularly rewarding was supervising clinical psychology trainees on a training course in Myanmar remotely. Knowing that I was indirectly involved in the care of children receiving treatment for cancer quite far away from home felt pretty powerful.

As I have briefly mentioned, training for me does not come without its challenges. Halfway through the Supervisor training, I was diagnosed with breast cancer. I did not want the course to go unfinished, so I made sure all assignments and my portfolio were submitted prior to starting my treatment. One year later, treatment was over and I had my first "all clear"... forget the night sweats from treatment, the sweats were coming under graduation robes in the middle of a heatwave! My number one piece of advice? It sounds so cliché, but life is short. Do whatever makes you happy- personally and professionally.

My experience of training and the interview process for DClin (and THAT question- "But what is your formulation?") has definitely shaped how I offer placements and provide supervision for Assistant Psychologists and trainee psychologists. I am keen to support skills development as a clinical psychologist and provide supervisees with an understanding of various aspects of the role and processes. And so, I think it is invaluable for supervisees to not only shadow, but experience and participate in as much as they can with colleagues in clinical psychology and also other professions or reflect on observations at a later time whether in supervision or with colleagues.

Before signing off, I would like to share my top tips for applying for the DClin.

1. Shadow and participate in as much as you can, and if possible, as many sessions as you can. It would be great if you could see a case through from start to end, and whether there are any interventions that you can deliver with supervision.

2. Practice doing formulations or attend formulation meetings.

3. Practice writing case notes and letters and get feedback on this.

4. Ask a clinical psychologist about a week in their diary, rather than a typical day. Clinical psychologists have different hats. Although days/weeks may look similar, each day, meeting, client or session can be very different.

5. Watch Disney films. Want to understand how fears can lead to safety behaviours? *Frozen!* Interested in

cavemen and survival? *The Croods!* Need a reminder of living life? *Soul![14]*

I should add, please do not feel pressure to know everything for the DClin interviews. The whole point of training is to learn. If you already know everything, what is the point in training further? In an interview for a qualified post, I was asked how I would implement NICE guidance for a specific disorder (it was a generic post). I started answering, wondering how I could give an answer that made me look like I was familiar with it... then I stopped and said "well, first I would read the guidance". Instantly, I felt more relaxed, and my response flowed more easily.

In a nutshell, that is my story. As I said at the start, my skills are constantly developing, I am learning new skills, and my role continues to change. Although it has its challenges, I love the work that I do, and I feel grateful that I am in a position to provide psychological support to those who are seeking it. I hope sharing my journey with you has helped you with yours, and I wish you the very best for your path. Good luck!

Dr Sanjeet Ghataore is a clinical psychologist working for Healios, providing innovative digital mental health care for children and young people.

---

[14]Editorial note: A review of this was done for the British Psychological Society's magazine, The Psychologist - see
https://thepsychologist.bps.org.uk/soul-searching-and-simply-living

Email from: Dr Marianne Trent

To: Dr Sanjeet Ghataore

Hi Sanjeet,

Thanks so much for your submission to The Collective.

You absolutely take everything in your stride and I'm so pleased that your cancer diagnosis had a happy outcome.

I think you're incredibly inspiring and thank you for including the examples of how you create bespoke and meaningful interventions for the children and young people who are lucky enough to have you in their world.

Keep being you and thanks for your behind the scenes support, encouragement and enthusiasm for the project, it's been invaluable. Very much looking forward to that cup of tea soon!

Marianne

10

Hari's Story:

Prejudice and Discrimination

I have stumbled my way into becoming a Clinical Psychologist in Training. This is not a normative account of one's journey into this profession, but a blunt reflection of how traumatic experiences have supported my growth into becoming the psychologist I am today and strive to become. Your experiences are yours; that is what makes you unique. Take care of yourself when reading this account.

I was raised on a council estate in Bulwell in Nottingham by parents who love me dearly. In the '90s, we were the only Indian family living in Bulwell, which had an emphasised population of White people teetering on stereotypes; low socio-economic scale, high teenage pregnancy, school dropouts and lack of employment, to name a few. Being the only Brown person in the town and at school who also identified as religiously Hindu meant that we were different from the norm. My first encounter with racism was in the second-to-last year of infant's school. We were sat on the floor, and as the teacher called our names, we were allowed to go and sit in our designated seats at the tables. My name was called, and as I steadily walked to the front, I was called a 'Paki' by a Black boy in front of the teacher; sadly, she remained silent, and life carried on. Being that young, however, I could not comprehend the magnitude of what that word meant. The issue remains that being the only Brown Hindu child in the school, and with one peer having already started this with no deterrence, provided ample grounds for further racist taunts by other peers. I can still remember my mum taking me to meetings with the principal each time an incident occurred, to no avail. I learnt that I was different from that age, and within the norms of what is acceptable, I sadly was not.

Most reminisce about their childhood and adolescence, at secondary school and college, with high degrees of sentiment and emotion. Usually, one's adolescence provides ample opportunities to push boundaries and question authority, learn about social norms from peers and spend time with them, flouting rules and regulations, and just being carefree. Infrequently, we would see the effects of prejudice and discrimination. Still, due to its infrequent nature, it seemed to be less poignant. Our house is on the corner of the estate facing a vacant car park. The big white naked wall became an open goal for the young people in the neighbourhood playing football. The concern was that each time that ball hit the wall of our house, it would replicate the sound of thunder as it shook the very foundations of the house. Sadly, highlighting the effect of this to the young people catalysed an aggravation of targeted incidents. Every day we would be taunted in the streets, our windows smashed, and our fence kicked in. There are two incidents that I still have flashbacks of. The first, it was 22:32, and I stood looking out of the window as I heard a noise. As I looked out the window, I saw a man run across our front yard with a boulder the same size as my head as he threw it at the window. My eyes watched it as it pierced the window - thank goodness for double glazed windows. The second, I was revising for a GCSE physics exam, and it had reached 02:30 in the morning. I heard a bang outside and rushed to the window to see what was happening. I witnessed more than five men run into our garden to kick our fence, and then they dispersed – the next day, the policeman said they were intoxicated; they weren't. These incidents became normal.

Despite being expected to do well in my GCSE's, I didn't. I wanted to do sciences at college but was declined at enrolment because my grades were poor; I was one mark off the required grade. I arranged a meeting with the associate principal. Our community police officer came with me to support my narrative of the difficulties we were facing. They allowed me to enrol if I could prove my worth by attending night school to improve my grade. I enrolled at night school for over six months and later enrolled at college. Despite this attempt at proving my worth, I was informed I had to achieve grades higher than a 'C' to remain at the college. Sadly, my first results of three U's and an E did not seem so inspiring. I managed to acquire DEE in my first year of A Levels, which was predominantly below par of requirements. By talking to a drama teacher and providing the narrative of my experiences, I remained at the college. Throughout my two years at college, the attacks on the house worsened. We spent every night awaiting the next incident. My dad would work nightshifts, so it would just be my mum and me at night, when the incidents were likely to occur, which also affects my ability to sleep to this day. I memorised the questions asked by 999 operatives. During incidents, this would theoretically allow the police to arrive sooner, yet the perpetrators would have left by the time they would arrive. With the effects of our environment at the time, how was I supposed to concentrate on my A-Levels?

My tutor at college became concerned and referred me to the college counsellor. At one point, she was highly worried about me and made an appointment at the GP. The GP diagnosed me with stress and sent me to Counselling in the city, which I attended for two years. In a last-minute attempt to pass my A Levels, I sought tuition in biology, psychology, and philosophy and achieved CDE. I trawled through the Clearing website to be accepted at the University of Northampton to study Psychology and Criminology; I wanted to understand why people do bad things to others.

I achieved a first-class honours in my undergraduate degree. During my time at university, I decided to leave my religious faith, started my own society to support students that might find themselves in the predicament of leaving their religious faith, and joined the national student organisation for this too. I was later elected as President of Humanist Students and provided the title of President Emeritus thereafter. Moreover, I volunteered at the medium secure hospital and was also employed as a healthcare assistant, in addition to working in retail at the weekend.

Near the end of my degree, I applied for the MSc in Forensic and Criminological Psychology at the University of Nottingham. I was placed on the reserve list for an interview. A day before the interview, I was asked if I would attend. I was later accepted onto the course. During my MSc, I worked with organisations in understanding the plight of people who leave their religious faith. Normatively, people who leave their religious faith are open to being abused by the people they love; my experience appears to be an anomaly as my family still love me. This motivated me to research this issue with a worldwide population of hidden victims; the study was later published in 2020.

Moreover, to gain experience within applied psychology, I would consistently ask every guest lecturer whether they knew of anyone who could provide voluntary experience. After numerous attempts, I succeeded. A guest lecturer gave me the contact details of a forensic psychologist at a low secure hospital. I worked as an honorary for a year-and-a-half and was later employed for over two years. Thereafter, I worked at a children's home for boys with problematic sexual behaviours.

I applied for the Doctorate in Clinical Psychology twice; the first attempt was a spectacular failure. I was provided with one poignant piece of advice. I was told that "they only know you by what you have written. Reflect and tell them what makes you unique". So, I did just that. I reflected on my experiences and how they have shaped me to become the psychologist I am. I spoke candidly about being diagnosed with ADHD to watching videos of golden retriever puppies as a coping strategy. I spoke about my activism work, my publication, and the various talks given on YouTube. Reading that application gave them an insight into who I am. I received an offer to interview for one programme. Sadly, as my long-term partner left me abruptly, I had a mental health breakdown at the start of March 2020. I couldn't eat, drink or sleep out of pure sadness; I felt the depths of despair that our clients report feeling. I paid for therapy more times than I can remember and continue to work through my difficulties. As such, I was in no state to attend a Doctorate interview, and it showed. The University of Liverpool emailed me thereafter to say I was 10th on the reserve list for an interview. I thanked them for considering me and was later accepted for an interview. Following this, I was placed 16th on the reserve list for a place. I called the programme and asked an administrator what the chances of securing a place would be. I was informed it would be unlikely and alternatively accepted a job instead. After a few weeks, Health Education England increased places by 25% on Doctoral programmes, and I jumped from 16th to 3rd. That week on Thursday, I was offered a place.

My journey into Clinical Psychology was not planned. I feel hypocritical to provide anyone with advice on how to get the magic Willy Wonka ticket of acceptance into Clinical Psychology. My journey so far has taught me how to live with failure, make mistakes and how to appreciate those experiences for what they are. They have given me a unique insight into the distress, fear, and depths of sadness many of our clients may feel. I thank those perpetrators for such an experience. Sadly, I live with the remnants of my experiences; it seems that my brain may have adapted itself with somatic markers to detect threats in a hypersensitive manner. I constantly live in battle with a brain that infers doubt into my existence each day. This account is not known widely; however, my experiences facilitate my critical stance of cognitive therapies that deem the individual at fault. My account provides an example of how distal factors have impeded me at each point. More must be done to challenge the norm of believing that the person is at fault when in actuality, environmental factors are.

Email from: Dr Marianne Trent

To: Hari

*Hari, you and I first crossed paths in May 2020 on LinkedIn of all places! I recall that what stopped me in my scrolling tracks was your lovely face because someone had taken a new photo of you, and you'd used it when you were talking about your research into working with the Apostate population. I commented on your post to say that I'd never heard of the word 'apostate' but that I was going to read your research and come back to you! Well, it ended up in us having a Zoom chat about your incredibly important work and I would urge everyone to read it or listen to our chat about it on my YouTube channel. From that first chat I saw just what a unique, special and talented person you are. I was confident that you were ready for training and that you would get onto training that year. You were less sure, but I just felt that you were **absolutely** ready, and were doing such important work that the world needed to know you! I also had no idea about the background to your experiences or that you had been so heartbroken so recently before we met. I am so lucky to have you in my world and in this book, I will watch your development as a Trainee Clinical Psychologist and beyond with eager enthusiasm.*

Here anytime,

Marianne

11

Jess' Story:

Reflections on my journey to becoming a Clinical Psychologist

I sometimes tell people that I became a Clinical Psychologist due to an intractable stubborn streak; when I was choosing my A Level subjects, aged 15, each pupil in my year had a "meeting" with our headmistress to discuss our possible choices. I had already made my decision; I was opting for Biology, Chemistry, and Religious Studies because I'd done them at GCSE, enjoyed them, and was good at them. My fourth choice was Psychology, because it sounded interesting, and I thought that was a good basis for choosing a subject I'd have to spend two years studying. My headmistress took exception to this, suggesting that as I had two sciences and a humanity, I ought to choose Physics – "a proper science" – or at the very least, Maths, as my final option. I, in turn, took exception to her trying to change my mind, and doubled down on Psychology as my fourth subject. This turned out to be a good choice – I did indeed enjoy my two years of A Level Psychology.

Not long after starting my A Levels, I applied to study Psychology for my undergraduate degree, thinking that a career in Clinical Psychology sounded interesting and rewarding. I knew that I wanted to help people and was interested in the scientist-practitioner model; that was about as much thought as I had given it. It was also the only option I was really aware of for a career in Psychology... Somewhere in the three-year degree course, I lost my direction a little - I think it was a combination of being told repeatedly how competitive it is to get onto training (true, but not a reason not to try!) as well as developing interest in other areas of Psychology as I learnt more about them. Either way, at the end of my degree in 2012, I applied for a Master's course in Applied Cognitive Neuroscience at the same university.

I loved my Master's; I found it immensely interesting and enjoyed all of the modules. I wondered for a while about doing a PhD in something related to Neuroscience and/or Psychology, but never quite found anything that ticked all the boxes for me. Eventually, and perhaps inevitably, I came back to the idea of Clinical Psychology - I was working in a temporary job in retail after my Master's, but I moved to a role in the dementia unit of a local care home, to try to gain some more "clinical" experience. I started volunteering with a charity for adults with acquired brain injury (ABI), which was a hugely valuable experience for me. And I began applying for the much-coveted Assistant Psychologist posts.

I didn't keep track of my applications, so I don't know for certain how many I applied for, but I'd estimate it was above 100. Plenty of these were unsuccessful, but I did also get a good number of interviews. I went to interview after interview, up and down the country (literally from Carlisle to Cambridge) and got similar feedback from most - they had liked me, I had interviewed well, I would probably be good at the job... but they had chosen someone with more experience. This frustrated me no end. To my mind, there was nothing I could do about other people's experience, and so this was not helpful feedback. I wanted to know what I could improve on for future interviews, and "another candidate had more experience in the area" did not give me that information. Eventually, through sheer persistence (did I mention my stubborn streak?), I was successful in getting an honorary Assistant Psychologist post in a local Child & Adolescent Mental Health Service (CAMHS) team. I started working in their Tier 4 inpatient unit one day per week, alongside my care work in the dementia unit and my volunteering with the ABI charity. Days off became a thing of the past!

I have to recognise my immense privilege in being able to do this – although my working-class family were far from well-off, I was able to live with my parents and pay minimal rent whilst working all of these jobs for quite a low wage (care work is barely above minimum wage, despite the skill and dedication it requires, and of course voluntary and honorary posts do not pay at all). My health was also a privilege – I was young and relatively fit, and could just about sustain working 13 days straight, with every other Sunday as my only day off. I know that many people are not so fortunate, and many of those people would make excellent Clinical Psychologists.

Alongside all of this, I continued to apply for Assistant Psychologist roles. Eventually, I dropped lucky – a role came up in a local Physical Health Psychology team and I was successful. I started that post in July 2016, almost three years after completing my Master's. It had been a long road, and I was absolutely thrilled to finally have taken the next step towards becoming a Clinical Psychologist. I loved that job; the team I worked in was brilliant, full of incredibly skilled and knowledgeable clinicians, and I found that I loved the clinical area too. We had two fab Trainee Clinical Psychologist on placement within the team who encouraged me to apply to the Clinical Psychology doctorate, although I did not necessarily think I was ready. In the end, I decided to submit a "practice" application – so that I'd know what the application form looked like, and maybe even get an interview for some practice and feedback. I planned that the next year would be my first "proper" application, and this was just a dummy run.

I was lucky to get an interview and hugely surprised when they offered me a place! I had not been expecting this and panicked a little that my less-than-one-year of experience as an Assistant Psychologist would not be "enough" to see me through training. I was reassured a little to learn that several others in my cohort had similar amounts of experience, and some had even less. Nonetheless, I turned up to our first day of training in September 2017, utterly convinced that I'd be told there had been some kind of mistake. I know I was not the only one with this particular fear, and I am happy to report that it turned out to be unfounded...

Clinical training was definitely a steep learning curve for me. The placements themselves were challenging but I rarely felt out of my depth. The academic aspects, too, were harder than anything I'd done before, but they did feel manageable – the real struggle for me was managing the placements *alongside* the academic work whilst still having time for myself, which I knew was essential for my mental health and wellbeing. This balance became increasingly difficult to manage, and then in March 2020, midway through my final year of training, COVID struck. I went from juggling a busy and rewarding placement (back with the Physical Health Psychology team I had been an Assistant with!) and the challenges of thesis, to working from home full-time.

Already slightly behind schedule, my thesis project was derailed by COVID-19 and I lost several months' worth of work as I had to re-design my project and more or less start over. My placement continued remotely, working with clients by phone and video link – the clinical placements had always got me through the tougher parts of the course, and I felt that I had lost some of that now that I couldn't even sit in a room with the people I was working with. The last six months of training were a massive uphill battle for me, and it seemed never-ending. I finished the course at the end of August 2020 with my thesis outstanding and spent the next six months working full-time in a qualified role without being qualified, alongside trying to finish my thesis. Days off became a thing of the past once again, and my health did begin to suffer as a result of the stress.

Finally, by the end of March 2021 I had finished my thesis, passed my viva, and submitted my amendments which were thankfully accepted. I don't think I have ever felt such relief! I had finally reached the point I had been working towards for nearly 12 years and could relax a little into a Qualified Clinical Psychologist post where my evenings and weekends were once again my own. I didn't know what to do with them at first; I was just giddy with the possibilities. As it happened, my partner and I bought our first house together the day after my amendments were submitted, so we spent quite a lot of my new-found free time working on the house... (I found myself asking, "Why am I like this?" quite a lot, those first few weeks!)

I am now four months post-completion of my thesis and coming up to a year post-completion of the rest of the course. I'm working in that same Physical Health Psychology team. My role now is within the Neuropsychology service which is a varied and incredibly interesting area of clinical practice. I use my clinical skills daily to support people with a variety of neurological conditions including Multiple Sclerosis, Stroke, Epilepsy, Parkinson's disease and more. I find the work fascinating and rewarding and am passionate about the role of Psychology within physical health conditions.

My top three pieces of advice to anyone interested in a career as a Clinical Psychologist would be:

1) Persevere; the journey is rarely straightforward, but the path that you take will likely make you a better Clinical Psychologist in the long run. For example, I learnt skills in care work that were not taught in my clinical training, and yet they are invaluable to me in my daily work.

2) Try to get as much varied, relevant experience as you can – voluntary or paid – during your degree. I do think that part of my struggle to get an Assistant post was due to having very little relevant experience during my time at university. I'd suggest checking out relevant charities, your university's Nightline or similar, part-time care or support work, research work, voluntary opportunities at your local hospital, and mentoring.

3) Finally (and I realise this is far easier said than done) try not to take rejections personally; Clinical Psychology *is* a hugely competitive career path and it is almost inevitable that you will be unsuccessful in applying for jobs, training places, or more likely both. This is not because you aren't cut out for the job, or they didn't think you were good enough; it is often purely because there are *so many* brilliant candidates that someone does have to end up disappointed. Try to see these let-downs as learning opportunities and reflection points; think about what went well, as well as what you can improve next time, and what your next step should be.

The other side of this is that there are, of course, many other careers which can be equally rewarding, if for whatever reason Clinical Psychology doesn't work out for you. Some people do reach their limit with the process and that is okay – you can do just as important a job in lots of other ways, whether that is in an unrelated field, through voluntary work alongside an unrelated paid role, or through related professions (mental health nurse, CBT therapist, and social worker are just some that spring to mind). At the end of the day, Clinical Psychology is just a job. Yes, it is a hugely rewarding job and one that I am immensely passionate about and proud to do. But it is still just a job and there are plenty of other options – as much as we can put it on a pedestal at times, it is not the be-all and end-all.

Dr Jess Smith is a Clinical Psychologist working in a Physical Health Psychology team in Cumbria.

Email from: Dr Marianne Trent

To: Dr Jess Smith

Dear Jess,

Thanks for your wonderfully balanced and compassionate submission.

I'm so pleased that you stuck at it and it definitely feels like a race that we have no idea if there will even be a finish line for us and yet, still, we want to take part!

I hope that you are able to relax into your new home and do some stuff you enjoy now that you have the benefit of time off!

Take care of you and thanks again,

Marianne

12

Joey-Claire's Story:

I just love Clinical Psychology!

My journey into Clinical Psychology started very young. You could say that I've always been a bit of a deep thinker; a true Virgo - introverted and analytical. People have always described me as very calm and 'quietly confident'. I had a good childhood in many respects; I grew up in Nottinghamshire in the Ashfield district, which has a large ex-mining community. In fact, both my sets of grandfathers were miners, and my dad even had a stint at mining before eventually training to be in the Fire Brigade.

My mum was from a working class background too and worked in a chemist's shop until she finally got into a position where she could do her nurse training. Although she had always wanted to be a general nurse, she took the 'psychiatric nursing' route because it was funded, and she was newly married with two young children at the time. I suppose this is what sparked my interest in mental health issues, as I'd always find it interesting to listen to her stories about her patients and I'd always be wondering 'what makes a person end up with these problems'.

119

Back then in the 80's, however, the medical model was dominant, and the 'Schizophrenia' diagnosis was *en vogue*. So, I didn't really get any satisfying answers to my wonderings.

And then there was *'Casey'*, my best friend in secondary school - Matthew Holland Comprehensive – though it's long changed its name. Well, let's just say school wasn't really a learning opportunity for me. Being just an 'average' student in most subjects, and being so quiet, I'd often get missed by the teachers, as they focused their efforts on trying to calm down the 'bad kids'. I think I came across as not very bright because I almost wasn't even there (I think I must have been dissociating quite a bit during my teenage years!), so I got placed in 'set 3' (out of six) for most things, and even 'set 4' in maths. Well, this just perpetuated the problem as a lot of unruly kids get placed in these sets. So, it's almost as though your opportunity to progress is stilted by being in a crap set, even before they have started trying to attempt to teach you something!

Anyway, I digress. *Casey* and I became best friends at 13. We were typical 90's early teens. Our lunch often consisted of a trip to 'Joan's ice cream van to purge on as many sweets as 50p could get you. Or on a good day, you could go to Kwik Save's café and go halves on a ham and pineapple pizza. We did our fair share of naughty things, nicking some sweets from the local shops, drinking cider on 'the hills, progressing on to a bit of weed smoking down the woods.

I remember being intrigued by *Casey's* situation, as her mum was so strange to me, I had to try and figure it out in my head. See; *Casey's* mum did have a schizophrenia diagnosis. I doubt she'd receive the same diagnosis these days; from what *Casey* said, her mum developed psychosis following the birth of *Casey*, her second child and before that there had been some trauma involving a motorcycle accident prior to this. I doubt any of this had been considered in her diagnosis or treatment, however.

She was medicated up to the hilt and every time I saw her, she presented as an old lady with dementia rather than a 40-something woman who'd had a breakdown following some stressful life experiences.

I can't say we didn't use this to our advantage, sending her down to the local shop to pick up fags and booze for us on a Friday night. But if you stopped to think about it, it was sad, sad for her and sad for *Casey,* who'd effectively lost her mum, never to recover from this 'mental illness'. So, then my curiosity was really sparked. What can I say, people just interested me! Of course, at the time, I'd never even heard of psychology, only going on to choose it at A Level because I didn't really enjoy any of the traditional more 'mainstream' subjects, like maths, science, history etc.

Well even though I loved psychology A Level, I didn't go on to do my BSc (Hons) in Psychology until some years later, having a stint at office work and living abroad doing waitressing for a bit, before I decided I'd better get serious about something.

Fast forward 10 years and I'd done it all, the BSc, the MSc, and the Doctorate. The volunteering, the honorary Assistant posts, the research posts, the shadowing; everything I could do to get there. I remember someone once saying to me, if you want it enough, it will happen, and it did.

But don't get me wrong, it didn't come easy. You go through the whole range of emotions on this journey, from frustration to envy, disappointment, hope, exhilaration and back again. Clinical Psychology training pushes you to your limit and you become a master at managing your own anxiety (this is what Clinical Psychology training was to me in a nutshell!).

And I often wonder if it was worth it. Because the jobs at the other side of training aren't the fantasy I'd imagined. Working in NHS mental health services will also take you to your limits;

there are no fancy offices with your name on the door. It's hot desking, it's over-working, it's managing four year waiting lists in the service. It's stressful and it takes your energy until you feel you have nothing left to give. But I love it. I love learning about people, I love helping others and I like to confirm that things and people can change for the better. It sounds like the ultimate cliché', but for me, it's true.

So, I'd like people to know that Clinical Psychologists come from a whole range of backgrounds, some of us even went to comprehensive school, and old polytechnics, like my beloved Nottingham Trent. But whatever our background, we are just people, people with the experience of being people, who are using this to empathise and support others to be the best versions of themselves. I remember being told never to say this on a DClinPsy course interview, but I'll say it now; I just love Clinical Psychology!

Email from: Dr Marianne Trent

To: Dr Joey-Claire

Hi Joey-Claire,

Thanks for taking the time to write your story for us. It sounds like you and 'Casey' had gone through some very important moments together.

I'm so pleased you're in love with our profession, it really does feel like the best thing in the world to be paid for what we love. It's also very important to highlight that it was worth the access route and that you were able to break down what might have been barriers to your accessing the profession to get to be where you wanted to. I'm confident that many people reading your account will find it very heartening indeed.

Thanks again,

Marianne

13

Becky's Story:

"Pizza tastes good regardless of your job title."

Dear Reader, I've wrestled with what to write to you for this Collective, in the same way as I find it difficult to marry up the authenticity of my own experiences with offering encouragement to the prospective Clinical Psychologists that I encounter in my day job.

Before telling you about my journey to qualifying as a Clinical Psychologist, I'd like to share this quote, entitled "Pizza", which I feel encapsulates some of my ambivalence about how I got to where I am:

> *The sky isn't more beautiful if you have perfect skin. Music doesn't sound more interesting if you have a six-pack. Dogs aren't better company if you're famous. Pizza tastes good regardless of your job title. The best of life exists beyond the things we are encouraged to crave.* (Haig, 2021, p. 51).

In today's language, it could be said that I experienced at least five Adverse Childhood Experiences (ACEs) as I was growing up (four or more ACEs are associated with significantly poorer mental and physical health outcomes; see e.g. Zarse et al., 2019, for a review). While I acknowledge my privilege in other areas of my life, these challenges inevitably left an enduring mark on my mental health, my attachments, and my relationship with achievement and perceived failure. For these reasons, it is perhaps not surprising that I chose Clinical Psychology as a profession.

For my undergraduate degree, I tried, unsuccessfully, to get into Medicine, with the aim of working in Psychiatry. Psychology was my 'back up' subject but in truth, I don't think I knew enough about either profession to make an informed choice. I attended careers talks to learn that getting into Clinical Psychology was a hugely competitive process. Although I don't like to admit it, if anything, this may have been part of the appeal for me. Getting onto Clinical Psychology training became my ultimate goal.

Friends and family would question my hours of voluntary work, minimum wage care work roles and the distinct lack of hobbies I had during and after my undergraduate degree. I justified this in the name of getting relevant experience, in order to get onto training. Looking back, the relational aspects of these roles was my meaningful activity. I was so focused on my goal; I wasn't able to fully embrace the enjoyment I got from arts and crafts on residential holidays for children with additional care needs. A 15-minute visit to assist an older person living alone to get into bed was a positive social interaction for us both – and the stories I heard!

In the name of getting onto training, I moved all over the UK. I worked in a prison, running CBT-based offending behaviour groups before moving into NHS Assistant Psychologist roles in a forensic mental health service, and services for older people.

Becky's Story:

What I learnt from these roles professionally is that we all want to feel understood and if it feels safe enough, people will tell it like it is. What I learnt personally is that it is not worth sacrificing your own health for a job.

As an Assistant Psychologist, I had a warm, empathic supervisor, from whom I learnt what I believe this profession is all about (spoiler alert – clinical work is only one part of it). She was invested in my progression and development. She taught me to hold more reasonable expectations for myself and that there will always be more work to do. Within the appropriate boundaries of a working relationship, she may have been my first experience of a secure attachment figure. In narrative therapy, there is a concept known as our 'club of life' (White, 1997). In this metaphorical club are the people who have shaped our experiences, helped us understand ourselves and made a positive difference to our lives. We channel the concept of these people, their values and their opinions to our future challenges. Among a number of other strong female role models, I have been lucky enough to have in my life, that supervisor remains in my club of life today. Who is in your club of life? What would they say about the journey you're on?

Anxiety, anticipation, tears. Interviews, reserve lists, rejection followed by rejection. After four applications in five years, I finally achieved my goal of getting onto training. Right, then I actually had to do the training.

Full of enthusiasm, my first year was OK, albeit a bit of a culture shock. I found the learning and conversations intellectually stimulating. Generally, my clinical placements were supportive and rewarding, and supervision was a real strength of these roles. Now, I feel well rounded for the variety of clinical work and placements I did but essentially changing jobs every six months was a whirlwind. I was extremely worried about what my placement with children and young people would elicit for me.

For my own mental health, I wouldn't choose to work in this area now, but the placement went much better than I thought it would.

As I continued to progress through the course, the feeling of being constantly evaluated, rarely feeling competent and often feeling guilty whenever I wasn't doing University work or relevant reading became too much. Before training, I think I would have gladly accepted a place even if I'd been told I would have no annual leave at all. While this was not the case, I began to resent not being able to go away for a long weekend without a lot of late nights, prior-planning and approval from at least three people. Perhaps tapping into some of my difficult past experiences, I started to feel trapped. I had invested all this time and effort and felt that I couldn't leave half-way through training, as I had no skills or experience in any other areas. The absence of a clear reason as to why I wanted to go into the profession made it difficult to sit in the library at 11pm on a Friday night learning about the assumptions of a two-way ANOVA. I thought getting onto training was hard, but this was all encompassing. The most helpful thing a Clinical Psychologist said to me at that point was that I didn't have to stay on the course, and it was OK if the profession wasn't for me. She pointed out my transferable skills. After this conversation I felt as if I was making the choice to stay, which helped.

On the last day of training, my cohort and I were asked to contribute an inspirational quote to a book for future trainees. Maybe the idea was to reference famous psychologists or philosophers, but my remaining intellectual and emotional capacity would only stretch to Disney characters. I would reiterate this advice today:

> *Just keep swimming. Just keep swimming, swimming, swimming.* (Dory, Finding Nemo, 2003).

Becky's Story:

I felt quite burnt out for a long time after qualifying. Thankfully, I have my evenings and weekends back and I can read all the non-psychology related books I want. My dogs are still great company, although they always were. I have more money and my options for career progression seem relatively good, if that's the route I choose to go down. I went into forensic services where I enjoy supporting service users, colleagues and those considering entering the profession. There are also plenty of difficulties too; a lot of responsibility, vastly complex dynamics within systems and things I feel woefully under skilled for. Overall, I enjoy my job, but I don't know if I would reminisce wistfully and say it was all worth it. I would encourage anyone considering entering the profession to do so with your eyes wide open and strongly reflect on your motivations – that is what will get you through this journey. Lots of the things I like about my role, I could have done via a number of other careers, with potentially less of a detrimental impact to my mental health along the way. However, I'm also not sure if I would have listened to my own advice about this before training. I may have dismissed it, telling myself "yea, but I *really* want it though". Don't forget to ask yourself why, and then try to find out if Clinical Psychology is the best way to achieve this, for you. For me, Matt Haig was most definitely right when he said:

> *Pizza tastes good regardless of your job title.* (Haig, 2021, p. 51).

Wishing you health and happiness on your journey, whichever path you go down,

Dr Becky Grace
Clinical Psychologist

References for Becky's Story:

Haig, M. (2021). *The Comfort Book.* Cannongate Books Ltd: Edinburgh.

Stanton, A., Unkrich, L. (2003). *Finding Nemo* [Film]. Walt Disney Pictures & Pixar Animation Studios.

White, M. (1997). *Narratives of Therapists' Lives.* Dulwich Centre Publications: Adelaide.

Zarse, E. M., Neff, M. R., Yoder, R., Hulvershorn, L., Chambers, J. E., & Chambers, R. A. (2019). The adverse childhood experiences questionnaire: Two decades of research on childhood trauma as a primary cause of adult mental illness, addiction, and medical diseases. *Cogent Medicine, 6*(1), 1581447.

Email from: Dr Marianne Trent

To: Dr Becky Grace

Hi Becky,

Thanks for your story and also for your references and wonderful quotes – I love that!

You've managed to really nicely reflect that what you enjoy about the role could also have been fulfilled by other roles. I think that can be really important to bear in mind, whilst Clinical Psychology is wonderful, that happiness, and achieving places on Clinical Training are not mutually exclusive concepts!

Thanks again, Marianne

14

Melissa's Story:

Many ways up the mountain....

I was 17 years old and really struggling. I was exhausted, anxious and overwhelmed. In an effort to cope, I began making lists which would include everything; unnecessary details like 'get the bus to school.' I was taking caffeine tablets in the mornings to find my energy and, for a while, I just kept going. My mother did not want to admit there was a problem, she was worried about having these difficulties stored on my medical record. When I started to develop panic attacks, I insisted that that I needed help. Looking back, it makes sense - I had been suffering the debilitating effects of glandular fever right in the middle of my A Levels at a high-pressure academic school. The exhaustion was scary. I had always been so physical and had spent most evenings and weekends riding and competing. At that time, I had a few sessions of Cognitive Behavioural therapy (CBT) but this did not touch the sides for what I was feeling and experiencing. I guess this has influenced the importance that I place on emotion and sensory experience in my therapy work now.

In the end I got better by myself. I have always been driven by a desire to understand and work things out. My father has an engineering brain and I applied that to my own experience. When I say 'myself'... of course I had help from family and friends. I pushed myself to do the things that scared me, and I was lucky enough to have people around me that I could trust.

I could be open about how scared I was, and they made it just about safe enough...I understand now that is learning through exposure...

It was around this time that I decided to become a clinical psychologist. Maybe I was influenced by my own experience, maybe I wanted to do it differently to the therapist I had seen, maybe it was just a drive to make sense of human beings. I always wanted to be able to live and work somewhere rural and I was quite strategic in thinking about how it could work and what was important for me.

I had heard about the difficulty people can have getting on to training courses, so I made it a mission and focused on anything that might help me get there. During my degree I chose a dissertation that would help me at interviews. I trained as a counsellor for a youth charity – this was a great foundation. I got to see real people and learn and practice all the basics of person-centred therapy.   Looking back, I   feel astonishingly privileged that I was let loose on the public so early in my journey and I hope it is always helpful to have a listening ear that doesn't judge.

I left university in 1998 and did a series of jobs to get the experience I needed. I worked in a residential home for children in care. That was intense, with sleepovers, relationship dramas and social injustice. I delivered sexual health education in youth clubs with the help of a plastic phallus nicknamed 'Rob the Knob.' I counselled young people with drug and alcohol difficulties and worked in CAMHS as a family support worker.

In 2001 I applied to Bristol. I was amazed and delighted when I found that the hard work had paid off - especially as I had expected to have to try a few times. It didn't go to plan. At that time my partner was not able to move with me because of his own career. We were best friends. We had met at 15 - he was my world, and I later married him. Going away and living hundreds of miles apart, may as well have been going to the moon. I got cold feet, but I pushed through.

One week later I dropped out. I couldn't hack it - being alone and isolated in a strange city; at that point living in an hotel. I had been too scared to commit to a contract in one of the grim grey rental houses I had found. What stays with me is the kindness of the other trainees who gave me a 'goodbye and good luck card'. I remember the bafflement at being given that card and wondering what had made them think to do it. It was a sort of consideration I had not experienced from peers before, and back then it would never have occurred to me to do that for someone else.

So, I escaped! I was relieved and devasted – I want to say disappointed because it sounds healthier and more proportionate, but it was a really big deal to let go of that dream. I knew I would probably never have the chance to do it again. The Bristol course were so supportive, I remember 2 members of staff whom I would love to thank in person if I had their consent – it was their genuine listening and understanding that gave me the permission to stop.

I didn't know what I was going to do next. I took a voluntary sector job setting up drugs and alcohol counselling in schools. At that time, the government was beginning to invest in addiction services in a way that they had not done before. Opportunities opened up for me which took me on a 10-year career trajectory that I had not foreseen. I worked commissioning and planning the delivery of drugs and alcohol services across six local authorities and two primary care trusts. From there I moved to a regional role at the National Treatment Agency in government office, and later at the Department of Health.

But the dream had not died.

It is exciting to think that you one can influence how money is spent, how services are planned and delivered, to make things better for those who need the help. But the higher I progressed the more disconnected I felt from the reality of delivering what was needed. It seemed that those with the knowledge lacked the power to influence policy and those with the power lacked the knowledge to make meaningful change. I felt, in the end, like a cog in a wheel looking at plans and targets and was not adding value in the way I wanted to. So, in 2009 I started a postgraduate diploma in cognitive behavioural therapy (CBT) and reduced my work hours so I could volunteer in an NHS trauma service. I re-applied for clinical training in 2010 – no offers. Then in 2011, I was offered places at Plymouth and Oxford.

My 3 years at Oxford were challenging! It felt risky to go back to being a student with people ten years younger than me - starting again at the bottom of the ladder. I was in a dilemma about whether it was the right thing. Halfway through the course my marriage fell apart. It was completely unexpected and agonisingly painful. I couldn't concentrate, my sleep was all over the place and I was flooded with adrenaline. Special thanks to Dr Sue Clohessy who could see the bigger picture, gave me my reference and who helped me to hang in there!

I qualified in 2014. I trained in EMDR and Schema Therapy and specialised in Post-Traumatic Stress Disorder (PTSD). Now after spending several years in an NHS specialist trauma service, I am a lecturer in clinical psychology at Reading University where I did that first degree all those years ago. I teach and supervise the CBT trainees. I've been a clinical lead for Healios who provide digital therapy and am joining Oliva – an exciting digital start up providing quality therapy for employees. I have a practice. I have the variety, freedom and choices I hoped for all those years ago. I never let go of the dream, the journey was tough, and I am so thankful I had a second chance.

So...what have I learned so far from this journey....

My early instinct that this fits me was right. My 10 years in the 'wilderness' gave me knowledge and perspectives I would not otherwise have. If I hadn't made it, that wouldn't be the end of the world! There are other great jobs, other careers and many ways up the mountain to either get there or get to somewhere you never expected at all. I have had to accept that some dilemmas defy explanation – just because it's terrifying doesn't mean it's wrong. I have learned the most from the hardest things. It's okay to be human, to have vulnerabilities and if you are brave enough, to say them out loud sometimes, it can help other people.

Dr Melissa Snaith is a Clinical Psychologist, trainer, and supervisor. She works as a lecturer in Clinical Psychology for the University of Reading and as the Team Lead for Oliva providing proper mental healthcare for the workplace. She uses a mix of different therapy approaches with an experiential and emotion focus. She specialises in trauma, anxiety, and OCD. For more info head to
www.drmelisssnaith.com

Email from: Dr Marianne Trent

To: Dr Melissa Snaith

Dear Melissa,

Thank you for your wonderfully honest story, I am so pleased to hear about the compassion you received from your first cohort.

It sounds like you had built a really varied and helpful array of relevant experience and I am sure that has paid you and your clients rich rewards in your qualified life. I do feel like I want to ask whether you got to keep 'Rob?'

You sound so busy but still so energised by what you do. Well done for talking about your difficulties and being honest with yourself and others too. It has clearly served you well and I hope it will continue to do so in future too.

Thanks again,

Marianne

15

Natasha's Story:

A pathway to determining your future job from your current reflections.

F irstly, I'm excited that you are at the beginning of a career that can be intellectually stimulating, varied, meaningful, give purpose and allow you to make connections with others.

I am a Chartered Principal Clinical Psychologist who decided, aged 13, that I wanted to be a Clinical Psychologist after considering and discounting only one other career (Psychiatry). I followed a practically textbook route to qualification where some aspects that I found really rewarding were:

- Volunteering in mental health charities and on a mental health ward in my late teens and as an undergraduate. This provided excellent training, brought me in contact into those in distress and gave me some insights into the functioning of the mental health support systems.

- Choosing A Levels strategically based on the criteria of the number one university for Psychology (Oxford). The choice of university also meant that I could meet Clinical Psychologists whilst still an undergraduate and integrate into research groups researching developments in psychological processes in those in distress.
- Applying for Wellcome Trust research bursaries in university holidays and specialising in mental health in my final undergraduate year. I found this invaluable as a summer job and again this can expand your network of colleagues and your specialist knowledge.
- Writing individual letters to Clinical Psychologists in local services to ask them if there is anything you could help them with. This feels much more personal than a group e-mail landing in a busy inbox, and offering help is likely to get you further than asking to shadow someone.
- Getting involved with your local Assistant Psychologist group which can be a great support and network during the stresses of the application process. It also often involves hearing talks from invited local Clinical Psychologists and finding out about areas that other people work within.
- Working as an Assistant Psychologist and actively pursuing all the opportunities to learn from your team (be helpful - offer to organise or reformat the self-help materials, offer to photocopy the handouts for the group and then sit in on the group, take on clients under supervision from your team specialists in new models, ask to borrow books etc). Obviously gaining an AP post is extremely competitive and experience is required to get the experience in a strange double bind. You could consider a Research Assistant post first or volunteering for a few hours a week as an Honorary AP alongside another paid post. I recently offered an HCA and a member of the admin staff honorary contracts as an AP

137

and, with the only change being a reference from a Clinical Psychologist, within a few months they had secured a trainee PWP and trainee CBT therapist post.

- Volunteer with the BPS Division of Clinical Psychology (DCP) at their annual conferences so you can sit in the workshops for free.
- A relevant Master's degree will gain you points on the application form. You can research training in which you are paid to train, less common but possible.
- Research the differences between the Clinical Psychology courses with the BPS DCP alternative handbook and www.clinpsy.org.uk/forum,
- Prior to interviews, research commonly asked questions and write down your answers using a relevant theory, model or evidence base (e.g., Gibb's Reflective model to frame reflections on a challenging time at work).

I got onto my favoured doctoral course on the first year of applying and have worked as a Clinical Psychologist ever since, subsequently completing further clinical and leadership qualifications. I personally have found it a pleasure to train and work with groups of such kind and thoughtful people, to have been paid a salary throughout my training, to be able to craft my own career from a diversity of job roles, for my profession to be valued and in demand, and to be able to adjust it to transitions in my own life and family.

It has also been my experience that you will be welcomed into Clinical Psychology whatever your background and whatever the factors are that make you unique. The richer and broader the range of perspectives we have as a group, the more relevant and effective we are in advocating and encouraging others. I have interviewed on Clinical Psychology Doctorate panels and truly the people that stand out are those who think carefully about how they can apply their own qualities and resources, with developing knowledge, to the benefit of others. This is far more important to the profession than the boxes you may tick on your equal opportunities form, so please consider the career and representing yourself for those who may follow you.

On reflection however, when deciding on my own career path, I didn't have the knowledge of other jobs and careers that may have brought me in contact with the same types of clients, the same types of teams or the same types of skill bases that I have come across as a Clinical Psychologist. As I have progressed in my own career, I have also been exposed to many more options in which I may also have had a fulfilling career.

In Clinical Psychology you incorporate many different job roles together; you are at once a clinician, a therapist, an advocate, a leader, a trainer, a supervisor of others, a mentor, a mental health specialist, a researcher and a policy writer. You hold knowledge on every age bracket, the range of mental health and neurodevelopmental difficulties; you assess, treat and evaluate; you are viewed as a key voice in your team. You may work in a hospital, clinic, prison, business, university, offering home visits or working from your home office. The list of permutations is endless.

On considering other permutations of Clinical Psychology, I realised that you could also:

- Work in a Multi-disciplinary Team (MDT) in the NHS (e.g. as a Psychiatrist, Cognitive Behavioural Therapist, Cognitive Analytic Therapist, Psychodynamic Therapist, Family Therapist, Counselling Psychologist, Counsellor, Occupational Therapist, Specialist Mental Health Nurse, Addiction Therapist, Dietician),
- Work with individual clients on their mental health, well-being, or self-knowledge (e.g., coaches, mentors, mindfulness teachers),

- Work with systems and organisations (e.g., Occupational Psychologists, Forensic Psychologists, Management Consultants, Occupational Health),
- Helping people (e.g., police officers, podiatrists, Opticians, Audiologists),
- Influencing others (e.g., PR, marketing),
- Educating others (e.g., Educational Psychologist, SENCo, school counsellor),
- Facilitating others to make changes to themselves (e.g., surgeons, yoga teachers, make-up artists, hairdressers, personal trainers),
- Focusing on audit and research (e.g., University researchers, Accountants, Statisticians, market researchers, work at organisations such as NICE),
- Innovating change (e.g., artificial intelligence in health care, politicians, campaigners), or
- Being involved in leadership (e.g., as team managers or C-suite executives).

This is a random, diverse and incomplete list. Perhaps as I now know and recognise that the full range of potential careers also isn't known to you yet. I really enjoy working with clients in my private practice and the full range of options, occupations and roles that would fulfil them isn't apparent to many clients that I meet with either, regardless of their age, status or wealth. I would recommend that you pause and reflect on this yourself and think carefully about Clinical Psychology and whether it is just one of the multi-faceted aspects that interests you.

Perhaps consider what gives you purpose, what lights you up? What might you want in ten- or twenty-years' time from your job? Who or what do you want to work with? What is your natural skill set? Do you want to be a member of a team or lead it? This may lead you further towards Clinical Psychology, with more clearly articulated reasons why, or throw up some alternatives that may suit you equally or better.

Regardless of the outcome of your reflections, I hope that you value your journey and experiences along the way; it is a long road, but no experience or knowledge is wasted. I wish you the very best as you navigate your career and I'm excited for the innovations, insights, and industry that your contributions will bring.

Dr Natasha Sayer is a Chartered Principal Clinical Psychologist and Executive Coach. Further details of her clinical practice can be found at www.versionyou.co.uk

Email from: Dr Marianne Trent

To: Dr Natasha Sayer

Dear Natasha,

Thank you for your wonderfully thoughtful and thorough advice. It's going to be so useful for those looking to take their initial steps into the world of psychology and beyond.

I love how focused and driven you have been from such an early age, and I absolutely have the sense that you can move mountains for yourself and your clients if needed.

Thanks again,

Marianne

16

Nicki's Story:

My meandering path to clinical psychology

My journey to clinical psychology almost started at the end of my undergraduate degree, when the university scheduled clinical and educational psychology careers talks at the same time in two adjoining lecture halls. Having decided in primary school that I wanted to be an educational psychologist, after hearing what they do when a relative was referred to one for an assessment, I steadfastly picked the door on the left and took my first steps on the path to educational psychology. Having completed a BPS accredited degree in Education with Psychology, I accepted a place on a PGCE course in order to gain teaching experience before applying for the Doctorate in Educational Psychology. The PGCE was intense: it felt like a never-ending cycle of planning lessons for children aged 3-11 years, then spending evenings and weekends marking mountains of exercise books for English, Maths and other subjects each day. Although I didn't end up as a primary teacher, the PGCE and subsequent supply teaching enabled me to develop a range of skills. I learnt how to plan creative activities (often by trial and error), how to assess children's individual needs, and how to manage challenging behaviour. I also learnt how to strike a balance between maintaining professionalism whilst also being playful with children, and I learnt how to engage learners who found school challenging. At the time I didn't appreciate how useful these skills would be as I trained as a clinical psychologist, but I certainly relied on these assessment and engagement skills on the DClin, and playfulness was certainly used on my child placements.

Despite being offered a job in the school where I completed my final placement, I felt I hadn't quite finished with university life. My undergraduate degree offered the best 3 years of my life – I loved learning and enjoyed all social aspects of being a student. As I didn't feel ready to start a 'grown-up career' I declined the job and spoke to my undergraduate tutor about returning to university for a Master's. She suggested that I should apply for a paid PhD instead of paying fees to complete a Master's. After conversations with different lecturers, I decided to apply for an ESRC scholarship to investigate pupil motivation from a socio-cultural perspective, as previous cognitive models of motivation were predominantly individualistic, and I wanted to consider the broader context that children are situated within. This research was undertaken in underachieving locales which had higher rates of poverty and social and economic disadvantage. This taught me to reflect on privilege and the barriers that many have to overcome in order to access things many people take for granted. This fuelled my commitment to social justice and my interest in systemic approaches to understanding people's difficulties. Ultimately, this influenced my desire to apply to DClin courses that offer additional qualifications in systemic practice.

The PhD equipped me with research skills that I later relied on during the DClin. The first year of the PhD programme required all students to undertake a postgraduate diploma in research methods, i.e., the taught components of the MSc in Research Methods without the Master's dissertation. Whilst some may think a year of research methods might be boring, it was a fun year, mainly due to the wonderful cohort (in the same way the DClin cohort get you through the challenges of clinical training). As postgraduate students we were considered more equal by staff and were invited to departmental socials where there was never a short supply of wine and general merriment! It's hard to believe but even muddling through SPSS with peers offered laughter as we desperately tried to find ways of making SPSS less tedious [top tip: Julie Pallant's easy-to-understand SPSS survival guide was responsible for getting us through the year]. During the PhD I learnt the usual processes of applying for ethics, searching for literature, fine-tuning methodological decision-making, learning to provide the rationale for different aspects of the research, in addition to trying to remain within the word limit when writing-up empirical chapters – sadly this last skill is one that I am yet to fully master. The PhD experience also taught me how to overcome barriers (such as having a year's worth of data stolen when my car was broken into), the importance of saving data on multiple devices, how to stay motivated when thesis writing is the very last thing you want to do, and how to try and manage a healthy work-life balance while studying and working as a tutor and then lecturer – the stolen research set-back meant I then had to find paid work whilst writing-up the thesis. Although it felt like a marathon, gaining the Dr. title and celebrating with family at my graduation seemed to make it worth-it.

During the latter stage of my PhD, I accepted a part-time job as a personal assistant to a lecturer with a visual impairment. One day she asked me to wait in her office whilst she popped to the loo and her roommate (an eccentric lecturer I had during my undergraduate degree) was there and had just received an email from a former colleague who was asking if he knew anyone suitable for a lecturing vacancy at a neighbouring university. He looked and pointed at me and said – "you!" He persuaded me to apply, and I was offered the role of Lecturer in Developmental Psychology. This started an 11-year accidental career as an academic. Had I not popped to his office at that moment I would not have known about the job or applied for it! I loved researching and learning about the latest studies so I could deliver evidence-based lectures and seminars. I loved supervising students and offering pastoral care to those who needed it. I was less enthused about the endless marking and increasing demand for administrative paperwork. This role offered opportunities to teach abroad (in Hong Kong and the Netherlands), write academic papers and present at international conferences. These were definite perks of a role that required long hours and effective time management. Again, experiences that helped me endure the DClin journey.

Several years into this role, the psychology department established a Master's course in child therapy and, with a need to have qualified staff teaching students, the university offered to support two staff members (including myself) to undertake therapy training. The 2-year programme involved completion of 100 hours of clinical practice, 50 hours of clinical supervision and 60 hours of personal therapy. Having never considered a career as a child therapist, I loved it. I was fortunate to receive exceptional supervision and the mandatory personal therapy helped me to learn what it is like to be a client, firstly with a terrible therapist and then with a wonderful, empathic, and skilled therapist. This helped me realise the type of therapist I wanted to be. The clinical work with children was also hugely rewarding; helping children to navigate a range of difficulties through play (i.e., their natural language) and seeing the positive outcomes of therapy was both humbling and satisfying. The university supported me to do pro-bono work offering therapy to children in a local hospital, where I was supervised by a brilliant clinical psychologist. Whilst this demonstrated university outreach work, unfortunately for them it was the moment I realised I actually wanted a career involving clinical work, particularly in paediatric health. I subsequently applied for and gained a place on the DClin and resigned from my lecturing role.

Nicki's Story:

As I approached the process of applying for the doctorate, I viewed it as a learning experience rather than an immediate goal to accomplish; this helped me to be more relaxed for the interviews. I never expected to gain a place but was thrilled to be offered a place at my preferred university, having been declined from the other university where I secured an interview and rejected from my other choices. Prior to the interviews I benefitted from speaking with friends who were clinical psychologists, who emphasised the importance of reflecting on past experiences. As I approached interview preparation, I listed the skills of clinical psychologists from job descriptions and noted experiences I had that matched those skills, and I also thought of important past experiences and listed all the skills and qualities used in those situations. This helped me to bring to mind past experiences and link to relevant skills when trying to offer reflective interview answers. Initially I wasn't confident as I knew I didn't have the traditional experience of being an Assistant Psychologist. However, my diverse non-traditional experiences helped me to answer the interview questions. For example, I remember being asked about working with challenging individuals and was able to reflect on non-psychology situations including a challenging supply teaching experience where a child tried to jump out of a second-floor window (yikes- not what I expected on my first day as a supply teacher!), and another where I was required to diffuse a situation when a parent with a drug addiction came to school and caused a disturbance. The DClin interview process helped me to realise that none of my past roles had been wasted; each offered opportunities and skill development that would ultimately help me to be a clinical psychologist.

Although it was almost 15 years since I chose the door on the left that almost resulted in a career in educational psychology, and I had somewhat accidentally meandered my way through a career in teaching, lecturing and child therapy, I realised that clinical psychology offered a dream role that offered all of the things I loved: clinical work, research, supervision, and continued professional development (CPD), while also making a meaningful difference to people's lives. Despite initial hesitancy and worry about changing careers as a mature student, I have not looked back - the choice I made to apply for the clinical doctorate was the best thing, career-wise, to have happened to me. Although my DClin journey has been quite a bumpy one (due to health issues and a bereavement) that resulted in an extension to training, I near the end of training feeling fully prepared for my qualified post, thanks to the diverse knowledge and skills acquired over the past three years and thanks to the outstanding pastoral support from the DClin staff. I am excited to be starting a career that I have dreamed of in paediatric health. I was genuinely surprised to be offered my job, especially as I applied so early, but I should, perhaps, have had greater confidence in the reputation of my course. The interviewers valued the additional BABCP, and family qualifications gained as part of the DClin. It appears that the hard work to complete the extra systemic assignments was worth it, and I am glad that I will have opportunities to use these skills in my role working with families who are navigating the complexities of childhood illness.

As I am still a work in progress, I will welcome opportunities to practice and engage in CPD, with the hope that it will benefit the young people and families I meet in my qualified role. When considering what type of clinical psychologist I want to become, I hope I am skilled in offering evidence-based interventions while remaining compassionate and empathic. I also hope I am supportive to colleagues in an increasingly stretched NHS, and an advocate for those who need it. When reflecting back on the DClin experience, instead of regretting that I had not picked the clinical psychology door 15 years earlier, my meandering journey has helped me to realise that no experience is wasted and I have benefitted from an indirect route to clinical training; my experiences have equipped me with the skills and resilience to reach the end.

Nicki's Story:

17

Richard's Story:

A Bear Arrives in the Lions' Territory

The Clinical Psychology course has been more than a doctoral course for me. It has and still continues to be akin to a school of life. I moved from a place near London to South-Western England, an unfamiliar area for my training. I thought such a fact was interesting alongside being in a predominantly White area. Deep down, I had my fears. For unknown reasons at the time, I struggled with my IAPT training. No matter how hard I tried, concentrating in an open floor plan office was a struggle. To be fair, it was also a time where I came out as queer to my family and friends, losing 99% of them. I recalled one time when I was a trainee Psychological Wellbeing Practitioner (PWP), and my supervisor and I awkwardly discussed the reasons she would **not** give me a reference. She said something along the lines of, '*If you are struggling with PWP training, what makes you think you would be able to*

149

complete a doctorate?' That stayed with me. And she was, in many ways, right. Conversely, I remembered the other challenges and hurdles I had gone through since relocating to Southwest England and believed that if I overcame such, then the DClinPsy course would not be any different. I believed in myself because I initially did not envision myself going to university to complete an undergraduate degree and two rigorous MSc programmes. But I did them anyway.

In the first week of my course, I saw how the cohort was different to me and I thought to myself, *there was no way I could or ever could be friends with these people.* There was a Black girl on my course who I chatted to on the phone a few times, and a guy who was in the year above me. That was good enough for me then. Even more so, for some reason, when I had moved to a new place or work setting, I tended to struggle with my stammer. And I am just *different.* In hindsight, the more I tried to be *normal,* the more I *stood out.* I thought people would not want to get to know me – however, I still made a couple of friends from my cohort.

Because of my experiences of clinical supervision from my Improving Access to Psychological Therapies (IAPT) training, I was nervous about working alongside my first placement supervisor. However, she was fantastic. Even despite feeling completely out of my depth in the placement area and the steep learning curve, it turned out my supervisor and I had things in common and we got on really well. Lectures were A LOT. Whilst stimulating, I was unsure how well my brain was taking in the information. I was so scared of failing the course that I engaged in my perfectionism behaviours, which ended up leaving me tired.

It was in my CAMHS placement that I would say I grew up. Learning systemic theory and practice taught me that just because something made sense, it did not make it automatically

150

true. So, it was important to maintain a position of curiosity. All my life, I have been attacked and discriminated against because of aspects of my identity. Being the opposite of a White, female, heterosexual, neurotypical and middle-class person brought those insecurities to the top of the surface. Sometimes, I wanted to quit the course. The profession and course is an interesting paradox from personal experience. First, a majority of people from the course and profession started to treat me differently when I *came out* about my neurodiversity. Second, for a profession that is meant to support people with various psychological difficulties and disabilities, which a key factor is due to social inequality, it sure feels cold and impersonal. In many ways, the profession has parallels with its explicitly corporate counterparts. I still remember my horror when I was a Trainee Psychological Wellbeing Practitioner and went to my first wide Trust meeting. *Business* and *competitors* were spoken about!

The pandemic started, quickly followed by the end of in-person teaching and of course, in-placement learning was gone. To say how upset, depressed, anxious and disappointed I was, is an understatement. My excitement of getting to know my cohort better and shadowing my supervisors on placement, as well as doing all these amazing things as a Clinical Psychologist, had disappeared almost overnight. These factors, alongside the uncertainty of when lockdown would happen, pushed me to dark places. Before that, I observed my supervisors who were just excellent: dealing with a range of tasks that were complex and many without breaking a sweat. I was always thinking to myself; *how could I be able to get to such A Level of efficiency?* From working in isolation and with significantly reduced opportunities for learning, the course was turning out to be exactly what I did not sign up for. I struggled to focus on Zoom, and Microsoft Teams lectures and I was always tired. However, over time, and with the purchase of electronic gadgets, I found 'my groove.' I then started to see the benefits of not having to commute. My uncomfortable feelings were substantially eased by a supervisor telling me it generally took about five years post-qualification to settle as a Clinical Psychologist. She also taught me self-compassion (Paul Gilbert's Compassion Focused Therapy), a practice I still adhere to now.

My Saturn return started in December 2020 (fascinating stuff, look into it!), a time that people well-versed in astrology dreaded. I found out that I was neurodiverse in January this year. Despite about five existential crises and oceans of emotion, everything started to make sense. It now made sense that, for most of the time, I found people as odd in how they communicated and vice versa. Like when I asked a people how they were, I *really* meant it. You can imagine the awkwardness when such a situation was the reverse - when I overshared because I thought people *really* meant it when they asked how I was. My life had comprised trial and error, which was a mixture of emotional pain and wonder. I unconsciously expected people from the profession to meet my unmet needs from childhood. Both the course and society did not seem to be measuring up for me in terms of fairness, empathy and unconditional positive regard. This, unsurprisingly, had the potential to make me quite miserable. My second year of the DClin has been akin to Usher's Confessions album and Adele's 21 album (those who have listened to those albums will know what I mean). It has been a time where I confronted myself, letting go of childhood ideas and facing reality. It is interesting. I always told my friends that eternally, I was 19 years old. In many ways, I was and felt like a child in a grown man's body. However, I cannot blame myself too much because the pre-frontal cortex (Brain's executive function) starts to mature fully from one's late twenties into their early 30's. I was entitled, judgmental, idealistic and overly simplistic in my thinking. Through the painful but transformative lessons in coming to terms with my intersectional identity and reality, I feel, for the first time, *I am now an adult.* As a Black, queer and neurodiverse person, I have come to the acceptance that I would deal with racism, homophobia and ableism from a majority of the society and the Clinical Psychology profession, for probably most of the time. Silence is a convenient armour that people can hide in.

The question now, is that how much do I fight the 'isms' and phobias? Do I fight at all? However, the inevitable experience of discrimination because of my intersectional identity, is a fundamental aspect of reality that I have now come to accept. But I will prevail. I'm not quite sure how to yet. Diversity, decolonisation and anti-racist/discrimination are currently *in vogue* in Clinical Psychology. But sometimes, I question the underlying motives of the people that advocate for such. Do people really care? Is it because it is popular right now? *Should I care?* Is it *really* my business? I am still in search for answers.

I have criticised everybody lately, from the Clinical Psychology profession to my training program, to supervisors, to my cohort and society. But, right now, I cannot imagine doing anything else. I am, as cheesy as it can be said, having the time of my life.

Perhaps on an unconscious level, if we are adopting a psychoanalytic lens, I regarded the DClinPsy course as a mother. My training as a Clinical Psychologist is akin to being in the gestation and infancy stages. As much as my training program has been tremendously helpful, the reality is that it cannot meet all of my professional and personal development needs. I have found having mentors, personal psychotherapy, as well as forming relationships with trainees from other courses, to be instrumental in my journey of growth and self-discovery. In myself doing such, I have graduated from being a child and adolescent, to now an adult (*well mostly! I hope!*), who is in control of their destiny.

Richard's Story:

Richard is on track to qualify in 2022. You can reach out to Richard Digbori on LinkedIn and on Twitter @richiedigs

LinkedIn Message from: Dr Marianne Trent

To: Richard Digbori

Dear Richard,

Thank you so much for your wonderfully insightful and thought-provoking account. I absolutely need to head straight to google now to check out some of the recommendations you have made! When I first read your account I mis-remembered it as Usher's second album so I listened to 'My Way,' which incidentally didn't hold my attention and made me switch off in favour of Chris Brown's first album so I'll have to ask Alexa to play me Confessions!

I'm so pleased that along your journey in Clinical Psychology that you have been able to make sense of the world and the body you find yourself in and that is has added clarity for you.

We crossed paths on LinkedIn, and I love having you as part of my virtual clan. I'm so looking forward to following your journey from this point forwards and you're so wonderfully supportive for helping drum up participants for trainee's research projects and sharing the campaigns across your network. It is something that I know the trainees and researchers will be very grateful for. I hope people do the same for you when it's your turn. I am certainly happy to share to my networks.

Keep doing what you do and thanks for being part of my world and of course part of The Collective.

Thanks again, Marianne

LinkedIn message from: Richard Digbori

To: Dr Marianne Trent

Thanks for the wonderful opportunity, Marianne. You are doing something very, very monumental!

TODAY

Richard Digbori · 7:40 am
Hi Marianne, hopefully this makes you laugh

I had the most bizarre dream

I was housemates with Kim Kardashian who received my copy of the book on my behalf

Richard Digbori · 7:42 am
Apparently, you came to my house weeks before and planned it with Kim when to show me. And then she put all the comments of praise on a Whiteboard!

Dr Marianne Trent · 7:43 am
Ha ha. Can I add this in to the bc ⁻ᵗ⁻⁰
Genuinely howling 😂

+ Write a message...

Richard Digbori · 7:43 am
Yes!!!

The dream was so fabulous that I didn't want it to end. She took the book and my participation seriously, like a best mate would

Dr Marianne Trent · 8:25 am
Well of course. Who are we anyway without an A lister as a best friend! Thanks for sharing your dream with me. I too as a z lister take your participation seriously....

+ Write a message...

18

Rob's Story:

Loving the journey so much that holiday seemed an inconvenience

I always knew I wanted to have a career helping people, but it was after my first AS Level teaching session on psychology when I first fell in love with the idea of being a clinical psychologist. I found myself being completely captivated by the differences between the cognitive, psychoanalytic, biological and behavioural approaches, and loved the idea of applying these theories to help individuals overcome psychological difficulties.

However, looking back I was completely naïve as to how difficult the journey would be, and after completing my degree in psychology, I applied for Assistant Psychologist posts and fully expected to gain full-time paid employment straight away! After about the 5th rejection letter, I finally caught on that I need experience in order to get the experience of being an Assistant Psychologist, so I immersed myself into volunteering experiences to finally help me achieve this. Yet years passed by, and I was still waiting for that elusive Assistant Psychologist post, and I put off the idea of completing a MSc in Clinical Psychology as I was told I did not need it to get on to clinical training (which, is actually factually correct!). However, my patience finally wore thin, and after applying for and completing my MSc in Abnormal & Clinical Psychology at the University of Swansea, I was finally offered an interview to be an Assistant Psychologist and was fortunate enough to gain full time employment.

During my time as an Assistant Psychologist, I loved the variety of experiences I was able to be afforded. I loved working so much, my line manager called me into a meeting and told me that I needed to start using annual leave as I had accrued so much! However, my time as an Assistant Psychologist was certainly not without its troubles, and I even had to go onto a competency development framework as it was determined by my line manager that my technical skills were not up to the standard expected of me. Strangely, even though I found this markedly upsetting and I often ended up crying on my way to work, my confidence in myself never wavered, and I had full confidence that the limitations identified by my supervisor would eventually be overcome.

In time, I was finally able to reach my competence level, and a year later I was offered a place on the Cardiff clinical psychology doctorate course on my seventh attempt! Looking back, I'm so glad it took me all seven times to get onto the course, as when I did go into training, I found the transition between being an Assistant Psychologist and a trainee clinical psychologist not too steep of a jump. Yet I would consider that many of the trainees whom I trained with found this jump to be quite profound and were perhaps not quite as ready for clinical training as they previously thought. I also found myself to be particularly jealous, dismissive and rude when I would speak about colleagues of mine who got onto clinical training before me, as I found the anger and jealousy associated with this knowledge to be too overwhelming.

Rob's Story:

During clinical training, I loved the variety of clientele that I was able to work with, including older adults, children, individuals with intellectual disabilities, adults and I chose my final placement to work with individuals with eating disorders. I found myself growing both personally professionally, and even met my wife during my second-year placement at Noah's Ark children's hospital!

Currently, I love my current role as a clinical psychologist for the Torfaen team for people with learning disabilities and love how my working day is never the same day to day. Overall, when I look back on my journey to being a clinical psychologist, I'm very proud of the fact that I started off completing on my own, knowing absolutely no-one in the field of clinical psychology, but with determination, hard work, sacrifice and the financial backing of my parents, I was able to finally obtain my dream job, and look forward to doing this for many years to come.

In regard to advice, I would encourage any aspiring clinical psychologist to join local Assistant Psychologist groups. However, I would caution such individuals by saying that that the competition element of being an Assistant Psychologist can bring out people's negative traits (it certainly did with me) so I would encourage people to be patient during their respective journeys, as I have found that people on the whole tend to be 'ripe for plucking' so to speak, and ready for the demands of clinical training when they are offered a place. You also do not want to get onto a clinical psychology doctorate course before you are ready, as clinical training is stressful enough without not being ready for it!

Kind regards, Rob

**You can reach out to Dr Robert Searle
(Clinical Psychologist) (Seicolegydd Clinigol) at:
Tîm Cymunedol Torfaen i Bobl ag Anableddau Dysgu/ Torfaen
Community Team for People with Learning Disabilities
Canolfan Fusnes Torfaen / Torfaen Business Centre
Ffordd Paneg / Panteg Way
Tafarn Newydd / New Inn
NP4 0LS / NP4 0LS**

Email from: Dr Marianne Trent

To: Dr Robert Searle

Hi Rob,

Thanks so much for your account. Oh! The idea of you walking to work in tears really moved me!

I'm so pleased you persevered with it all and didn't let one bad review, quote or possibly one more difficult relationship alter your determination to become a clinical psychologist.

Thanks so much for taking your time to write for The Collective and wishing you all the best with your role in future too.

Thanks,

Marianne

19

Sara's Story:

Sometimes I still pinch myself: reflections on becoming a Doctor of clinical psychology

My name is Sara and I'm a principal clinical psychologist. I completed my doctorate in clinical psychology at the University of Southampton and I've been qualified since 2017. I currently work on an older adults' organic ward developing a completely new psychology service. I also work privately, mainly with children, families and young adults, so I utilise my training across the lifespan.

A strong interest in the subject led me into clinical psychology. I wasn't someone who always wanted to be a psychologist or work as a therapist. In fact, I wasn't sure what I wanted to be "when I grew up". I had a vague idea of wanting to be a medical doctor, or work in a caring role, but at college I felt torn between further developing my creative interests (like art and design) and going with a subject that hooked me from the beginning of my A Levels- and that was psychology. "Hooked" seems like an appropriate word. I was fascinated by the A Level textbook. We were encouraged to buy *and actually read* chapters before each teaching session, and because I remember feeling that I couldn't get enough of the subject, I actually did it!

The Research Route

I distinctly remember *knowing* that psychology was for me when I applied to universities, but it was only during the final year of my undergraduate degree that I finally turned my attention towards the future and my career. At the time, I was approached by my third-year dissertation supervisor who suggested that I apply to study a PhD. I don't know what it was about that meeting, but I realised at that moment that I wanted to do a clinical doctorate. Feeling quite proud of myself for having my work noticed, I happily and politely declined. I went home that evening and told my parents about the opportunity that I turned down - they were aghast: "Why did you make a decision so quickly!?" "This is a great opportunity!" - as I really had no plans for a clinical doctorate until that point, they suggested I have a think about the opportunity, whilst also considering other options moving forward. So, overnight I constructed a plan, and the next day, I went back to my supervisor to talk to him about starting this process of applying for PhD funding. Why? Because I had heard that research skills are highly valued by many universities, and there are lots of different routes to getting onto the course. Plus, with the competitiveness of training, I wanted a substantial career to "fall back on" in case the doctorate didn't happen. My PhD focused on cognitive psychology, and I conducted several experiments using a computer-based study to explore the cognitions and metacognitions of regular and non-regular gamblers. I obtained external funding from The Gambling Trust and published a paper. On reflection, I'm so pleased I took this route as my interest in research has continued in the real world, and it has helped me to understand the importance of service evaluation, outcome measures, as well as to feel confident in setting up research projects. I also continue to develop and use the 'scientist practitioner' skills in my current roles.

I should also mention that I also gained experience as a paid Assistant Psychologist in neuro-rehabilitation before I undertook training. My research experience helped me to project manage a randomised controlled trial and facilitate weekly groups of manualised memory intervention for people with multiple sclerosis who struggled with cognitive impairment.

Training and Parenting

I look back on training as a both a challenging and fascinating period, and I do miss it. Training at the University of Southampton consisted of completing four core placements (older adult, adult, child and learning disabilities) (LD) as well as a longer specialist placement during the final year. My cohort at the time I started training (2012) was small and friendly (n=13) and we all gelled together well, meeting every lunch break and planning nights out and weekends away.

I became pregnant a few months into the first year and had my first born at the end of 2013 - throwing another type of challenge into the mix! Taking a year off for maternity leave and discretely slipping back into year 2 of the clinical doctorate wasn't an easy transition. I was juggling sleepless nights, mum guilt alongside adjustment back into training with a new cohort. The experience led me to really focus my time on training. When I was home, I just couldn't focus on work when I wanted to be present with my child. It also influenced the topic I chose for my thesis which was *The Influence of Mindfulness and Mental Health on Maternal Sensitivity and Child Outcomes Across the Perinatal Period.* At the end of my final year, I had my second son, and so another pregnancy during training, alongside parenting and juggling case reports, assignments and the thesis, meant that I submitted my thesis a few months later than intended - and I clearly remember managing to submit it a week before going into labour - close call! So, another year off on maternity leave and during this time I managed to complete my viva with a new-born, submit my minor revisions, and subsequently secured a clinical psychologist position in an older adults Community Mental Health Team (CMHT). It certainly wasn't my best performance at an interview, being acutely aware that my husband was outside the hospital waiting for me in the car with our 3-year-old and 4-month-old that I was exclusively breastfeeding! I still cringe at some of my interview answers and can distinctly recall apologising for my "baby brain" at the end of the interview.

In all honesty, I thought I was set for work post-qualification with children and families with three of my five placements completed with that population (CAMHS, child LD, specialist paediatrics). Having completed the older adult placement with very little actual work with older adults (my placement was changed to a pain team due to a psychologist retiring and my case report was actually written about a 36-year-old woman – hardly an older adult) and knowing my love of neuropsychology which I did not develop as much as I wanted to during course placements, I was happy to gain additional experience post-qualification in this area. The other plus points for me included a job that was local, as well as the flexibility of the role and the opportunity to really develop my leadership skills. It also highlighted to me that we have a solid set of transferable skills that we can apply to a multitude of new contexts, even when there is always more room for learning and developing. The CBT, neuropsychological and systemic approaches that I developed throughout training have been invaluable to my work with individuals, carers, families, and healthcare teams.

Selling Apples and Private Practice

I was born in Southern Ontario, Canada, and when I was six, I was caught by my parents selling their delicious newly bought red apples door-to-door on our street. My parents weren't too impressed at the time, and I'm not sure why I felt the need to sell those apples – as I have no memory of needing money for anything at that age, but I can confidently say my strong entrepreneurial spirit started from a young age. I was one of those stereotypical kids you often see on American TV shows selling lemonade at the end of my driveway (which I often did), and I've always wanted to have my own business. Fairly soon after qualification, I heard about a psychological therapies company in Southampton looking for associates and I dipped my toes into part-time private practice and haven't looked back. The NHS funds the doctoral programmes, and I am aware of some psychologists holding strong opinions about other psychologists working in private practice after a heavy investment in training, which can lead to a lot of shame. I'm also incredibly aware of the lack of resources and lengthy waiting lists for NHS psychological services, and how many people and families just don't meet the "severe and enduring" criteria for access to a psychologist. To be able to shape my own practice and invest in my own training (i.e., I have just completed EMDR training) has been invaluable for my growth as a clinical psychologist, alongside my NHS work.

In 2019 I started a business with my best friend after we reflected on our parenting experiences and need for maintaining our own wellbeing. We developed *The Mindful Parent* (www.mindfulparent.co.uk), committed to supporting new parents with the transition to parenthood, and we have a growing community on Instagram (The Mindful Parent UK) that draws on evidence-based psychological approaches to encourage daily mindfulness and self-compassion as ways of maintaining mental health. As part of this project, we developed Mindful Me Cards which are 30 beautifully designed cards for new parents that are intended to be drawn one per day across the course of a month, and feature in our gift boxes perfect for the arrival of new babies.

More recently, I launched *Find My Psychologist* (www.findmypsychologist.co.uk) in March 2021, which is an online directory for finding HCPC registered psychologists in private practice. The business is set up with my husband (a business lecturer) and brother-in-law (who previously worked for IBM, so he has the technical and marketing knowledge).

Finding the right psychologist is a time consuming and daunting task for most people. It can take a long time to find a psychologist on the web, and quite often it's the case that people find a psychologist they like the look of (based on their webpage) and find out that that psychologist is full, only to have to start the process again. On top of this difficulty, the majority of people don't understand the difference between professionals offering therapy, and so we provide accurate and transparent information about qualified psychologists on our site, including our extensive training. We encourage psychologists registered on our site to list their services in a jargon-free way. Importantly, our target for psychologists registered on our site was reached quickly and I am so excited that the site is actually now being used by the general public!

My role in NHS Older Person's Mental Health has also developed. I initially gained a lot of older adult experience as the only psychologist within a multidisciplinary community team, mainly focusing on a caseload of therapy and neuropsychological assessments. I've gained valuable knowledge and specialist skills working with older people, including understanding the main issues affecting this population (e.g., the impact of retirement and loneliness; the interaction between physical and mental health) and how to adapt therapy for increased understanding and engagement. Since November I have been developing a psychology service on an organic inpatient ward (mainly dementia patients), and I'm proud of how well psychology has been accepted and embedded within the inpatient team to date. I've definitely needed to adapt to unfamiliar territory, and I've had to learn a completely new way of working with patients due to their significant cognitive impairments. The majority of my work is with carers and families, and staff members. My leadership and supervision skills have developed considerably, especially as I've been fortunate enough to have assistants and trainees. Older adult mental health services are generally very underfunded and there are usually very few psychologists within mental health teams (if any). I am passionate about continuing my work in this area and advocating for this population.

Final Reflections

Despite all my experience to date, do I still pinch myself about gaining a place on training? Yes, sometimes. My journey to become a clinical psychologist – the pre-training Assistant Psychologist experience, studying for a PhD and then swiftly onto clinical doctorate training, has developed me in many ways (both personally and professionally) and it has pushed me to my limits at times, particularly in terms of juggling childcare with training and work, and continuously stepping outside of my comfort zones. The 'bottleneck' of training is difficult to get through, which requires intense persistence and patience, but it is very much worth it for the variety of my roles and the endless possibilities ahead.

Email from: Dr Marianne Trent

To: Dr Sara

Hi Sara,

Wow, I just loved reading your story and I know that as the mother of 2 young children this reference won't be lost on you "you sound busier than Miss Rabbit!' It sounds like you're managing to strike the perfect balance of NHS and private practice alongside Mummying and keeping yourself energised with very exciting projects!

Wishing you all the best with your 2 ventures, I find that rather like children that ventures can multiply so I'm excited to see how your story unfolds. I'm also keen to learn more about those apples and how and when you moved from the States!

Thanks for being part of my world and of course, The Collective, I know people will find it really inspiring.

Thanks again, Marianne

20

Shona's Story:

Able to be authentic

I left university with a psychology degree and a fascination with people. I had no clear direction aside from that. One of my favourite uni modules had focused on mental health and was led by a clinical psychologist so I thought maybe that would be a good place to start. Naively, I had no idea about the process or how competitive it was!

So, I started looking for jobs. Assistant Psychologist roles were plentiful but having applied for about 30 across the south of England with no interviews, I was getting a little desperate. I went through a contact my mum had, to speak to a local psychology lead about routes to training. They told me I had no hope of gaining a paid AP job without doing one voluntarily first. They offered me a full-time unpaid role which I had to decline...I needed to be able to afford to eat! I eventually decided that I could do 2 days unpaid, work 4 days in an admin job and then have a day off a week. Looking back now as a qualified clinician, I hate unpaid AP jobs. They privilege those who can afford to not be paid, or risk poverty for those who really can't afford it but are desperate to gain the experience. And they significantly undervalue the skills and experience people bring to the role.

Luckily, I actually bagged a job as a graduate mental health worker in an IAPT team, a week before I'd agreed to start the unpaid AP role. So maybe the psychology lead wasn't right after all! However, it wasn't all roses. I couldn't be fussy about location, so I'd taken a job that was a 2hr commute from my family home. I couldn't afford to move out and didn't want to commit to a rental and risk hating the job. So, I spent a year commuting 4 hours a day to a high-volume, high-pressure role. I experienced a lot of anxiety including panic attacks and really had to overcome that in order to actually be able to manage the commute, let alone do the job! One benefit of working in a CBT service is you can't help but learn the theory of how to manage anxiety. On the flip side, I had the best bunch of colleagues, all young graduates, many of whom I remain friends with to this day.

We survived the wheel of IAPT with Pizza Fridays, being taught belly dancing by our lovely administrator and playing jokes on new incoming supervisors, convincing them the old supervisors had always provided weekly cakes. After a year I was promoted to a band 5 role in the same team, moved closer by and then did my first Clinical Psychology application. I met some brilliantly inspiring psychologists who helped me think about the kind of psychologist I wanted to be and that really helped me with my application form and preparation for interviews.

Looking back on what was important that helped me get onto clinical training, I can tell you one thing. I was lucky. To be fair, I had a really positive reference. Our clinical lead seemed to really value my work and he was reasonably well known and respected. But (as I later found out), it just so happened that the person reviewing my application form actually trained with him, so knew him personally. That meant that particular good reference carried more weight than another 'good reference' and saw me through the application process. I was on the reserve list for an interview and got called the day before to take an interview space. I got a lucky question about private healthcare providing NHS services which was a real interest of mine and so I spoke about it until they (politely) asked me to shut up! When I got the call to say I'd got a place I was stunned. And also devastated for my many colleagues who hadn't got places who I honestly thought were more ready than I was to start training.

And then there was training. I think getting on first time helped me. I had few expectations. Training wasn't the be all and end all for me. I rolled with it, some stuff I knew a bit about, and some stuff was totally new to me. For some of those who'd been trying for years or who had been set on doing it since they were young, training seemed a disappointment. It was too rigid for them; they'd already got a huge amount of experience and seemed to feel restricted and like their existing skills weren't valued. They also went on to become great Clinical Psychologists, but I don't think they enjoyed the process much.

In our final year you got to pick a placement. I chose a CAMHS team that worked solely with families where there are safeguarding concerns. What's the phrase, art replicates life? I was knowingly drawn to a team that had echoes of my history in it. I was open with my supervisor about that and honestly, it was the best decision ever. It freed me up to work with the knowledge of my own life experiences but without those getting in the way of the work I was doing. It meant I had a deeper connection with the work but, through supervision, it was a safe connection. I've worked in other areas since training but have gone back to safeguarding work. It feels familiar and I love the families I work with. It's really the opposite of my pre-training experience at IAPT, which suits me well. But I could probably manage in an IAPT service tomorrow. That's the beauty of being a Clinical Psychologist for me. You can really do pretty much anything, pretty much anywhere.

What do I love about being a Clinical Psychologist? I love being able to be authentic. I bring my humour, my life experiences and my values into my work. I share personal experiences of mental health difficulties and how I overcame them, when it feels appropriate, and I really think that adds value to what I do. I also value the life experiences of those I work with and how they can weave that into their work. I always suggest completing mutual genograms with my supervisees and supervisors, so we get to know our social GRACES and find points of similarity and difference. My personal (and professional) view is that being authentic is one of the most important aspects of the profession. We can't expect others to be honest and vulnerable with us if we won't with them. We all have rough edges to our personalities; well, I certainly do! And I think if you are yourself in an interview and that uni/job don't want you, well then it probably isn't a good fit for you.

Dr Shona Lavey-Khan
Clinical Psychologist

Shona's Story:

Email from: Dr Marianne Trent

To: Dr Shona Lavey-Khan

Hi Shona,

Thanks so much for your story. I couldn't agree more about the importance of being your authentic self. I just love the sound of the ruse you guys came up with getting the supervisors to buy you cakes! When I was an Assistant, we used to do AP meetings with 'payday cakes' but managing to convince the 'qualifieds' to pay for them would have been the cherry on the Bakewell so to speak!

I think we'd get on well, I'm also a massive fan of genograms and always like to do them with new assistants I meet as well as with clients too. I think it's a CAMHS clinician thing – it just works incredibly well!

I'm glad you've found a qualified position which also allows you to be genuine and to help the families and clients you work with so effectively.

Thanks again,

Marianne

21

Kate's Story:

My Journey to DClin: I Did It My Way

One GCSE a year early, extra GCSEs in year ten, awards and merits, I was a highflyer. There was no question of my academic ability, A Levels were the natural next step.

Sitting in another boring psychology class I started to question why I had thought my interest in people might have developed into anything. The A Level Psychology teacher dictated, and we scribed...no discussion, no debate, no soul. I lost interest and gave up on this A Level, leaving me with just two, Art and French, the first rungs on the ladder of my journey. I was already working in the make-up industry, felt I had a trade, and was earning good money outside of my studies, *who needs A Levels anyway,* I thought?!

I got B in Art, and E in French but I enjoyed my work and had a good lifestyle. *I'm just not the academic type,* I surmised, *I*

173

must be arty, as if the two were polar options. After A Levels I started a degree in Fashion Design but left in the first term, lured by my ability to earn well *and* have a fun life. I realised that for me Uni was just a great excuse to get my own place, so I just did that. With my decisions fully supported by my artist parents, I arrived at my A Level leaver's evening excited to tell people about the recent turn in my career. Teachers quickly altered the mood telling me they were 'disappointed' and I 'could've achieved so much more'. My confidence in academia was rock bottom, my focus was on proving to these people that I could succeed without qualifications.

A colourful career followed. I worked all over the world, met people, spent money and had a really good time. My interest in people was always there and as my career moved into the events industry, I immersed myself in learning about and being able to connect with people. My work introduced me to a spectrum of different people, from the UK to America, celebrity houses to the biggest council estate in Europe. I encountered different cultures, religions, personalities, ages. I managed teams of people who all had their own needs to support. I trained and negotiated. I hired and fired. I learned and I listened. My resilience and boundaries were strong, and my ability to think of others and lead from the front developed. My work taught me daily the need to understand what different people needed and wanted, to create atmospheres and environments conducive to a brief, to get into the mind of others and make their day enjoyable and interesting. I worked with a variety of disabilities and mental health, but I also worked with a lot of mental health in the context of the 'normal world', misunderstood, undiagnosed, unrecognised. Reflecting back, I can see how important working in this way has formed the way I work now.

My work took me to every corner of life, into people's lives, and their minds. I needed to reassure and understand, and get to see what other people wanted, and deliver it for them. I was charged with creating atmospheres in different environments on a temporary basis. In all my time working in mental health I have never encountered anything as complicated as getting a number of artists and performers in the right place at the right time in the right frame of mind to perform. I was a problem solver for others. I worked on risk and motivation for others, as well as the never-ending demands from marketing and brand managers. The brief could change quickly, and my problem solving would adapt. I learned that you never know who you are talking to, secret bosses and potential new clients are everywhere. I worked with families, older adults, different communities and cultures, I learned about different celebrations and what matters to others.

In my late 20s I was offered some make-up work with the military. With an apparent never-ending supply of energy and drive I took this because the work interested me. I worked with amputees and different forces from around the world. I attended military briefings and familiarised myself with the language. I worked with all ranks, forces and nationalities and had some of the most resilience building experiences of my life. I encountered medical terminology, suicide, banter, pain, emotions, and observed those who were professionally pressured to their maximum. I experienced things that I felt privileged to be a part of. I experienced things which will never leave my mind. I was excited by these opportunities and experiences. Standing in the middle of the Brecon Beacons in the middle of the night or jumping on helicopters was pretty invigorating. This was the hardest physical and emotional work I had ever encountered, but also the most fun and fulfilling. I felt the comradery and liked it. I used my already open-to-anything mindset and pushed myself to learn things. I did not always enjoy what I learned, but I learned to work with those uncomfortable feelings and situations and achieve where I could, even if these were small successes. On a practical level I developed my dynamic risk assessment skills and learned to speak out appropriately if needed. My love for spending time with people was fulfilled daily, hearing stories, comforting and understanding, and hearing about rehabilitation and life experiences. I also learned where people struggle, how they suffer, where mental health is not prioritised. Trust was key in this work, I built trust and sometimes my trust was abused.

After some years this work ended and I went back to the 'normality' of my previous life, but my interest in psychology, in particular rehabilitation had been resuscitated from somewhere deep inside me. It was a feeling I couldn't shake, and I started to consider my life choices. I knew nothing about the world of psychology, qualifications, pathways or the dreaded 'journey'. My mum had just completed a degree in her fifties so I thought maybe if I do a degree, it might satisfy my interest, then I could go back to my work and get on with my life.

Despite my pleas to the admissions team, I was offered a foundation year due to my A Level results. At 32 years old I skipped off to my first day looking forward to learning. Already having aim and purpose, I found some of the explorative science overwhelming, I scraped through my biology but kept focused. I worked hard running my business alongside my studies. By my second year I was hooked on psychology. This way of learning where you could discuss and learn together, no dictation or scribing. I was already convinced; this is what I want to do. I made major financial decisions and closed my business, I moved close to the university and immersed myself in university life; talks, science fairs, libraries. My choices had reduced my earnings drastically, and therefore my lifestyle. I continued to study and worked multiple jobs which would replace some of my income, enough to live but also leave my mind free to study. I was aware of the age differences between me and most of my cohort, but I had spent all my life socialising professionally with people older and younger than me, so I joined in and found common ground. I met other mature students and enjoyed discussing different life journeys.

Although I enjoyed my degree, I still had an internal narrative that I wasn't academic. I took a summer research post so I could learn more about doing research. I took part in numerous studies so I could really immerse myself in what others were doing and how they approached their learning. It was the way I had always learned, find out about people and see what makes them tick. I attended talks and science festivals and read and read and read. I often felt I was working backwards. I had experienced so many of these theories, I just didn't know they had names, it was fascinating.

At a Uni career's talk, we were told the realities of 'the journey' to DClinPsy; 'Only 4% of people who apply get on, think carefully about your journey.' I just thought *I can be 4%* and carried on reading and didn't think much more of it.

While I was at Uni I volunteered at Headway while also working three jobs. I used every opportunity in my different jobs to practice my non-judgemental stance, my compassionate thinking skills, and my listening skills, in the hope that one day these skills would be used clinically. I used my work time to think about my studies.

Working so many different jobs wasn't all a bed of roses. I was bullied at one job. I was dismissed and ostracised at another, but I kept focused. My work in the events industry had conditioned me to keep a strong and confident 'face' even if I was paddling hard under the surface to survive – the swan. This seemed to get me through but my actual confidence in my abilities was low. I spent a lot of time trying to understand why I felt this way, but my realisation was that this is how graduates are treated. A shocking reality of the system. This saddened me.

I had a new supervisor at Uni, and this was enlightening. When I come away from my supervision, I would have great reflections. While cycling home I would often stop at a park bench and just think about what we had spoken about. Thinking time is precious, I had never had it before, and I was learning a lot.

I finished my degree with a 2:1. With the 'you're not academic' narrative beautifully reinforced, I was pleased to get this chapter behind me but was facing a whole different working world to the one I had imagined when I started my degree. While self-deprecating to one of my peers who got very high grades, he replied, 'but I'll struggle to get a job, you have people skills already' and I held on to this compliment for the next part of my journey.

I wanted to put my previous career behind me and move on to my new career in psychology. I approached this with a secrecy about my past and a feeling that I needed to close a chapter. At 36 years old I had never interviewed for work before. Even the jobs I had done while at Uni had been taken through word of mouth. I set up my business from leaving school, I had interviewed people to employ, but I had no experience being interviewed. My sister helped me write a CV, myhousemates helped me with interview advice; reflect, reflect, reflect. I contacted people and asked for advice, every word being heard and considered. I always remember being so grateful for people's time and advice and promising myself I would pay this forward when the opportunity arose. I applied for jobs, and I was certain of my areas of interest: veterans and neurorehabilitation. The rejections came over and over again; I started to really self-reflect. The turning point came when I saw what I thought was my dream job as an Assistant Psychologist in a military veteran charity. I was offered an interview but not the job. I came away thinking, *do I really know enough to know where I might work best?*

I widened my net. I decided that I would leave some of this up to the interviewers to see what they saw in me. After 6 months of applying for many roles, I was offered an AP role in a private company working with children with Complex Trauma. Children! I never wanted to work with children! I was nervous and excited; I would do it for a while then move on. I moved across the country again.

At the end of my first week my supervisor asked how it felt having finished my first ever 'employed by someone else' working week and I amusingly replied about how refreshing it felt to only work eight hours of the day! I had come from a completely invalidating work life; most people think that 'work from home' means lounging around all day. In reality, it means there is no end to the working day. Being told to finish at 5pm and a department to deal with IT issues was like a dream, all the rest of the hours in the day were my own, what a treat! To top that, having come from an industry where there is no 'working week', all days are chargeable, I hadn't had a weekend in 20 years. I am still thrilled to have one every week, and annual leave is just the best!

This AP role was mainly consultation-based work. My 'we can do it' attitude from the past was really useful in this. I was proactive and used to mentoring others to achieve their needs, so this fitted well with my working style - although I secretly resented that this is where my skills came from as I had not come to terms with the merging of my careers yet.

While in this job I also undertook a number of projects in my personal life. I renovated a house; having to sofa surf with my brother for some of that time, I struggled with my drop in finances and had to ask for help from others, I lost family members and experienced my own grief. As I had always been the person people went to, I learned to tell my supervisor when I had things going on outside of work so they could be considerate with me. Moving to an industry where personal distress and overload is acknowledged and accepted was alien to me. From an industry where the ethos had always been *'get through, move on.'*

Kate's Story:

I applied for DClinPsy each year because my Uni supervisors had always advised I do. I also had an internal ongoing maths equation, *'If I don't get on soon, I will be over 40 by the time I qualify'*; race, race, race. I wasn't ready, I felt that but ignored my intuition. I found the yearly cycle of anticipation and rejection had become a part of my circannual rhythm.

I have had some great supervisors. They have always given me great advice, but I have also always embraced my supervision. Be vulnerable, let them guide you, trust the theories. Sometimes it was hard, and sometimes I felt like a star pupil. When I mentioned parts of my previous work in discussions by supervisors, they wanted to know more about it, and how that is a part of me. They told me they started to understand how I worked from this. I struggled to merge the two careers. One supervisor told me I was 'too confident', and it took me months to even tell him about my past career. When I did, we really connected and the advice in that supervision was really useful for me because it was tailored to me; my openness was key to that. Being resilient in my work and vulnerable in my supervision became my focus. One supervisor helped with my internal narrative. I used to say, *'if I get on course'* and he would say *'when you qualify'.*

Work in private healthcare was busy, fast paced, autonomous. This played to all my strengths, but I had an underlying feeling that I could do this because of my past and not because of my future. My supervisor suggested I look at NHS roles, but I stayed in private healthcare because I still really struggled with a fear of interviews.

I rarely encountered other APs but would hear about them within the company. I started an AP group. I have always valued peer supervision, and this is a great way to learn and reflect. I booked myself onto training and workshops wherever I could. Free ones, naturally. I also took every opportunity to attend training offered at work. My focus was widening from clinical contact. I would sit quietly in training, my imposter syndrome always overwhelming me. I would wait for someone to storm in and kick me out as an imposter to the world of psychology. This wasn't always helped by the qualifieds I encountered. I went on a workshop where everyone was chatting to people next to them. The person next to me asked my job title and refused to speak with me after finding out I was an AP. I'll never forget how sad that made me feel. The systemic prejudice can be strong enough at the bottom of this ladder without the people who are halfway up reinforcing it.

I heard that some research was being done within the company I worked in and asked if I could help. This would be great for my CPD (continuing professional development), but I was told no by my supervisor. This, combined with some unpleasant work dynamics I was encountering, prompted my search for new roles.

I got an NHS job. I have always been proud to wear my blue lanyard. Me, who had spent my early career revelling that I didn't need a qualification or to work for anyone else, was a junior in the NHS, at nearly 40. I never did anything to the norm! I felt proud, and I loved my work. This job was as an AP in Children's Community Learning Disability, *children must be my thing,* I thought. Used to supervision now I connected and learned quickly. I slowed down, became more considered, could see my strengths, and was challenged.

I had started to develop an understanding of the applications system and the world of psychology in general. I was also very passionate with my supervisor about my concerns about 'the journey', the lack of inclusivity, the age discrimination, the lack of solid guidance for applicants, the over competitive nature of people being pitted against each other. He said, 'get involved!'

Kate's Story:

A BPS DCP pre-qualification group (PQG) workshop day had been advertised on social media so I booked on for some CPD hoping it would satisfy my need for some psychology chat outside of work. This day changed my world again. I met like-minded APs who spoke openly and networked. The open discussion about competition which wasn't apparent in behaviours was refreshing. I made solid professional friends and offered to be part of the committee that day. Joining the PQG as the Children Young People and Families faculty rep allowed me a space to really get involved and form my own identity in psychology. Not just what work was telling me to learn, but my own interests and passions. I listened and learned. I didn't like everything I heard but I started to understand a lot and learn where to challenge. I got involved in research, published a paper, contributed a talk to the Group of Trainers in Clinical Psychology (GTiCP), hosted and participated in webinars. Maybe I could do this academic stuff, not only was I doing it but for my own passion, on my own time, my confidence in myself started to grow.

At work I met a trainee and we connected. We still speak and she told me that she felt I would be good at this job and that helped with my confidence too. We had a talk in AP group from a Clinical Psychologist who had qualified in her 40s. I had never met anyone who had qualified as a second career before. This motivated me too.

Even though I had been applying for DClinPsy every year I finally felt ready to apply. This was no longer a practice. I felt confident. At the test stage I mucked up a test. It was my own fault, but I spoke about it, reflected on it, and saw my peers get on course that year. I was motivated for the next year already. As the year passed, I reflected a lot on my entire career.

I changed my job again, a challenging role working in Forensics, with adults! For the first time I drove away from the interview and said to my mum, 'I hope they can see in me what I see I can do in that job'. I got it. I was nervous, I had labelled myself the AP who was good with children so work with adults gave me the fear. I came with humility, listened and learned, but all with my growing confidence in my own identity as part of the psychology world. In this job I really joined up the dots and connected my previous career skills with my current career. I encountered such different people. I had the opportunity to use skills from all my roles. I worked with veterans in one-to-one therapy where I used my knowledge from past experiences. I worked with people with learning disabilities (LD) and used adaptive communication skills from my time in the children's LD team. I worked with adults who had grown up in the private care system and reflected on the cases I worked with as a new AP. I encountered women my age who were struggling and realised that people can all be vulnerable. I recognised what it was like to feel you have to achieve - achieve at work, and in an industry where mental health is not considered and accepted. I used my skills of connecting with people and finding out about their environment, community, interests and family dynamics to inform my practice. I used my dynamic risk assessment skills to remain vigilant but remained relaxed and non-judgemental when working with offenders – we are all people. I realised that my work in mental health has been important but my experiences working with mental health in industries which don't understand or acknowledge mental health is even more important. This helped me to understand why others may struggle to understand, accept, and work with the issues they experience. I gained respect for myself in this job, and in turn respect from others. I will always wonder if one preceded the other, or if they coincidentally collided.

There wasn't an AP group in this trust, so I set one up. Opening up a place for peer supervision is still important to me, and I also wanted to give others this space. During this role I continued to have my own personal experiences, illness, finances, a house flood. I had learned to share things with my supervisor and let them know where I am at. This allowed me to continue working by adapting my expectations and prioritising each time. I watched and learned from colleagues' working styles.

I have always been supervised by people the same age or younger than me. They regularly contextualised my questions in comparison to them and where they were in their life. We always got on, but the advice was sometimes, 'I wouldn't at your age'. The first question I asked my supervisor in this job was 'am I too old?' She said a clear 'no'. I had two supervisors in this role. One was a Counselling Psychologist. I found this different supervision really useful. I developed my psychotherapeutic skills, read a lot, and continued my own self-reflection. I continued to grow. My supervisor helped me to explore my own working styles with different people and consider new approaches. My 'we can do it' developed into a 'sometimes we can't and that's okay'; acceptance of my own abilities. The pandemic gave me the opportunity to slow down and self-reflect. I followed my own advice. I looked at my own biopsychosocial balance and focused on my own soothe system. In this job I also had loads of opportunity to get involved with the wider psychology team. I volunteered to do research, literature searches, and use the skills which had lay dormant since my undergraduate degree. This helped with my confidence.

During my five years as an AP, I applied and got a place on four different Master's courses, because I have felt some inadequacy of not having any postgraduate qualifications. My understanding of the system and the difficulties in what is good to have on your application has always sparked interesting conversations during supervision. I have always found myself back to the same thinking place, if I could afford to do a Master's or see one I am particularly interested in then I should do it. Every year I would cancel the place I had gained. In all honesty this was always a decision of justice. Universities keep saying that a Master's isn't needed, and I couldn't afford to do one. Instead, I focused on taking opportunities to build my research skills at work.

Working with other APs and younger practitioners has been interesting to me. I have always tried to connect with the people I work with. I have shared my work, reflected and enjoyed that shared experience. What I have received and observed has sometimes been competitive and distant. The system seems to pit pre-qualifieds against each other, and everyone seems to buy into that. I took choices to pursue this career because I wanted to. Times have been hard; I financially support others, and this can make it complicated for me. I know I am capable of earning more, but I choose this. There are many assumptions within the world of psychology, and too many times I have observed that we seem to help others and ostracise our own.

While going through this self-reflection and writing a paper about barriers to application I started to resent the DClinPsy application system. I decided I would not let myself be downtrodden any longer. I started to look at different qualifications, maybe I could get back into the events industry, maybe I am an occupational psychologist, maybe I need to work in HR. I applied for various things and was offered an interview for DCounsPsy. I didn't enjoy it; I saw other people who were so right for it. I didn't get a place, but this jump off the DClinPsy road only made me feel more connected with it. I returned with a fresh confidence. Despite its twists and turns and closed gates everywhere it felt *right* for me. I came back even more focused.

I spoke to my PQG peers and they helped me to reflect. Also, my supervisors really believed in me, and I spoke openly with them about my confidence issues. I felt ready. Even my family started to tell me they felt I was changing, becoming more 'whole' and contented with my plans, even though they could see how hard they were. I had found peace with my application and the process. Despite the difficulties I no longer felt it was a battle, just a wait for my time, *I can be 4%* came back to my internal narrative (even though this statistic was now more like

Kate's Story:

2%). I asked for application mentoring which really helped me to understand myself in my application.

I have always toiled with the question; do I include my own lived experiences in my application? I chose not to for two reasons. I can't find links to my application; it is part of my life but not my reasons for applying. The input would be minimal, 'I know how people can fall through the cracks in the system'. It doesn't inform my application, it does, however, continue to inform my practice and my understanding of people.

I was offered a reserve interview. My confidence knock was huge, *why am I a reserve, maybe I am not right for this, am I delusional?* I spoke to my peers again and they helped me to refocus. The mantra of my supervision became *you only need one.* I connected with myself again. I prepared myself in a way which felt natural and not studious. I maintained my calm, and my understanding of myself. I didn't need to revise, I needed to 'be'. I was offered an interview with two weeks' notice so I maintained my balance and told myself I know what I am doing, I will be fine. I prepared by revising my CV, and therefore knowing and reflecting on myself better. I upped my self-care and sheltered myself from all distractions.

After the interview I wasn't sure. I felt like I didn't muck it up but if I'm not what they want then that's okay, I showed them what I have. My colleagues were dropping rejections, one colleague gave up psychology all together after multiple interviews.

After 19 rejections and one reserve interview my offer email arrived. I was thrilled! The feeling of validation was so real. All I kept repeating to my mum was 'it's not even a reserve place it's a real one'! My supervisors were not as surprised as me but equally thrilled. I have kept in contact with all my supervisors, so I emailed everyone, right to my Uni supervisor to let them know that he was finally free of writing my academic reference now! Weirdly, when I started to tell my peers I was surprised by how many of them told me how 'lucky' I was. I felt invalidated again. I felt I had earned my place but the narrative of 'the journey lottery' is so strong it was seen as a 'win' rather than an achievement. This stopped me from telling people, I wanted to enjoy the feeling.

My respect for the course is so strong that this is a small celebration, and I have now started to tell people. I am blocking out the rumour tree at the moment, I have always done things my way and I know what my gut tells me. I am not able to take a month off before I start the course; financially I can't afford to, but I can't wait to start and work towards the next step in my journey.

All I know is that in all the experiences I have had in work, I have never felt as comfortable as I do in this one. The experiences aren't quite as exciting, or stories you can tell, but I love it, it is me.

I'll be 41 when I start my doctorate and I also love that!

If I had continued that A Level, I wouldn't have been a good psychologist, I am doing it my way.

Kate Cudmore is about to start her Doctorate in Clinical Psychology at Staffordshire University and is on track to qualify in 2024 when she will be aged 44.

Connect with her -
Email: katecudmore@hotmail.com
LinkedIn: Kate Cudmore
Instagram: @katecudmore
Twitter: @katecudmore
And connect with the BPS DCP PQG on Instagram - @DCPPreQual

Kate's Story:

Email from: Dr Marianne Trent

To: Dr Kate Cudmore

Hi Kate,

Thank you for your wonderful submission, you have had such a varied career to date. I am confident that your cohort will really benefit from your wide and diverse experiences and they will of course serve you well too.

Thank you so much for taking the time to share your story with us. I know it will be incredibly powerful for those who are looking to get started a little later than many.

Your story reminded me of one of my favourite books: Angela's Ashes; lots of rich detail about smaller aspects and then a quick overview of grief and natural disasters, I enjoyed it very much and was left wanting more!

Wishing you the absolute best (not of luck, you don't need luck!) Let me know if you need anything over the next 3 years of study!

Thanks,

Marianne

22

Karen's Story:

A Letter to You.....

Dear Aspiring Psychologist, If you are reading this, you're probably thinking about a career in Psychology. I hope my story will give you some insight into the process of training as a Clinical Psychologist, some reassurance that you do not have to follow a certain path to get there, and perhaps some ideas of how to get helpful experience.

I don't know what stage you are at, so I'll start from the beginning...

I first studied Psychology at AS and A Level, alongside Biology and Maths. This was, apparently, an unusual combination and did cause some scheduling difficulties with exams. However, the other subjects helped me in my ongoing study of psychology. I felt I had an advantage when it came to understanding the different statistical tests used because of my Maths A-level. Biology has also been helpful when working with the biopsychosocial model.

Karen's Story:

After my A-Levels I studied for my Psychology (BSc Hons) degree. I found it a bit 'dry' – undergraduate psychology is a very academic subject and the course I did was mainly lecture based. The assessments were a mixture of coursework and exams. I had hoped to complete a placement year as part of the course to gain some practical experience of the application of the psychological knowledge from my degree, unfortunately this was not possible as there were no local placements and the lack of funding meant placements further away were not affordable. However, I was able to gain some experience supporting one of the lecturers with a research project during the summer between the second and third years of my degree. I completed my degree with a 2:1 and moved back to live with my parents[15] while I searched for a job that used the knowledge and skills from my degree.

I worked in retail during the final 2 years of my degree and continued this after graduating. I spent the next few years applying for Assistant Psychologist jobs. I was unsuccessful and was repeatedly told I did not have enough experience. I sought out voluntary opportunities working with people with mental health difficulties and was able to gain some experience working with the local branch of the charity Mind.

After a couple of years, I had managed to save enough money to do a Master's course[16]. I only applied for one course (in Health Psychology) and was surprised to be offered a place! I opted to complete this part-time so I could continue working part-time in my retail job in order to support myself financially. I loved studying for my Master's - I felt the topics had more relevance to supporting people, however there was no practical

---

[15] I recognise my privilege in being able to do this, and that this is not something that everyone is able to do.

[16] See above.

190

element to this course. After completing the course, I remained in contact with some of the lecturers and was able to gain some experience working on a research project they were conducting. The lecturers heard about an opportunity for psychology graduates that was being advertised by the local NHS Trust, and kindly let me know about it. I applied for the position and was fortunate to get it – my first post in the NHS!

The role was on a neurosurgery ward providing additional support to people displaying behaviours that challenge as a result of the brain injury they had sustained. I was part of the ward team, so I gained a great insight into working in the NHS and seeing how different professions all work together in a multi-disciplinary team. After a few months I started applying for Assistant Psychologist positions again, hoping that the experience I was gaining would increase my chances of being successful.

Unfortunately, it did not appear to make much difference as I struggled to get interviews for Assistant Psychologist positions. I noticed that lots of Assistant Psychologist posts asked for experience of certain activities, which I didn't have, so I sought out opportunities to gain these experiences. I approached a Clinical Psychologist within the Trust and asked if there was any way I could do some voluntary work with them to gain experience. I also found a local charity who were recruiting volunteers to facilitate peer support mental health groups. I was lucky that both the Clinical Psychologist and the charity were willing to let me volunteer with them and gain very valuable experience. However, this did mean that I had two voluntary roles in addition to my full-time paid role within the NHS, so I was working around 50 hours per week[17]. I continued to apply

---

[17] Once again, I recognise my privilege in being able to do this, and that this is not something that everyone is able to do.

for Assistant Psychologist and Research Assistant positions that would help me gain the 'relevant experience' needed for applications for the Doctorate in Clinical Psychology.

With the extra experience I was gaining from my voluntary roles, I started to be invited to interviews for Assistant Psychologist and Research Assistant positions. I lost count of how many interviews I attended before being offered a position as a Research Assistant. I think this reflects how competitive these posts are as well as the fact that I'm not very good at interviews (I get too anxious).

I loved this position! The team were amazing and incredibly supportive. I enjoyed knowing that the work I was doing was contributing to increasing the knowledge base and improving people's wellbeing. I left after about 18 months as I had been living away from home during the week (going home at the weekends) and I was missing my dog!

I had applied for the Doctorate in Clinical Psychology whilst I was working in my first NHS post. Unsurprisingly I didn't get any interviews, but it was good experience of completing the form. I applied for the Doctorate again when I was working as a Research Assistant. The first time I applied, I was offered two interviews but was not successful that year. I applied again the following year and was again offered two interviews. The first interview didn't go well and by the time I left I was not expecting to be offered a place. Sure enough, a few weeks later the letter arrived confirming that I had been unsuccessful.

The next interview was a couple of months later. It felt like everything went wrong before the interview, but I think this actually helped! I didn't think anything else could possibly go wrong which helped me relax and be myself. I thought I'd done my best but didn't know if that would be good enough. So, I was surprised when a letter arrived a few weeks later offering me a place!

I loved training! I moved to do the course and I fell in love with the city and area I trained in. Living locally helped me to understand the local context of the people I was supporting. Training had its challenges: I had moved away from my family which was difficult at times, there were some stressful times when there were academic deadlines relatively close together, and I had a difficult experience with a supervisor on one of my placements which knocked my confidence. However, I feel I was well supported by the course team and my fellow Trainees. We had a study day every week (which was occasionally used as a self-care day) and had a group reflective practice session once a month. My cohort were very supportive, and we had a good blend of strengths. The placements gave me the opportunity to work with different client groups and this helped me discover what I enjoyed most and wanted to specialise in.

Unfortunately, the Covid-19 pandemic broke out not long after I qualified so I have not had the opportunity to experience 'normal' qualified life to compare with training. I have found working clinically during Covid very challenging as I experienced mental health difficulties of my own during this time (due to a number of factors). I also noticed I really missed undertaking research, which was one of the main reasons I chose Clinical over other types of psychology.

I am due to start a new role as a Clinical Tutor on one of the Clinical Psychology training courses soon. This has more research and less direct clinical work so I hope this will allow me to focus on my own mental wellbeing for a while. I plan to return to doing more clinical work in the future and would like to get a balance between clinical and research work. This isn't the direction I thought my career would take, but I'm excited about the opportunity to support Trainees and help to shape the future of the profession.

I managed to qualify as a Clinical Psychologist with determination, persistence, and a lot of luck (being in the right place at the right time). Looking back, it was not an easy journey, and I made a lot of sacrifices along the way. If I knew then what I know now, I would have tried to get a part-time role working within healthcare (rather than retail) while doing my undergraduate degree as this would have helped me gain experience at an earlier stage.

Good luck and best wishes for your journey in psychology!

With my best wishes,

Dr Karen Coalford

If you have found this story helpful, please consider making a donation to Changes, Bristol at https://changesbristol.org.uk/ **to support them with providing free mental health support to people in Bristol.**

Email from: Dr Marianne Trent

To: Dr Karen Coalford

Hi Karen,

Thank you so much for the speed at which you put this together for us, you saw me mention it on the Saturday morning and 'whoosh' it was with us by the Sunday afternoon!

One of my favourite things about Clinical Psychology is the diverse experience of everyone and the sheer number of skills and aptitudes practiced each day and at different stages of our career. You have most definitely demonstrated that within your letter. People will find it very helpful to read the different ways to think about accessing experience. You must have been utterly exhausted before you started your doctorate, but I bet it's only with hindsight that you can truly appreciate that! So pleased you enjoyed training – I did too!

I'd like to wish you all of the very best in your new role at the university. I am sure the trainees will most definitely appreciate your mix of academic and clinical expertise.

Thanks again,

Marianne

23

Charlotte's Story:

Jumping ship? Or just finding the right path!

My journey to clinical psychology hasn't been the most traditional. I think it truly started at A Level: I'd sat some GCSEs and A Levels early which left me with the option to do an A Level in a year. Everyone suggested psychology and I said *'nah, I'll do theology.'* I'd already decided to study speech and language therapy (SALT) and given that I already had a random set of A Levels (Maths, Biology, French, Health & Social Care & Art) another random subject wasn't going to make much difference. I was sure that I wanted to work in Sure Start once qualified with families and, in my mind, my career was sorted. However, this was in 2011 – the year we got the coalition government and as I progressed through my four-year degree, Sure Start quickly started disappearing. However, this wasn't what led to the move away from SALT. Around halfway through my degree, I was growing increasingly frustrated whilst being continuously marginalised in a profession where I rarely saw another person of colour and was exposed to

196

microaggressions (racist, classist and ableist) on a daily basis. The lack of safe spaces as well as space to reflect on how our identities impact the work we do, began to impact on me to the point that I started contemplating what other career options are out there for me. I knew that I still wanted to be in a helping profession. Taking some time one evening to reflect on what I truly enjoyed and valued about my training, I ended up with the following list: helping people, working creatively, research, understanding behaviour, making sense of people's experiences and service development. The penny dropped for me when not long after this evening, I took a clinical psychology module. I have to say I both loved and hated this module for very different reasons. I was enthralled by the material, it really changed how I positioned my practice and the way I positioned myself as a health practitioner with living experience of trauma. However, the downside of that module and being in such a small class (26ish) meant that when people decided to whisper stigmatising remarks about your mental health, you and everyone else in the room could hear it. No one ever said anything to challenge it and at the time I did not have the energy. Silence is violence. And the stigma I experienced sitting in this room is where my mental health activism began.

Getting through the remaining half of my degree would have been impossible without the mental health society I set up in the students' union with an amazing team of women with lived/living experience and my days spent in the student newspaper office laying up the beauty pages every week and working as a blogger for a designer men's wear brand (at this point I was considering a career in lifestyle journalism; it was great while it lasted).

July 2015 – graduation. I'd been applying for all sorts of random jobs in the run up to this and was lucky enough to be offered two: a full-time graduate internship at a disability charity in London and an apprenticeship at an arts charity in Manchester that was only two days per week. Of course, me being me, I took the apprenticeship.

You're probably wondering at this point what has this got to do with clinical psychology? At the time, having had four very tough years, I just wanted a job that I would enjoy that would be low stress and wasn't too concerned about how 'relevant' this would be to my long-term career goals. I worked there on and off for 4 years and in between I worked in schools, I did National Youth Theatre, wrote a few plays and most importantly did a lot of work on healing myself and reminding myself of what the *why* was for pursuing clinical psychology. My arts job has turned out to be one of the greatest learning experiences of my career to date, and despite the mainstream perception of it not being the most relevant sort of role when pursuing psychology, I think I learnt more about mental health, power and social inequality than I ever did anywhere else.

After applying for my conversion and then deferring I was finally ready to start in 2016. I had initially deferred because I wanted to be sure I really wanted to go down this career route so delaying my conversion felt like a sensible decision. When I started my Master's, I was toying with becoming an educational psychologist, however about 7 weeks into the course this idea quickly disintegrated. Pretty sure I was sitting in a neuroscience lecture when I just thought 'nope, ed psych is not for me' and began making a detailed plan of how I was going to get onto the clinical psychology doctorate. I'm the kinda person who loves a very 'detailed plan' so I made a list of every job/experience I ever had (I won't list them all here, my master CV is not something that will ever see the light of day) and identified the gaps in my experience. The obvious ones were getting experience as an AP, getting research experience beyond speech and language therapy (I helped one of my lecturers with testing a new linguistic analysis tool) and making sure I worked as hard as possible on my Master's in the hopes of counterbalancing my 64%/low 2.1 from undergrad.

The perfect research job popped up when I was sat in the library with a friend – a project using participatory action research to explore inequalities in mental health experienced by people of Black, Asian and Mixed backgrounds. With only 48 hours 'til the deadline, I had to make a start. This was quickly disrupted when I saw a mouse run across the library and flew into a panic (that's a story for a different book), but once I'd got out of the building, I had a plan and I fully intended to give this application my best shot. To tell you I was overjoyed when I got this job was an understatement. It gave me the confidence boost I needed following coming out of Uni the first time, feeling quite 'academically incompetent' (an academic on my course did actually call me this in a meeting and I never quite managed to shake it off). But this job nurtured my love of research methods and helped me to see if the DClinPsy didn't happen, I could be quite happy with a back-up career in research.

As my Master's drew to a close, I started looking for AP jobs, I was rejected from the first 17 that I applied for with no interview offers. Then I saw an advert on twitter to be an AP in a social enterprise working for someone who I really admire as I follow their work. Once again, I spotted this job near the deadline except this time I only had 3 hours! Whilst I had a lot of AP applications on my laptop, I was aware that none of these had gotten me an interview, so I decided to just start a fresh personal statement. I really wanted this job and so I decided if I was going to get it, it would be by being myself, not by writing what I think I'm expected to write to get to interview. I was very surprised to get a phone call inviting me to interview and the rest is history. Working in a psychology role where social justice and anti-racism is at the heart of everything we do, was good soul food for reminding myself that I do not need to compartmentalise myself or sacrifice parts of my identity to work in this field.

When the time came to apply for the doctorate, I was in two minds about applying. This was largely down to clinical psychology's diversity problem. As a Black-mixed, disabled, working class woman who was a young carer and has lived experience of mental health difficulties, I was well aware that the odds were massively stacked against me. I did myself a deal to take the plunge now and knowing that if I don't get a place, it's because those courses are not right for me rather than me not being right for them or me not being 'good enough'. I stretched to taking a gamble and applying to a course where I didn't quite meet the academic entry requirements in the hope that they may take my mitigating circumstances into consideration. One application turned into two interviews and one offer. To tell you I was completely in shock about this is an understatement. The shock probably remained for two months after getting my offer. The application process was brutal, and I decided halfway through that if I did not get in, I would need to take a break for a year or so before applying again. I also made the decision I would apply a maximum of three times as this process is incredibly draining.

I think clinical psychology has fostered a culture where the norm is to apply again and again year on year and to always be trying to level up. I have always said I never want my life to revolve around psychology and for a part of this application process it did. I also made the error of spending more and more time with other applicants during the process and whilst peer support is great, too much peer contact can lead to all sorts of toxic, competitive dynamics. I knew I needed to remind myself of who I was and that this was a job, so I started attending more regular life drawing classes, doing my nails and watching more French crime dramas. This helped ground me again.

Getting onto training came for me at a time when lots of things had shifted in my life and I was ready for my next big adventure, having done so much work to move through trauma and emerge as myself,

Dr Charlotte Maxwell
Clinical Psychologist

Email from: Dr Marianne Trent

To: Dr Charlotte Maxwell

Hi Charlotte,

*Thanks so much for your story. I am in shock that anyone in any job could have the gall to call anyone 'academically incompetent!' What a dreadful, disempowering and traumatising statement to hear from someone in a position of power. I was also saddened to hear that grownups could be so mean about anyone's mental health; it sounds a lot like primary school **not** university! I'm so glad that you used these experiences and others to fuel your fire and to still strive for the right path for you but also whilst maintaining your sense of self and not at all costs! The manicures and crime dramas sound like the perfect antidote!*

Thanks again,

Marianne

24

Clair's Story:

When things click into place!

I was sitting on the bed in a bamboo hut, on stilts, on the edge of one of the most beautiful beaches in Thailand. There was a gentle breeze, the sun was shining, and I could hear the waves lapping against the shore. I was feeling peaceful and still. It was here that I first realised I wanted to be a psychologist. I was 19. I'd finished my A Levels but had no clue what it wanted to do at Uni, or even if I wanted to go. So, I decided to spend a year travelling around Australia, Bali and Thailand. I realised on this trip that I wanted to help people. I had no idea what this would look like. All I knew was that I didn't want people to feel alone in their pain.

So, my plan on my return to the UK was to do two more A Levels: in Psychology and Business Studies, which would lead me into a Psychology degree. But when I got back, I found myself getting distracted with working, and my Psychology plan fell into the background. One job to another and I ended up progressing in an advertising and marketing career. But as the years progressed, I was becoming more and more unhappy in that world, knowing that it wasn't the career for me. So, at 24 I decided to make some life changes, quit my job, and applied to study Psychology as a "mature student". I was so excited to finally be learning Psychology!

I saw lots of students working part time jobs in shops and bars, but I knew I wanted to have time to *actually study*. So, I took a job as a Support Worker in a local housing association. I worked in a youth hostel for young people involved in the criminal justice system. It was a night job, so I would spend time supporting the young people in the evening, and then stay overnight to be on call if any of the young people needed help during the night (e.g., from emotional difficulties, to police involvement, to young people absconding out of the window!) Luckily, most nights were uninterrupted, and I would go straight from the hostel to Uni. This gave me my days free to study. And my hard work paid off, I got a First.

After Uni I started to apply for Assistant Psychologist and Research Assistant roles within the NHS. It was tough. There were only a few local posts, and there were a lot of people applying for them. At this point I joined a local group of Assistants. This was pivotal. It was a source of support/camaraderie, and also of shared information. Even though we were often going for the same posts, it felt like we were all rooting for each other. It was here that I learned a lot about the process of applying for posts, and also applying for clinical training (i.e., the Doctorate in Clinical Psychology, otherwise known as the DClin, which qualifies you as a Clinical Psychologist).

There seemed to be a hierarchy of which roles usually led to the Assistant being successful in applying for clinical training. This seemed to be due to the role itself (offering a range of experiences that the DClin courses valued), as well as who the lead psychologist was (and hence what type of supervision was offered). Both of the Assistant roles I did were primarily research focussed. The first role I did on an honorary contract (i.e., I wasn't paid) in a service for adults diagnosed with a personality disorder. I did this to get my foot in the door and gain some experience. This helped me to secure my second role, in a service for adults with drug and alcohol addictions, which was paid.

Then I made my first application to clinical training. I had access to examples of previous application forms (at one of my posts they had kept a file), which helped me to know where to start. I then asked the Consultant Psychologist supervisors for their feedback on my form, as well my Assistant colleagues in the group.

I was not successful that first year. I was disappointed, but I also knew that it was really normal for people to try a few times before getting a place on the DClin course. I decided to balance my primarily research focused roles by getting some clinical experience. So, I started a role as a Graduate Mental Health Worker (which is now the IAPT service). Within that role I did a Postgraduate Certificate in Mental Health, which was essentially a CBT course for anxiety and depression (before IAPT brought in their own PWP training). In my role I saw clients for individual therapy sessions, and I also wrote and delivered group programs.

I then applied again for clinical training and was offered an interview with all 4 courses that I'd applied to. To prepare myself for these interviews I asked a couple of Consultant Psychologists if they would 'mock' interview me. This helped me practice my answers, and more importantly, practice calming my interview nerves! I believe this was pivotal in helping me navigate the real interviews. And this time I was successful! I attended three of the four interviews and was offered a place by two of the courses (which is why I cancelled the fourth interview – I knew I would accept one of those places and hence I wanted to enable someone from the waiting list to go to the fourth interview instead).

I was so happy to finally be living my dream of getting on the DClin! I just hadn't thought much about what was going to happen after that! But I was looking forward to learning and applying that to help clients.

My cohort was a small cohort of 13 people, and we were split into three smaller groups (depending on region) for some tasks. It felt like we were a team. The course was split into teaching, placement, and academic work/research. I felt lucky in that I enjoyed all three elements (and that there were no traditional exams!). I also enjoyed learning a range of therapeutic models. I knew I wanted more than the CBT course gave me and I began to be drawn towards the systemic, attachment-based models.

But even though clinical training seems to take over people's lives, my private life remained important to me. I didn't want to put my personal life on hold. So, I got married one year into training, and in my second year I was thrilled to fall pregnant with my first child. I completed the second year of clinical training before going on maternity leave for a year. I returned to finish my final year, joining a new cohort of trainees. However, I knew I didn't want to work full time anymore so I agreed with the course that I would complete the year 3 teaching within that year, with one cohort, but I would only work part time hours. So, I spread the required number of clinical placement hours out, meaning it would take me two (part-time) years to complete my final year (which would normally be full-time). But it was important to me to have my children close together in age, so I fell pregnant again, with my second child, one year into the two years. I took another year off on maternity leave and returned for a final time to complete the second part of my final year, this time solely on clinical placements. I thoroughly enjoyed my final year placements. I worked in services seeing couples, perinatal clients, families, and children who were fostered or adopted. Due to the way I completed training these placements began to feel more like how an employed position would be, rather than

Clair's Story:

a trainee on clinical training, which was great preparation for finishing training as a qualified Clinical Psychologist.

Doing clinical training in this way brought challenges (reaching placements targets, changing placements, having to change research supervisor) but it also brought a wealth of personal growth and development. Having children enabled me to understand some aspects of Psychology in more depth, and understanding those things helped me to be a better parent. I also had two important small people to think about, so it put some of the academic pressures into perspective (P.S I went on to have a third baby one year after qualifying!)

Completing the course definitely gave me a sense of achievement. I was so proud of myself for navigating my placements, finishing my research, successfully presenting my viva, and ultimately walking across that stage to hug Baroness Floella Benjamin at my graduation!

I am so grateful for all the learning – both personally and professionally. The course teaches you the things you may expect, and it also teaches you things you don't expect. The learning is both personal and professional. It is a journey into a deeper sense of yourself, and into what it means to be human, as well as how we heal and grow.

It was during the course that these things began to 'click' for me. But it's not a one-time thing. Things have continued to 'click' into place. Through further trainings and also from my clients. It's truly an honour to be welcomed into another person's inner world. To be present with them in their inner exploration. To know that they are not alone in their pain. And to witness the human ability to heal.

Dr Clair Burley is a Clinical Psychologist, offering trauma-informed and attachment-focused therapy. She runs a private

practice in Dorset, specialising in relationships – both with the self and with others, from the past and in the present.
www.drclair.com

Email from: Dr Marianne Trent

To: Dr Claire Burley

Hi Claire,

Wow! I am just in total awe of you smashing it out the park with your First whilst sleeping in a workplace too! Also, would fully have loved to hug Floella and I definitely think you ought to return to that Thai Bamboo hut now you're qualified and a smidge older and see what other cracking ideas come to you! I expect as a mother of 3, such hedonistic time to contemplate feels like a dim and distant memory!

Thanks for being part of this process and for checking in with me regularly, it's been lovely to be in touch with you and you've been so supportive. It's been a massive project and having you cheer it on and be enthusiastic about it has been very much appreciated.

Wishing you all the best with your work and until you can get to Thailand, I'd say that Dorset is an excellent second choice!

Thanks again,

Marianne

25

Shabnam's Story:

Learning from rejection and re-writing the script for acceptance

S ometimes we tell ourselves stories about ourselves that are incomplete, unreliable, or simply misleading. These stories have the power to keep us stuck in a mental place that is unfulfilling or frustrating, a distorting lens on the world and ourselves. Their constant retelling determines which aspects of our lives are reinforced, and which parts of our history are forever left out, when those might have been powerful and valuable factors that changed our lives in positive and progressive ways, making us the person we are.

Here is how I started rewriting my story and my life, and how it led me into clinical psychology training.

From the start of my educational journey, I was an average-grade pupil. I was not a very confident child and probably came across as a quiet learner without anything remarkable about her. I was therefore not seen as someone who needed the teachers' attention – if I was really *seen* at all. All I knew was that I had to do well. It was a lonely pursuit and one that felt unique to me. One classmate was a bit of a bully, and he got attention; as I got older, I noticed that my academically bright friend was praised consistently by teachers and peers alike. I learnt a limiting narrative at quite an early age.

LIMITING STORYLINE 1: Average does not get noticed. It is not good enough.

This was a strong cultural message I received: both as the daughter of Pakistani immigrants, and as a girl growing up in the society of the '80s and '90s, when I was at school: to live a comfortable life, you need to be a professional, a white-collar worker. I happened to be good with my hands and was able to fix sockets and mend a VCR (Video Cassette Recorder, that was *the thing* in that era!) But that did not fit with contemporary expectations of a girl or a future professional, so once again I knew intuitively that there was no point in pursuing skills which weren't valued.

Looking back, I was always destined for a job somewhere in the field of healthcare. As a *good* Pakistani girl, I assumed it would be medicine. I wanted to please my parents and practise a profession from the Holy Trinity of medicine, law, or accountancy.

The problem was that I hated secondary school, and I chose subjects that would get me into medicine instead of the ones I enjoyed and had a chance of doing well in. I can say now (thank you, therapy!) with some conviction that my feelings about school were not explained by a lack of academic ability. It's just hard to do well in something you dislike so much. This is where I learned another limiting storyline.

LIMITING STORYLINE 2: Regardless of whether you like something or not, just power through any emotional incongruence. The goal always justifies the means.

My confusion about my actual abilities and dislike for that learning environment become easier to understand when I think about the teachers' perceptions and how they expressed them. My English teacher remarked how surprising it was that I managed an 'A' in my GCSE, having assumed my family spoke a different language at home – which apparently should have hindered my ability to learn. So, would she have expected that 'A', after all, had she known that we only ever spoke English at home?

Then, just as I was embarking on the torturous journey into A Level Chemistry, I was informed by the teacher that I would never do as well as my only other Chemistry classmate (it was a small school), since she had got a double A* at GSCE, and I only had a double B. Another one who already knew how my story was supposed to end. Cue another limiting belief.

LIMITING STORYLINE 3: I'm not good enough.

For a child who was quiet, respectful, unremarkable, her whole life ahead of her, to be *seen* in this way was, frankly, damaging. But, like a good girl, I just laughed them off and persevered. Stress-filled. Supressing anger. At times dissociated. After all, they were the teachers and they must know best.

Luckily, *my* best was not good enough to get into medical school and I ended up choosing to study for a psychology degree. I didn't know it at the time, but this was when I committed to rewriting my script for the first time.

One transformative moment for my scriptwriting in those transitional teen years came when I was in the final year of A-levels, feeling burdened by the realisation that medicine was not going to be an option for me. A motivational speaker was brought in to help the Year 12 and Year 13 students feel more confident about our imminent exams, and for the first time I experienced the power of words and the positivity they can offer – and, crucially, the intense, overwhelming emotional impact that the right words can have on your view of yourself. I was harbouring a fear that my future was set to be ruined by my average abilities, as I pushed through the pain that came from not understanding Chemistry and other Science subjects because I was 'not good enough'. But that day something magical happened: despite the situation seeming so dire, I started to feel less anxious about my future. I had the feeling that I was able to think clearly for the first time, and sensed that maybe, just maybe, it would be possible to feel more secure in myself if I just looked at my situation from a different point of view. It lasted no more than a few seconds, and went as quickly as it came, but I have never let go of that moment. It became the basis of why I do what I do now, and the reason I can believe in it so strongly. So, here is my attempt at rewriting the narrative.

STORY REWRITE 1: Feelings matter + Words matter = Positions can change

➔ **What things do you feel and say about yourself, out loud and internally? How do they shape your relationship with your life goals?**

As I embarked on what I would later realise was my psychology career, I was better able to balance what I felt, the choices I was making, and where I was heading. It turned out this was exactly what I needed to excel at university and ultimately to graduate with a first-class degree. I put this incredible outcome for such an average, unremarkable pupil down to some key factors.

I remained a 'persevering student' because it was all I knew how to be. But somehow, I started to feel more able to shape what I was doing and colour it with more emotional content, which led

211

me to have more open and authentic conversations with myself and others. And people started to hear these conversations. They were heard by my Personal Tutor, Bryony Pulford, the first teacher who actually and profoundly helped me believe in myself. She pointed out my strengths, which changed the game for me. Apparently, I had strengths that I didn't know about. Apparently, I had missed some important parts of myself that needed nourishing. Apparently, I needed to think about all this as part of healthy personal development. So, I did. And it helped me to rewrite that second limiting belief for the first time.

STORY REWRITE 2a: Perseverance and hard work are necessary skills to succeed in whatever you do. They are not a guarantee (you need other skills, too), but together they are important ingredients. What's more, perseverance gets a turbo-boost when you view yourself in a more balanced way.

➔ **Do you know what your strengths and challenges are? Do you review them regularly?**

In my final undergraduate year, I decided to work on a project about the choices among South Asians/people from South Asian backgrounds to study towards a 'Holy Trinity' career, and the authenticity of those choices. Unsurprisingly, the data that emerged suggested that many of the South Asians respondents were parent-pleasers. They felt that their emotional relationship to their choices were secondary to the expectations they felt. While this finding would form the basis for a book in itself, it was the feedback I received from my project tutor, Paula Brough, that sent me reeling. She said she had enjoyed working with me so much that she wanted to offer me a place on her new PhD programme... in New Zealand. I could never have imagined such a commitment to me from a teacher. Ultimately, I declined, but only after first sitting with the discomfort of self-belief, wondering what this offer really meant to me. By this point I had already committed in my head to becoming a

Clinical Psychologist. Having enjoyed the project so much, though, I did think about studying for a PhD in the UK, which was one possible route into clinical training. And, sensing that this route might be more enjoyable, I applied to do a PhD at a department which also offered a clinical training course. I started my PhD the summer after my degree. Now I had a lot of new material for my rewrite of those limiting beliefs.

STORY REWRITE 2b: Being average is actually OK. And there is evidence to suggest I can sometimes be more than average. It's important to hold on to this data.

➔ **Where is that evidence for you? Review it regularly. See if you can find more.**

Frustratingly, I discovered quite early on that a PhD is not necessarily the best route into clinical training, because clinical training requires skills that are much more sophisticated, self-reflective and adaptive than that one can get from research. As a *completer-finisher*, however – confirmed by Belbin's self-perception test – and with my history of perseverance and parent-pleasing, I endured the challenges of working on a PhD, several changes of supervisor and two applications for clinical training in the process! Needless to say, I was rejected three times in consecutive years (the third time after submitting my thesis) because I wasn't able to offer a good enough understanding of working in the NHS, or of the complexities of intervention that clients and their families might need.

After the second round of rejection which had cited identical reasons as the first, I had tried to gain some clinical experience by working as an Applied Behaviour Analysis (ABA) tutor for a young child with autism. While this gave me an excellent grounding and understanding of behavioural interventions, I lacked the systemic experience of working in a multi-disciplinary team and of being able to work with family factors. Unsurprisingly, I received a third rejection. Without NHS experience, my PhD and ABA work was not enough. So, I stopped applying for clinical training and got a research-oriented job. I used this time in my CV partly to lick my wounds, but also to see how I could prevent myself from repeating earlier mistakes that were holding me back.

A return to my first script rewrite really helped me here: how can I position myself differently in relation to the problem?

As you read this, I suspect you already know what conclusion I came to.

I decided to make contact with the local NHS service in the town that was hosting my research-heavy employed role and was asked to apply for what we would now call an honorary Assistant Psychologist to run CBT-based groups for adults referred from Primary Care settings. I think this was the first time I had a realistically informed plan to help me fully commit to getting into clinical training, so I took my plans to the Service Lead at the time, Liz Howells. She must have seen something decent in me that also suited her service, because when funding became available, she asked me to apply for the Assistant Psychologist post. I accepted a part-time role in her service so I could remain part-time in my research-based job.

I got onto the DClinPsy course that same year. Fourth time lucky, for me. But I can honestly say that it was the right time. What could I do then but rewrite my third and final unhelpful narrative?

STORY REWRITE 3: When I give myself space to reflect, I am good enough to be a clinical psychologist.

Clinical training had its moments of challenge and difficulty, of course. But for me, I had only reached that point by coming to understand my values, how I wanted to achieve in a way that felt authentic and finding ways to grow and develop personally and professionally.

I am sure I would have found training and post-training tougher had I not been able to experience, reflect and make changes during the lead-up to finally being accepted onto the course. The reflections, connections and support I experienced then have been crucial to sustaining me beyond training when, many would argue, the real learning begins.

It was making the connection with my authentic values that helped me realise I wanted to work with clients who have experienced life-changing injuries, and also to realise that the services typically available to them were crying out for a more psychologically informed approach. After years of watching and wondering, I developed PsychWorks Associates, a service I see as epitomising my academic and professional life experiences. Our case management and treating psychology specialisms make for a highly relevant service in the Personal Injury world. Using a unique case management and formulation-based model of conceptualisation, we can offer clients a litigation-sensitive service that supports them and their families through the trauma, loss, grief and adjustment that follow a serious or catastrophic injury, in order to optimise their rehabilitation and settlement outcomes.

It was important to me, too, that we provide those who work with us a supportive, reflective environment that allows for the best learning and development to happen... just as I was fortunate enough to have.

I'm not sure that I have completely re-written or written off my limiting beliefs, but do I know now that I have other versions of myself to draw upon that feel equally real and true. It is only by getting to know, almost befriending, those limiting beliefs that I have come to see that they have been helpful in some ways, but that their impact needs managing, or they can do real harm. This chapter of my story, then, ends here:

NEW STORYLINE

I can be the person and clinical psychologist I want to be.

So can you!

With my best wishes,

Shabnam

Dr Shabnam Berry-Khan qualified as a Clinical Psychologist in 2008 from the then Bristol/Plymouth course and worked in CAMHS in London upon qualifying. She started working in private practice in 2010, both as a treating psychologist for seriously injured clients and a Personal Injury Case Manager. Through the case management work, she set up the UK's only psychology-based case management and litigation-informed psychology services called PsychWorks Associates, *www.psychworks.org.uk* **She also has a podcast, The Psychology of Case Management, which is available via the website.**

Email from: Dr Marianne Trent

To: Dr Shabnam Berry-Khan

Oh Shabnam,

Thank you so much for your wonderful story. I just inhaled it – what a wonderful format and style idea too. I reckon there's a book idea in it all by itself!

We first crossed paths via LinkedIn, and I just love having you in my network. I'm also delighted to have been the one to introduce you to the world of the voice note function! You're wonderfully supportive and so kind and compassionate. You are absolutely great at your role and most definitely have done incredibly well to re-write those limiting beliefs because you're smashing it out of the park. People should definitely check out your podcast 'the psychology of case management' because it's so interesting and your passion and admiration for enabling the clients you work with sings out loud and clear.

Thanks again and wishing you all the best with everything you do,

Marianne

26

Marianne's Story:

Owning our story

I honestly think I have the best job in the world and sometimes I have to pinch myself to reflect upon the fact that I get paid for doing stuff which makes me really happy! When I was studying my undergrad course at Glamorgan University, I actually found the module on Clinical Psychology pretty boring. It seemed to only be about data and neuropsych testing and with only theory and textbooks to look at, it all felt a bit dry. I love learning from experience and learning about people and hearing them speak, for me, it just didn't appeal. I don't even really recall having heard of the job title Clinical Psychologist until the week before my undergrad finals. We all traipsed into the lecture theatre for a chat on 'different career options post-graduation.' One of the lecturers mentioned what a Clinical Psychologist did and how it was super hard to get into training. She said we probably shouldn't bother and should do something else instead. Well, that was enough for me......from that point forwards that's the career I wanted! The thing is I know that I'm not alone in that either. I'm in a psychologist

Facebook group of over 3000 people and in a recent post surveying why people got into the profession a staggeringly high number of us said that part of our motivation for becoming a clinical psychologist was because we had been told *just* how difficult it was. Seriously. What does that say about our dogged determination, our desire to prove ourselves? Maybe even our masochism, perfectionism, and ego? Well, there's a doctoral thesis topic for you if ever you needed one!

Speaking of ego..... I gained my first paid AP post at St Andrew's Healthcare, and they had the coolest name badges. They were gold enamel, and they said my name and job title. 'Marianne Durran, Assistant Psychologist." Honestly, wearing that little beauty for the first time and checking myself out in the mirrored walls on one of the wards in the cool new 'Assistant Psychologist clothes' I had bought to complement the gold badge, remains one of my proudest psychology moments to date. I wish I still had that badge. I wonder where it is. I think they made me give it back when I left. Maybe I should make myself a gold badge now. It probably wouldn't look nearly as snazzy teamed with my working from home PJ bottoms though! The thing is, I think I am *probably* much less of an arse now I'm qualified than I was when I was an Assistant. One of my pet hates is when people refer to themselves as 'psychologists' when actually they've 'only' done an undergrad. I wish Psychologist was a proper protected title so that everyone knew they were in safe hands. Confession time...I wonder whether it irks me so much because actually, that used to be me! I loved chatting to people and telling them I was a psychologist, when, actually, I was an Assistant Psychologist! These days I am proud to be a psychologist, but I don't tend to tell anyone who will listen that I am one! I think there's something to be said about the imposter curve, the less we know the more naïve we are to this and as we get more experienced, we become aware of everything we don't know, and we are more likely to stay within out limits.

Marianne's Story:

So, in 2007 whilst I was completing my form, it's fair to say that I wasn't having the best time of life. My friend Kara refers to this stage in life as that where I '*mainly ate carrots and houmous.*' At the start of August, I had decided to separate from a long-term partner which had not been easy. A few weeks later, whilst on my way to my first ever bootcamp class[18], a chap in a Jaguar crashed into me in my beautiful Yaris. My car was written off, I got whiplash in my neck and back and almost immediately after, I started studying for my Master's with Newman University College. This was all whilst working full time and being in pain whilst striving for my first ever NHS assistant post. I was applying for jobs all over the country. I recall at one stage crying on the stairs at home the day before an assistant interview in Nottingham. I was in pain. It was in the days before I owned a satnav, I wasn't sure how to find the interview and I wasn't even sure it was a job I wanted anyway but I really wanted it 'for the form!' My mum, clearly a bit shocked actually did pull it out the bag and say, "if it's too much then just cancel the interview, don't go!' So, that's what I did and instead spent my day off doing a bit of R&R and likely for me at that time, probably listening to a bit of R&B! So, other than listening to Chris Brown and Ne-Yo, it's fair to say it wasn't an easy time in my life. But it did give me lots of time to focus on my form. I recall laying half slouched on my parent's sofa with my laptop propped on my knee and stomach for what seemed like any spare minute[19] of the day in September, October and November. I was a woman on a mission with my form. This was my third time applying but the first I thought I might stand a chance. It was the year that I *just did me.* I didn't show it to anyone. I wanted to make sure it sounded like me, so, many, many times over, for each revision I made, I read the form aloud to myself. I'm sure I was quite

---

[18] I never did make it to the bootcamp class and have never been to one since either, it wasn't meant to be I guess!

[19] Genuinely the way I'm sitting right now except now I own the sofa.

annoying to my Mum who was watching Coronation Street or whatever on the other sofa.[20] My rule was, that if I felt embarrassed saying it aloud, or if it wasn't the way I'd actually speak in person[21], then it wasn't going in[22]. As a result, when it was eventually time to stand in the post office queue and dispatch it, I was absolutely thrilled with my form. Whilst far from ideal, this time in my life did turn out to be a useful reflecting point though. Seven months later after the accident, a fair bit of osteopathy and Pilates, and lots of partying with my assistant and non-psychology friends later, my back and my heart were in much finer shape. It was in my personal suitability interview for the course that I was asked to reflect on a difficult time in my life and that was it. Don't be afraid to be vulnerable. They need to see that to know that you can be human and that if required you are able to use appropriate help seeking too.

> *"When we deny the story it defines us, when we own the story, we can write a brave new ending"*
> *(Brene Brown).*

I was in the fortunate position that I was offered 2 places for doctoral training. I do often think now that if I had picked 'the other' course, that my life would be entirely different. Genuinely, some of my consideration for which course to choose at the time weighed up the fact that at interview one course had proffered a selection of my favourite herbal teas for

---

[20] Editorial comment: I am shocked, and even a little bit disappointed, that I have gotten this far into your story, and you have reigned yourself in with the swearing! None of your famous one-liners that I've grown to love either. Readers will just have to listen to your lives to experience the Best of Marianne – never a dull moment with you, being your EA makes me so happy!

[21] I did rein in my urge to swear.

[22] For projects like this one I still write in that style now too. If it's the way I'd speak, I'll start sentences with 'And' and all sorts. I'm sure I'm a nightmare for my EA Chrissie.

my delectation whilst the other had made me cry. Which did I pick? Simple, I'm a martyr - I picked the crying! Just kidding, I of course picked the course which felt like it was 'a bit of me'[23] from the moment I arrived. But had the course where I sobbed in my car as soon as I got back to at the end of the day, been my *only* offer then I would have accepted it and likely been on cloud 9 to do so!

The year I successfully applied was the year where the Bristol course was cancelled. I had done my Bristol selection test from home, been invited to do another test in Bristol and then been invited to interview. Then, due to a misunderstanding with the way a new university were planning on running the course as solely academic with no placements, without warning, the plug was pulled. This was because a taught only method was not going to churn out the type of clinical psychologists we needed to be - ones who were effective and practiced at being with clinical patients / clients! In turn, hearts were broken for people whose only interviews that year were on the Bristol course. I really fancied Bristol and had the course gone ahead and I'd been successful at interview I might well have ended up there as it was close to a number of my close friends from my undergrad days which would have just been lovely! As it turned out, my 'herbal tea' course was Coventry & Warwick, and I am delighted to say that I absolutely loved training. I felt like I went into it with my eyes open. Sometimes it would be hard. I would need to juggle my social life, academic life and placement commitments, and then at times it would be pressured and stressful. Sometimes it was, but largely, I found that by using my study days pretty much exclusively for study, that until my thesis rolled round, hand on heart, I didn't do any work in the evenings or weekends. I think what was useful for me personally and professionally that our course gave out *'pass or fail'* marks

---

[23] 40-year-old love island fan alert!

for academic work. There were no percentages. There was no direct way to compare scores across the cohort and so, as a result of this, my perfectionistic tendencies could be chucked out the window entirely. I aimed to pass and for all but one assignment in the 3 years, this is exactly what I did, and that was good enough for me. It did get a bit grim in my viva but that all turned out marvellous in the end too and happily I still managed to graduate with my cohort. Standing in Coventry Cathedral with my coat of many colours and my funny squashy hat, was genuinely a wonderfully proud moment, almost as good as the gold badge! I love reflecting that my dad was there watching because, fit and healthy at the time, sadly, just over 5 years later he died. I had been in the very fortunate position that he and my Mum had always supported my career although it's fair to say I don't think they understood what it was. My Mum really wanted me and my brother to go to higher education so that we would have different chances in life. My Dad was a boiler man, and I could not have been more proud of him, but 2 days before he died, I was holding his hand and he said to me, "I wish I'd tried harder at school." The idea that my kind, sweet, palliatively unwell 71-year-old father was having regrets of this kind was so sad making for me. But on the other hand, it's probably a life well lived if that's as big as your end-of-life regrets get[24].

My Top Tips![25]

Have loads of fun

Honestly, please do. It helps us to weather the storm. I have just the fondest memories of my assistant years. Many of my assistant friends are still some of my closest friends now and 2 even ended up in my cohort too.

---

[24] There's more of this story in *The Grief Collective: Stories of Life, Loss & Learning to Heal*, do check it out if you'd like more.

[25] Dr 'Robbo' if you ever read this, I can imagine you finding this Viz inspired title very amusing.

Marianne's Story:

Master's study:
In 2007, I started a distance learning, part time Master's course with Newman in 2007 whilst I was also working full time as an assistant across 3 busy inpatient wards for St Andrew's. If it's a possibility for you, I would say that distance learning, part time Master's are an excellent way to build academic experience because it also allows you to work full time at the same time. If you have kids, it would be more of a struggle too of course, although as I am learning with my book projects, when required, I can work when my kids are sleeping. At the time when doing my Master's, we had to travel in for exams and one Saturday of teaching per module, but I think the in-person teaching was later reduced to be more inclusive for distance students. Due to the appeal of the flexible nature of the course, there was a lady on my cohort from Ireland so do check it out if you'd like to add some more strings to your academic bow. I found it invaluable because it taught us how to plan research and how to pick it apart and discuss it analytically. These were strategies I then used for assistant, training and qualified interviews too.

CV gap plugging the creative way #1:
I was desperate to get my foot in the door and get my first AP post. I took 10 days of annual leave from my social rehabilitation work with physically disabled adults and sorted out an honorary post 1 day a week spread over 4 months, and it was enough! It gave me a Clin Psych as a reference and opened the door for the first time to being behind the clinic room door and discussing psychological terms, concepts and theories with a real-life clinical psychologist. I was hooked! Whilst it meant less annual leave that year, I think this is an excellent way of gaining experience without necessarily having to lose any money, so do bear it in mind. The unit loved having me too because APs are such a fantastic resource and they'd never had one before. I seem to recall after I left, they did go on to then employ one too,

224

so it paves the way and shows just how useful and essential assistants are! I finished this post in the summer and by October I was starting my first paid assistant post!

CV gap plugging the creative way #2:

By the time I was 6 years post undergrad I had experience working with physically disabled adults, working age adults, older adults and forensic. I'd also had a wicked time travelling around the world for 8 months and temping in offices and doing home caring[26] to fund it. I had zero experience with children and young people. I reached out to a local Brownie group and there followed 2 years of the most incredible learning and fun experiences as honorary 'Wise Owl.' It was so helpful to learn about the normal scope of children rather than just the clinical aspect I would later see. I could also totally fit one evening a week into my schedule too. Being able to speak about these children in my secure training unit interview for young people totally bagged me my first NHS assistant post too so it worked!

CV gap plugging the creative way #3:

Reach out to your local NHS trust and ask if there are research meetings / groups or any key researchers you can be put in touch with. I learned a lot of useful stuff for my thesis by going along to research meetings whilst I was training. If you don't yet have research experience you could also find some honorary stuff which will look great on your CV too[27]. When I was an assistant in exchange for being able to put 'honorary research assistant'

---

[26] No time or space to discuss home caring but I loved that job. Such a privilege and actually laughed a lot with my clients but also taught me a lot about dignity, respect and trust. Also gave me lots of opportunities to wonder at 3am in the morning whether I had remembered to lock 'Beryl's' door!'

[27] Editorial note: or get in touch with Chrissie and she'll keep you in mind for her next research article or any other psychology-related writing projects that come her way!

on my form, I helped a trainee out with some of her bits and pieces for data collection.

Create and count your publications:

When I was striving for training, no-one in my department was free to present their research at an upcoming international conference (In Nottingham!) So, I volunteered, and they were delighted I had, and so I did it! I put it on my form as it counts as a publication. I also wrote a vaguely amusing post-conference report and submitted it to a journal, it was accepted and published, and you've guessed it.... It counted as a publication! I also offered to write up the research for a journal because the qualified staff were struggling to find the time and then ended up as 3rd author for the project! Think about ways you can gain publication experience which might involve thinking outside the box and asking for opportunities. Can you get involved with a book? Research?

You do you:

Be you. You're great! Reflect and make sure the form sounds like you and shows your unique skills, talents, and interests. Consider using section sub-headings so that your form makes sense and flows well. In forms I have reviewed I often find that answering questions in massive full sentences is a waste of space. Be concise but easy to understand. Don't use fancy words which mean nothing. Don't leave that relevant experience section blank! Fill the space on your form but make sure it's easy to read. I also prefer to write in a present tense – you've not lost the skills just because you're no longer doing the job! These are some of the observations I made in a form I reviewed last year:

"This is page 6 in the application, and I currently feel I know nothing about you or what interests you or makes you unique. I feel like this whole section falls a bit flat."

> "Try not to just tick boxes for the sake of it. Be
> interested and interesting!"

It's often a good idea to get someone qualified to review your form. It's much better to get this feedback from someone *before* you submit your form, rather than it be thought by someone screening your form at your dream course!

No one is coming to save you:
Reach out to people. Create opportunities for yourself. Chance it. If you don't ask, you're much less likely to get. You literally have nothing to lose and potentially everything to gain.

Practice Interviews:
I absolutely cringed at the time, and definitely didn't want to do it. But in 2008 my NHS supervisor Charlotte did a mock interview for me ahead of my 2 clinical interviews. It was fantastically helpful and got my 'rabbit in the headlights' moments out of the way in a supportive and risk-free situation. This is something I've done for a number of assistants since too and they all universally cringe, but all say it was helpful in retrospect. Speaking of cringing. Charlotte was also present for my first ever 'therapy sessions' with a young person. Honestly, I was dreadful. So awkward. It was in a forensic unit and the young person was far cooler than me. To both Charlotte and the young person. Thanks, and sorry. I'm now much better at therapy but couldn't have got there without either of you!

Lastly, follow your dreams:
The other day my 8-year-old son asked me a question:

> *"Mummy, when you were younger, what did you want to be when you grew up?"*
> *"A Doctor and a journalist"* I replied.
> *"Oh, but that's not your job now, you don't read the news!"*
> *"Well, no baby, but I was on it once.... And I love that I help people to feel better in person but also through my writing!"*

I really hope that this book and maybe even my own story have been helpful for you!

Dr Marianne Trent is a Clinical Psychologist & lead author for *The Grief Collective: Stories of Life, Loss & Learning to Heal.* She weaves a compassionate approach through all of her specialist trauma, grief and eating disorders work with clients. She is also the creator of the 'Our Tricky Brain' kit, which helps professionals working with people who experience trauma and depression to understand their symptoms in a non-judgemental and validating way. She is regularly in the media and always has new projects in the pipeline. To sign up to her mailing list head to: www.goodthinkingpsychology.co.uk

Email from: Dr Marianne Trent on 31/08/202021

To: Dr Marianne Trent on 31/08/2022 via www.futureme.org

Well, hello future Marianne. Currently you are literally hours away from clicking publish on your second book baby. It has been quite the project and one which has been wonderful to be part of. It's also been one which has seen your team grow to include an Editorial Assistant (EA) too! Currently however, you're wondering whether anyone will buy the new book, whether they'll find it helpful and hoping that the contributors all like the way it looks when it is all done!

So, how has the last year been for you Marianne of 2022? Have you been able to achieve the goals you set yourself? Did the other book you've already made a start on get published? Did you manage to make more time in your diary for the media stuff you so enjoy? How's the pandemic situation? Currently both of your team have Covid-19 and here's hoping that by the time you receive this email that things are feeling less risky on a daily basis. This level of threat is hard to sustain, and we just aren't geared up for it as humans!

Currently your kids are both a week away from going back to school and you are already practicing the dance you will do on that first morning when you get home with empty hands. It's not been an easy 18 months for anyone and you're absolutely doing it well enough.

Keep doing what you do, even on the days you feel like no-one is watching or can't be bothered. People are watching and like what you do, and you have the messages from some of them to prove it!

Go forth and do great things. Or.... just get really good at sitting on the sofa playing Homescapes and Gardenscapes! x x

Reflections

27

Kim's Reflections:

'Failing' at gaining a doctorate place – or just not quitting?

So, my instant reflection on reviewing these collection of stories – where has this book been all my psychology life?! Just wow. So helpful, enlightening and surprisingly raw. I found the honesty and snippets of comedy (that made me chuckle out loud) extremely relatable and a lot of the experiences certainly resonate with me and my position, which I actually found very surprising, and also containing.

For some context, I am an aspiring clinical psychologist, currently working as an NHS Assistant Psychologist (the holy grail, right?!) within a Tier 4 CAMHS service. Despite my hard work, overall, I have tended to come out as academically average, or sometimes even below average which has not stood

233

me in good stead for achieving a place on training. Being an aspiring clinical psychologist is hard. I do not just mean hard work getting into the field or managing potentially challenging roles or environments, but mainly I think, the never-ending necessity for perseverance. I have had five unsuccessful doctorate applications, over seven years and am currently avoiding the reality that application number six is on the horizon.

The consideration for no longer putting my life on hold became very apparent for me during last year's application cycle. Although it had not stopped life from continuing, it had always hung over my head that the plan of qualifying in advance of starting a family was essential for me. I just could not see completing training any other way.

Although my desire to succeed is still as strong (if not stronger) than ever, it just no longer feels a reasonable expectation to continue with 'but maybe next year I will be on the doctorate' when considering life choices. I reviewed what I wanted in life and concluded that I needed to prioritise other things over training and not chase something which let us face it – ambition or not – I may not achieve. Not that the doctorate had taken over my life per se, but in terms of what comes first, it certainly felt that it needed to be completed first. I briefly considered not applying the following year, however, I just felt very unhappy and almost a lack of purpose if I were to just give up trying on something I still wanted to achieve so strongly. Failing is only when we give up trying right? Which of course is very different to choosing that this is not the right path for us or needing a break from this relentless process. I did, however, accept that I am no longer planning my life around the 'what if's'. For the first time, I am no longer being too rigid over life being in the right order. It is a career and a line of work that I am determined to achieve, but now I have accepted that it will happen when it happens and it will have to fit around my life at that time, whatever it may look like. I have realised that there are so many ifs and buts and uncertainties in life, that it just does not make sense to me anymore to plan for commencing training, which ultimately, I cannot entirely control.

The honest experiences shared in this Collective are a stark reminder for me that although getting accepted onto training and becoming a clinical psychologist are very privileged positions to be in, they can also come with their challenges. I found the reflections by the authors incredibly helpful and reinforcing which alleviates some of the pressure discussed above and a reminder to enjoy the process and for me, working on tolerating the frustration that comes with this competitive process. After all, we ask our clients to sit with uncertainty and discomfort so I feel I should practice what I preach. Also, my freshly graduated self would have done anything to be where I am now! (Cue some self-compassion and gratitude).

Reading the experiences of others who have been through this process, has certainly helped me feel much more relaxed about the prospect of juggling my personal and professional life for when I may get accepted onto training and when I have a family, as I aim to do both. When? Who knows? But whenever that may be, it is now with less pressure – which honestly, I was only putting on myself. It has also created an increase in flexibility and opportunity for other things. The excitement of considering and applying for different pre-qualified roles (which can without a doubt be other things to an AP) around doctorate application season (not my best idea) whilst also considering new elements of my personal life has been made significantly easier since I have 'let go' a little. I will keep applying, but I will also keep living by finding joy in other things and ensuring that I enjoy the process until I get there, as fulfilment along the way feels the most important. As who knows, like some have mentioned in their stories, if and when we get there – we may be even be slightly disappointed if training continues to be put on a pedestal! This Collective has really helped remind me that there is more to life and that our work and the clinical psychology ambition, although important, is only a piece of our life puzzle.

Kim Bayley is an Assistant Psychologist working for the NHS in a tier 4 CAMHS service.

Email from: Dr Marianne Trent

To: Kim Bayley

Dear Kim,

Thanks so much for your reflections. Honestly, the first line had me a little dewy-eyed! I hatched the idea for this book and kind of hoped it would be helpful and knew that I would have loved to read it when I was an aspiring clinical psychologist but wondered if maybe I'm just a bit out of touch? So, to actually have what 'businesspeople' term my 'ideal client avatar' read the book and love it has blown me away! So, thank you! I would like to wish you all the best for your application cycle this year and of course as a thank you just give me a shout if you'd like me to review your form!

Do keep me posted and so pleased this book has already been helpful for you,

With my best wishes,

Marianne

28

Ercan's Reflections:

The Barriers we face

As soon as I heard about this book, I was excited and envious. Excited for the brilliant information finally accessible to those interested in becoming a Clinical Psychologist and envious because I wish this existed for me years ago and many people graduating will have this excellent resource.

I'm sure this book will be recommended and even offered as a graduation present for aspiring psychologists for decades to come. I applaud and thank Marianne for spending the time to write this.

At the age of 10 I moved to Cyprus with my family where I completed my Secondary education until the age of 18 when I moved back to England for my Undergraduate in Psychology. I have spent the last 6-years in pursuit of becoming a psychologist. During that time, I started as many do, as an HCA within an inpatient ward. Over the years I made my way through different jobs until 2016, when I was offered a position at a substance

237

misuse charity working one to one with young people. It was from that I got first-hand experience working clinically with people, understanding, and developing skills in Cognitive Behavioural Therapy (CBT). By the time 2017 rolled around I was able to move into Improving Access to Psychological Therapies, (IAPT) as a trainee Psychological Wellbeing Practitioner, (PWP). Since then, I have stayed in IAPT - working across a variety of roles: a qualified PWP, Senior PWP and now as a trainee High-Intensity CBT therapist (HICBT) a role for which I am due to qualify soon.

I really appreciate my time having trained and worked within IAPT, and now hope to apply for the Clinical doctorate one last time.

In recent years I have been successful in being interviewed for the course twice with one interview resulting in a reserve spot which, unfortunately for me didn't manifest into a place on training. I recall how daunting and confusing the process to become a psychologist was. I am far more confident now but could not claim to fully understand the process. Over the years, through my own research and attending various events I began to piece together the necessary information to hopefully lead to me having the right skills and experiences for the course. To avoid others facing this daunting process alone, I have dedicated time to ensure information is shared widely through groups and webinars. In the recent years I have seen a real push from aspiring psychologists and trainee psychologists to widen access in the same way. I hope to see this continue.

That said for the 2022 intake, Health Education England, (HEE) made a surprising change. They announced that those who had completed other courses funded by them, such as the PWP training, were no longer able to apply for funding until they had been qualified for 2-years. While many of us understand the decision, I take issue with the sudden implementation of it with no warning. This has meant that many who are starting, or completing, these courses with the hopes of applying for the doctorate are now forced to stay in their position. Had they known about this change in advance, they would have been able to make an informed choice as to whether they wished to apply for these courses in the first place.

I write this less than 12 hours since the announcement was made, and as such, the repercussions from this change are yet to be fully experienced. However, I would anticipate a significant downfall in applications for these courses affected by this new restriction, unless the apprenticeship programs for the PWP training becomes the mainstream. I am concerned for those directly affected by this change and the implications this will have on their mental health and financial stability. Many people have had to make sacrifices in the hopes of applying for the doctorate. That choice has now been taken from them. This goes against what many have promised, which is widening access and increasing accessibility for those from Black, Asian and Minority Ethic (BAME) backgrounds, and / or those with disabilities. Many are not in the position to pay for an MSc or survive on a band 3 role, while desperately applying for an Assistant Psychologist post. Therefore, they would have applied for these courses to get a postgraduate qualification and increase pay. Unfortunately, many find the stress of these roles not worth the pay, and for them to hear that they must remain for an additional 2-years might well be heart-breaking.

There are many other issues from this sudden change that I haven't covered. I, and many others, have tried to push for reconsideration. While I don't know what the outcome will be, I know that many of us won't stop without having our voices heard. Psychology is about helping the people and moves like this just show us that Health Education England are not

Ercan's Reflections:

interested in recruiting people from diverse backgrounds which represent the people.

Ercan (Jason) Hassan is a High Intensity CBT therapist. He is an administrator for the Facebook group, UK Clinical Psychology Doctorate Applicants, please do come and join the group if this would be helpful. He has also launched a petition to ask for a reconsideration of the HEE funding decision. To read more information about the petition or to sign head to: https://chng.it/h2ZshBtpts

Email from: Dr Marianne Trent on 01/09/2021 18:50

To: Ercan (Jason) Hassan

Dear Ercan,

Thanks for your submission and for breaking the record for speediest turnaround of the project. I messaged you at 17:09pm as I was about to carve a roast chicken for dinner. By the time I was stacking the dishwasher at 18:14pm it was in my inbox!

My day has been pretty busy with writing a new chapter for this book but yours has been off the charts busy! I'm so sorry to hear how this has impacted upon you personally and professionally. It's all the more painful that if you'd been granted the reserve list place, that you'd now be days away from starting training. Instead, you're now not even eligible to apply for funded training in England. It's a lot to get your head around and I think there will be shock and tears across the country for some days and weeks yet.

Well done to you for doing everything you can to level the access to training for people. It's an incredibly admirable quality and hopefully a sign of change because certainly when I was applying it all felt a bit like closely guarded nuggets of wisdom kept close to chests!
I wish you all the best for the rest of your IAPT training and for your next few years too. Let me know if I can help with anything.

Stay in touch, Marianne

Ercan's Update 13/09/2021

On the 9th of September, HEE announced some promising changes which has given me hope for a better future for all clinicians, aspiring psychologists and those who benefit from the services we offer. They have now provided us a rough timeline as to when these measures will be implemented, giving some notice for those considering whether to apply or not. They also announced that these measures will not be applied retrospectively, meaning those who had already applied or completed these courses will no longer be restricted from applying.

This I believe is a great start, however, from my own views and feedback gathered there is still much to be done.

First and foremost, and I hope HEE will start inviting open discussion amongst all impacted by future changes. I also think the question needs to shift from "how do we stop people leaving IAPT services for the doctorate?" to "how can we improve IAPT so that people want to stay?".

Unfortunately, the attitude regarding those using these NHS-funded courses has yet to change. Much of the blame regarding retaining staff appears to be pinned on the idea that they are all using these roles as a steppingstone which simply is not the case. There are many who leave these roles due to the toxic environment from these services. It's also known that retaining NHS workers isn't just within IAPT services, but the entire NHS. The idea of a "steppingstone" also confuses me. It sends this message that it is wrong for people to aspire for greater things, something everyone in every job outside of mental health wants. The developments so far have been promising, I hope we can continue to move forward, not just to benefit aspiring psychologists, but to benefit the mental health services, the NHS- funded courses and the public we serve.

Ercan's Reflections:

On the 8th of September I hosted an open meeting for all to attend. There were a mix of Clinical Tutors, Trainee Clinical Psychologists, Clinical Psychologists, and Aspiring Psychologists. From their feedback I have compiled an open letter to HEE with our suggestions on things we would like them to consider going forward.

To read Ercan's open letter you can visit the link here: https://medium.com/@jason71291/an-open-letter-to-hee-in-response-to-funding-changes-feedback-7ecbef6306f2

Email from: Dr Marianne Trent on 13/09/2021 13:11

To: Ercan (Jason) Hassan

Seriously Ercan, I am impressed. You are doing great things! I can't know but suspect that your actions in starting the petition and facilitating important conversations has been a major contributory factor in the HEE's amended decisions.

I am confident now that there be some people, perhaps even reading this book, will now go on to access funded clinical training in the next few years who would otherwise not have been eligible to apply. I'd say they might owe you a drink at the very least!

I'm also very grateful to you for staying in touch and helping me get my head around these changes and what they mean for this book too!

Wishing you all the best, I watch your journey with very eager interest!

Marianne

29

Emily's Reactions:

Supporting Fair Rules or Moving the Goal Posts?

I am currently a trainee Psychological Wellbeing Practitioner (PWP) with aspirations of one day becoming a qualified Clinical Psychologist. Following my first application in 2019, I was given feedback that:

> "You are a promising candidate who needs more clinical experience to gain a place on the extremely competitive Clinical Psychology Doctorate (DClinPsy)".

It therefore seemed a natural progression to apply for the Postgraduate Certificate in Low-Intensity Interventions to gain this vital clinical experience. I felt confident that this, along with an MSc in Clinical Applications of Psychology, an Assistant Psychologist role, and numerous voluntary experiences, would make me a strong candidate for training the following year. However, on 1 September 2021, after I had started my

Emily's Reactions:

DClinPsy 2021 application, Health Education England (HEE) announced some changes had been brought in for applicants who have already received funding from them within the last two years. This change in policy affected a number of mental health professionals including both trainee and newly qualified PWPs. While I appreciate this change in policy will allow for a greater distribution of HEE funding and increase employee retention in selected mental health careers, I wonder if there are other factors which have a greater influence of high staff turnover; especially with regards to low-intensity work. The high number of required contacts and the relatively low recovery rates across IAPT (being approximately 50%) leads to increased vulnerability of staff burnout within these services. I personally have found this year extremely difficult, finding myself often feeling overwhelmed with the workload, emotionally exhausted, and working longer hours to cater for this. During these darker times, thinking *'this is good experience for the Doctorate'* was often a silver lining; but what now? Some of these integral components of the PWP need to be explored to both support staff wellbeing and increase employee retention longer-term.

This new rule immediately makes unassuming individuals ineligible for the DClinPsy funding after undertaking other training with the hope to pursue the Clinical Psychology Doctorate, with many of these individuals, like me, being strongly encouraged to undertake such training to support their application. Furthermore, I also had initial concerns regarding if this change in funding will create additional barriers to those from disadvantaged groups in the long-term, an example being that not all individuals can afford to fund a Master's or gain experience through unpaid work and thus, might have pursued a funded route to gain this experience. I appreciate that HEE made a statement on the day of the announcement that steps will be taken to mitigate any short-term unintended impact of this change on financially disadvantaged applicants. However, personally, I think it would be fairer for this change in HEE funding to be implemented in the contracts of low-intensity and other HEE funded training, which would allow individuals to make an informed choice regarding their career progression.

I am just one of the many voices affected by this announcement. However, I am trying to take into account strategies which we discuss during low-intensity interventions, focusing on what is in and what is out of my control. I cannot change that I am unable to apply for the Clinical Doctorate this year. Despite this, HEE have given me the gift of time, time to enjoy my new PWP qualification and my mid-20's without thinking 'I can't do anything February-March in case I am invited to complete the pre-interview tests'; and 'I can't book anything between April-May because I might get invited for an interview'. Unintentionally, I was letting the application process control much of my life. Being a Clinical Psychologist is an important goal for me, but being a Clinical Psychologist is not my only goal.

Emily Bridgwater is a Trainee Psychological Wellbeing Practitioner, who currently plans to apply for clinical training from 2023/24.

Email from: Dr Marianne Trent

To: Emily Bridgwater

Dear Emily,

You write so wonderfully. Thank you for taking the time to put this together for me on the very same evening that you and many others in the country are reeling from the HEE news. I felt like it was so important to reflect this very important update in the book. It adds further context to the human stories, and it will be one that I'm sure many readers can relate to, although of course I'm sorry they find themselves in this position at all. It reminds me of when the Bristol course I applied for was pulled. It felt like at the time that an additional year of the cycle was a hard blow for affected candidates. However, here what we are considering is not just one year, not even just 2 years because you need to qualify, get your certificate and then wait 2 years until the course start date to apply. I'm so sorry for what has happened. I know from when you worked with me as an honorary that you are quite brilliant and capable of many things. Please do be kind to yourself, enjoy that beautiful doggy of yours and keep doing the great work you are doing. Let me know if I can help with anything, Marianne

Marianne

30

Lauren's Reflections:

It's not about the destination but enjoying the journey

My journey is a little different to the others you have read about thus far as I am not yet a trainee or qualified. I am an Assistant Psychologist at the very start of my journey, but nonetheless I feel I have reflected and learnt a lot from my experiences so far. I hope others reading this also at the very beginning of their journey to the doctorate know that they aren't alone and maybe my reflections will be of some use.

Since the age of 16 I remember being very interested in psychology. It wasn't available as a GCSE at my school, so the first glimpse I had was during A-level. I absolutely loved it, especially the clinical components. At this point I remember stumbling across the job role of a 'clinical psychologist' and thinking *this is what I want to do!* I went on to do a BSc in

Psychology at the University of Warwick which I finished in 2018 and still felt sure I wanted to be a clinical psychologist. I then completed the MSc in Clinical Applications in Psychology also at Warwick in 2019 and this reaffirmed my passion and excitement about this career.

I was fortunate to have a six-month placement as an honorary Assistant Psychologist as part of the MSc. I had a very varied placement working at an independent child psychology practice. The client group consisted of private paying clients with work focusing mainly on anxiety management, ASD assessments and reports and working with foster and adoptive parents, children and professionals. I thoroughly enjoyed being able to do clinical work and finally applying theoretical learning to clients. Nothing felt as rewarding as being able to facilitate someone's recovery and improving their wellbeing. But sadly, the placement ended, and the course finished in August 2019. I very much had a *so now what?* moment. I knew I wanted to be an Assistant Psychologist if I could, but for the life of me I couldn't find any assistant posts being advertised. Due to the sheer number of applicants, the few that were advertised were closing within hours of the advert being put out. I'd finished my MSc but had no job and, to be honest, felt a little deflated. I was so keen, so ready to go out and use my degrees, yet of course this was exactly the case for most psychology graduates too! I realised for the first time just how competitive the clinical psychology profession is. I could almost feel how many aspiring clinical psychologists there were around me, all keen on applying for a handful of posts and places.

Cue my first big reflection *"it's all about who you know"*. Hard work and experience will get you far. But what can take you further is making connections. Most qualified clinical psychologists are extremely keen to help those just embarking on their careers. They know the struggle of getting on to the DClinPsy too don't forget! I was fortunate to be introduced to a friend's family member who happened to be a consultant clinical psychologist in an adult mental health setting. She managed to help me become an honorary Assistant Psychologist within her service. This is where I was fortunate enough to meet Marianne and had her as my supervisor for the 8 months I was there. I have been lucky that in the places I have worked, supervision for assistants has always been protected time (I know some workplaces are not as hot on doing this). If you can get regular supervision in the role you are in now or get some time to speak to a trainee or qualified clinical psychologist, please do! I have found being able to talk freely about lots of different things with Marianne and my other supervisors incredibly helpful. It has helped me to learn about what is *actually involved* in being a clinical psychologist, including those unpredictable moments and a space to working collaboratively to bring change. For instance, I worked with Marianne to pilot a compassion focused informed therapy group and most of this stemmed from discussions in supervision. We were both frustrated with the long waiting times for our clients and passionate about wanting to change this. We used my supervision to think about strategies to provide clients with an intervention sooner and so our pilot came to fruition. I was able to learn a great deal about the 'bigger picture', how clinical psychologists and other healthcare professionals (HCPs) fit into it and how long the process can be in triggering change and the barriers to this (such as financial and time constraints, but also differences in opinions and using evidence to support your case). I know without having supervision to facilitate such conversations, I wouldn't have as good an understanding on what it's *actually like* to be a qualified clinical psychologist, as some of these things just aren't mentioned in books. Supervision has also been essential for me to reflect on things that have gone well and not so well in my client work, research and also how to develop into a more well-rounded HCP. My first supervisor and I had a good relationship, however, I really bonded with Marianne and as a consequence, the supervision sessions were more authentic and we both got a lot more out of them (well I certainly did at least).

It is so important to be honest in supervision and to not be afraid of asking stupid questions. I remember that in the first few supervision sessions I asked Marianne about all of the different acronyms I had heard being thrown around. As a profession we are definitely guilty of using them a lot and forgetting that a layperson has no idea what ACT, CFT or EMDR are![28]

My experience as an honorary Assistant Psychologist in and out of the NHS undoubtably helped me to land my first paid Assistant Psychologist post. My first (and current) post is working within a Neuropsychology service, and I love it! This leads me to my third big reflection... *put yourself forward and if you can, do some voluntary work.* I was in a fortunate position where I could financially cope with being unpaid for three days of my working week as an assistant. But I know this is unrealistic for many, and to be honest it shouldn't be the norm as it's hardly promoting an inclusive and diverse profession – but that's a whole different book I reckon![29]

However, what I would say is if you can offer to help with projects, research or things like this, being a part of a book, will all help you to firstly gain more experience, but also strengthen your profile for the DClinPsy application. It's worth taking a deep breath, doing something which might feel a bit out of your comfort zones, use who you know and ask if there are any opportunities available. The worst that could happen (from my experience) is that they say no. But in asking, they will note that

---

[28] Marianne's note: it would seem inappropriate to solve this riddle for you at this juncture but if you're scratching your head do flick to the acronyms section on page 299.

[29] Marianne's note: this so made me smile as I wrote exactly this sentence just earlier today, my phrasing is clearly rubbing off on you my friend.

you are keen and motivated to undertake such projects and you will be at the forefront of their mind if an opportunity arises in the near future. Many of my psychology friends have done this and even gotten jobs out of it! So, it is definitely a worthwhile thing to do.

The last big reflection that I have learnt is... *to enjoy the process.* I remember a lovely trainee I met told me to enjoy being an assistant and not focus too much on getting onto the doctorate. I remember at the time thinking that was very easy for her to say. She'd just got on the course, she was going to be a clinical psychologist, meanwhile it could take me years to get on! It is only in recent months that I have really taken this on board and really appreciated hearing this advice. It can be hard at times to enjoy the process, because let's face it, it isn't the nicest of processes to endure *'just'* to get a job. I'd be lying if I said I didn't feel anxious when it comes to thinking about *'the dreaded form,'* but I am no longer putting extra pressure on myself. I have learnt to adopt the mindset of *"I will get on when I'm ready and it's the right time".* I have learnt that mostly we are out of control of the selection process. All that we can do is gain experience and complete the form and interviews to the best of our abilities. Beyond that, it is out of our control. Therefore, worrying too much will not change anything (perks of being in psychology is being able to apply approaches/techniques to our own situations). As part of learning to enjoy the process, I have come to learn that just because I have had another year not of not getting onto the doctorate, does not mean I have wasted a year. I previously felt a little bit like it was a race to get onto the course; that my career doesn't start until I get onto training and qualify. I have now learnt and embraced that this really isn't true. All of the fundamental skills I am developing and experiences I am having are helping to shape me and prepare me for one day being a qualified. Some of the experiences I have had have even been new for the qualified psychologists I work with – for instance, the most recent piece of work myself and consultant have been doing is a Section 49 Report. My supervisor has been qualified for over 10 years and this was her first experience with this type of work too. I am very happy in my current role and can see already in the 15 months I have been an Assistant Psychologist, I have developed and gained so much. It's acknowledging that this process never stops too. It continues throughout your whole profession, which is what partly makes clinical psychology such an interesting profession. We are led by research and continue to evolve and grow.

Lauren Milbourne is an Assistant Psychologist she will be applying for clinical training in the 2021/22 cycle.

Lauren's Reflections:

Messenger Message: Dr Marianne Trent

To: Lauren Milbourne

Lauren, oh lovely Lauren. I loved having you be 'my assistant' and I missed you every day after you left until I then left 14 months later. I'm so pleased that our work together was useful for you, it was also superbly useful for the clients we worked with who absolutely raved about our work. I see the job of an Assistant Psychologist as being about helping free up qualified time to be able to optimally function in their client work. Whilst doing this, assistants of course learn a heap of relevant and useful skills and approaches and often see how to apply theory in practice which can be invaluable. In your case, you did a superb job supporting me both practically with getting photocopying and outcome measures ready but also helping me with clients in the group so that I could maximise my clinical time by seeing a client each side of our group so we could minimise waiting lists. People told it wasn't possible to 'do 2 clients and a group within a 3-hour clinic,' but with your help we smashed it and proved it was indeed possible! When you told me you'd got your 'new' job it was my first experience of being simultaneously delighted and gutted! I was used to being the leaver not the left! I still recall our 'hot chocolate Tuesdays' in my kitchen after clinic and in between clinic base changes very fondly. Just after you left, the whole world stopped, and Covid-19 rocked the service and indeed the entire planet. The associated lockdowns with the kids saw me 'up my hot chocolate game' to include whipped cream and marshmallows so we'll have to make a date for you to come round again! I am so excited to see how your clinical journey unfolds. Here anytime!

Love from Me, x

31

Chrissie's Review:

2am Covid Ramblings

Marianne. Where do I even begin! I first came across your work when I saw an advert for your 5 Day 'Feel Better' Challenge on the Good Thinking Psychology Facebook page in April 2021 and, as it was free and having embraced the importance of self-care during the pandemic lockdowns, I decided to join just see what the fuss was about. I was wary, not sure if it was just another one of those salesy marketing ploys which some therapists seem to be doing on social media. I could not have been more wrong. Marianne, as a psychologist you are knowledgeable, friendly, funny but professional, present and personable - unlike many other psychologists (sorry not sorry). As a colleague, well you're nuts, in word and deed, especially your work ethic – and this is contagious (at least I hope your ability to jump from task to task and manage an intense workload - including clinic, media broadcasts and projects like

253

this one - rubs off on me even a tiny bit...and also not forgetting that one of my first memories is joining one of your live Q+As and hearing you talk about sheep – I'm sure there was a very valid reason why! Whilst I watched most of the videos on replay during that first Challenge and didn't fully engage with the tasks (I recommend that you actually do engage, they seem simple but work wonders), I was intrigued by the concepts and found that it aligned with my values; particularly normalising mental health issues. As some of the contributors of this book have mentioned, despite being in the professions they are in, a lot of clinical and counselling psychologists, counsellors and therapists alienate mental health, when in reality, everyone suffers from varying levels of stress and anxiety at some point of their lives, it is what makes us human. The more I engaged, the more they resonated and even after the Challenge ended, I found that some things had simply become a part of my internal monologue – for example, breathing through the time when I was on a project at a special needs school where a teenager on the spectrum had a tantrum and lashed out at 5"1 me and I was caught unawares when I should have been on guard. So, when the Challenge came around again in June, it was a no brainer and, as Marianne well knows, I really benefitted from it, and this led me to enrol on the Feel Better Academy course. I have also purchased *The Grief Collective* – a vivid compilation of short bereavement stories and learning how to heal from loss, I found many of these relatable in terms of reminiscing about the death of my grandparents, godfather, godbrother and uncles - and The 'Tricky Brain' Kit and Instructional Video – I don't use it on clients (yet), but I have used it on myself and I am due to use it on family and friends too; it really gets the message across and is an excellent conversation starter.

So, now you know how I 'met' Marianne, but how did I get into psychology?

GCSE Psychology wasn't a thing in my day, I think it started literally the year after (I was also in the last university batch before course fees doubled!), so I was first introduced to it as an AS Level subject. It was here, during secondary school, that I attended a conference and heard Professor Elizabeth Loftus and Christine Sizemore speak on Eyewitness Testimony and multiple personality disorder, sparking my interest in the application of psychological theory. I *needed* to know more.

During this time, my paternal grandmother succumbed to dementia; as we lived next door to her and my aunts and as she had in-house care until her death in 2006, I saw first-hand how neurodegenerative conditions impact the psychiatric element of many age-related illness. I also had the chance to babysit for a disabled infant and had the opportunity of sitting in on physiotherapy appointments and multidisciplinary team meetings. This is all in hindsight, as of course at the time, little sixteen-year-old Chrissie didn't really see the significance of these opportunities; they just seemed mundane but were in reality shaping me into the professional I was 'called' to be.

From a really young age, I was also involved in attending and later assisting in church creche which spurred me onto work with children - I had high hopes of being a Paediatrician although I've never really been great around blood, puke and broken bones and then, much to the dismay of my Sri Lankan parents, I got a double D in Science GCSE. They had high expectations after my two older sisters got A*s and As and went on to obtain First class English and Classics, and Politics, Philosophy and Economics degrees (now working as a Senior Consultant in Melbourne and very well-travelled and successful

Lawyer) – so that dream was shattered. I got 2Bs in English Literature and Religious Studies; 5Cs in English Language, Music, French, Maths and ICT; and 3Ds in History and Double Science and then my AS and A Levels were a shambles too, quite literally went through the alphabet; I knew I was good at English Literature (B) and Philosophy of Religion (C) which I studied at both AS and A2; but my attempt at ICT AS Level yielded an E and my attempt at Psychology AS Level yielded a D. I was also told that I needed Biology AS Level to study Psychology at university, but I got a U. This was gut-wrenching for me of course, having put all my eggs into one basket. I remember running upstairs and sobbing in the bathtub when I learnt I got *that* grade (essentially ungraded even though I did answer most of the questions!?!) and my big sister Nic banging the door down to see if I was okay (she gets a special mention as I haven't seen her since October 2019 because of the pandemic!).

When my dad's older brother founded a Christian charity school in Sri Lanka and invited me over to teach English to 5-12-year olds, and assist in other classes (I was very worried about Maths given my mental arithmetic anxiety in secondary school but that's another story), I eagerly embraced this opportunity to take a gap year abroad on an island I had grown to love; I held my "Honorary Educator and Mentor" title proudly. The opportunity to teach underprivileged children in Sri Lanka strengthened my aspirations and portrayed the significance of Bronfenbrenner's bioecological systems theory (by this point, my family and friends were well aware how nuts I was – about psychology at least – as I would always bring up different theories I had learnt; Pavlov's dogs being a favourite due to being a foodie). I empathised with how the tumultuous environment caused by the civil war influenced the growth and development of these children, predisposing them to other co-morbidities such as depression, anxiety and conduct disorder. I became more aware of the need for us to be trauma-informed in our work supporting children, young people and their families causing me to implement more integrative child-led approaches when volunteering with children suffering from neurodevelopmental and specific learning differences such as autism, dyslexia, dyscalculia, dyspraxia and global delay to ensure their physical and mental wellbeing. I treasure this time to this day as it is an experience I would not have been able to have at any other time; not only did it humble me but I got to spend time with a kind-hearted, generous soul that I could call my uncle (and ultimate hero); despite being the youngest in the family, and the most sensitive, he didn't find me a nuisance or attention-seeking – or a wet blanket in some cases! He had faith in me. I also forged lasting relationships with children and young people, some even orphans, who are now the same age I was when I taught them (18 or 19) and keeping in touch with me via social media! If anything, that experience forced me to grow up and gain some level of independence; a lot of family friends in England didn't think I'd stick it out for the full ten months (September to July; the academic year in Sri Lanka is January to December) and thought I'd be back within three months but I believed in myself, trusted the process (it definitely wasn't easy) and proved them wrong!

During my gap year (and years following), I was able to do diplomas in Level 2 Child Counselling and Level 3 Child Psychology (little did I know that years later I would be writing and tutoring on similar distance learning psychology and counselling courses for a college!) This enabled me to get an unconditional offer for the four-year BSc (Hons) Psychology and Child Development degree with Foundation Year at

Chrissie's Review:

Staffordshire University which gave me Graduate Basis for Chartership (GBC) with the British Psychological Society (BPS). These four years, like my gap year, were pivotal; during the holidays I managed an array of voluntary work including as a sessional playworker at a local special needs children's centre and shadowing an applied behavioural analysis (ABA) tutor with an autistic boy with acute deafness. I got a 2.2 in this degree. Some may say I probably shouldn't be as proud as I am about that, but I am – I am in awe of those who took on part-time jobs and still maintained 2.1s and 1sts, yet I passed those exam retakes (exams heighten my anxiety – so imagine having both my GCSE History and Maths exams on my birthday, and also struggling with what was diagnosed, ten years later, as adenomyosis cramps!) and I survived numerous sleepless nights for that dissertation. My final year supervisor was also a miracle; she found out exactly what made me tick resulting in my research topic and also helped me gain a place on the MSc Family and Child Psychology course at the University of Chester (the fact that I wanted to do a Master's was nuts in itself, but finding a uni that accepted my 2.2 was a miracle, and my family and friends were constantly rooting for me too – in fact, my entire family got together and helped me with data collection and dissertation proofreading which was very unexpected but very welcomed)! I only got a measly Pass mark, but this was where I expanded on my research and also gained graduate BPS membership which enabled me to volunteer at Society conferences. Also, these two student research projects later formed a paper published by the BPS Division of Health Psychology[30], which was disseminated in issue 18 of Psych2Go magazine (a small business that I currently provide pro bono

---

[30] Fitch, C., Provencher, JP et al. (2020). Do I Look Fat in This? When self-image, intuitive eating and childhood parenting practices

258

editorial consultation for) and formed the basis of a recent literature review published by the BPS Division of Educational and Child Psychology.[31]

After my Master's, I really struggled to find a paid Assistant role, so I made the scary decision of becoming self-employed (my aunt is my accounts advisor until I can actually afford my own accountant)! For a few months whilst I was finding my feet (and having the bright idea of emailing a bunch of distance learning colleges), I helped my dad with admin for his property development business; I hated it because it was so unrelated to psychology, and caused a few family feuds, but I did learn a lot of useful personal and professional skills – and I was getting paid! I did have an honorary one-year contract with the Pyramid Project funded by University of West London and really enjoyed it. The organisation conducts 10-week interventions in schools in social interaction. I used Maslow's hierarchy of needs, which explains the importance of friendship, intimacy, and resilience, as a model for my work with 13 Year 7 girls, providing an inclusivity culture and a sense of belonging, encouraging the forging of common bonds through shared interests, and increasing self-esteem through creative expression. We also addressed sensitive topics such as bullying (I was a victim of both physical and emotional bullying in primary and secondary school, so this helped me reflect and come to terms with it), to support the teens in considering and solving emotionally charged situations. From conducting analyses and drafting reports as per Goodman et al.'s Strengths and Difficulties Questionnaire (2010), I observed changes in

---

[31] Fitch, C., Susilo, D.K., Provencher, JP et al. (2021). "Who taught you how to hate yourself so much?": A brief literature review on body image in children and adolescents and the case for mindful eating habits and self-compassion. BPS DECP Debate, 178(1), pp. 7-14.

students' behaviours; they displayed reduced emotional symptoms and thrived in pro-social behaviour. I was slowly becoming the person I wished I had when I was younger.

From my initial decision of becoming self-employed until Covid-19 hit, I acted as seasonal editor for Go Teach Publications Ltd., a provider of biblical teaching material. Go Teach trains staff in their understanding, presentation and explanation of the Bible to youngsters from different backgrounds, enabling us to examine available and practical resources for children's learning; somewhat psychology related! As of November 2020, following several submissions to the magazine, website and divisions (I pestered them long enough, so they had to give in, eventually, right?) I am now an associate editor of the Culture section of the BPS magazine The Psychologist; I have had the pleasure of recently interviewing the lovely Dr Marianne Trent about her work for the magazine too![32]

You, like lots of my family and friends, may think I have lots of experience and am a qualified psychologist – nope. For a really long time, I was under the impression that educational psychology was my niche; I have applied for the doctorate three times, got an interview second time and reserve list third time (no interview) and no place. This scared me; I was turning 30 in April 2021 and fifteen-year-old Chrissie wanted to be a married, qualified psychologist by 25 with two babies by 30. Well, if I carry on with that train of thought, I will be focusing on my failed dating history, heartbreaks and losses and comparing myself to

---

[32] See https://thepsychologist.bps.org.uk/i-had-dream-what-i-wanted-and-gave-myself-permission-do-it

all the 24-year-old girls my family knows who had impromptu lockdown weddings – one married a man who I thought I was in love with (and then the guy I was actually dating moved away, why do all bad things happen in one go?) and another just told me she is already pregnant after seven months - so hey, I'm really not doing so good am I? But – things change, and we should most definitely not compare our journeys because, as my aunt says, "all five fingers are not the same!" (I am assuming your fingers are an analogy for people?) Not everyone has the same goals as you, some may have none at all! It will all work out better for you in the long run, you just may not see it yet!

I eventually realised maybe I'm clutching at straws, I'm not very good at applying legislation to my practice and I am more drawn to psychodynamic and mindfulness approaches like acceptance and commitment therapy (ACT) and being on the forefront of talking and helping people, particularly children and adolescents. What really is my niche? I started doing more research to find something more me; the BPS Qualification in Counselling Psychology (QCoP), the professional Counselling Psychology doctorate, training as a children's wellbeing practitioner (CWP) or an education mental health practitioner (EMHP)? Maybe even the Clinical Psychology doctorate? The options are endless, I'm enjoying the journey and I'll find my niche.

I am currently investigating the parental feeding practices and problems of primary school-aged children with and without autism spectrum disorder with Dr Danielle Ferriday (who absolutely gets a special mention, she's one of the most intelligent people I know!) at the Nutrition and Behaviour

Chrissie's Review:

Unit[33]; I endeavour to continue these themes future research as I believe they will influence my future assessments of children and young people with self-image and eating issues – when I someday get chartered – but there is no rush or timeline now. I am going to start a postgraduate certificate in Counselling Psychology next month, and plan to do other courses in order to increase my psychotherapy knowledge and get onto a clinical placement. Because of my research interests, I also really want to train as a psychometrician, but we shall see how that goes; don't want to bite off more than I can chew – what an odd saying, but it is also true![34]

Given my background in academia, I am more drawn to a PhD – I applied to one and didn't qualify for funding - but there's also such a thing as a PhD by Publication...so who knows what I'll get up to next!

Psychology is a constantly evolving discipline, and I am constantly evolving and honing my skills too with CPD; I have done courses in Mixed Methods Research Designs, Child Nutrition, Child Social Work and Child Positive Discipline and obtained certification in Safeguarding and Child Protection. I am continuing to hone my skills and work with the sensitivity and dedication a psychologist requires, ensuring that what I do will someday be useful in supporting children and young people

---

[33] Funny story actually; this research unit is based at the School of Experimental Science at the University of Bristol. I had no idea that Marianne wanted to go there too until reading her story; but I applied there FOUR times (Undergrad, Master's, Doctorate/Phd) and didn't make it - maybe that's simply because I was meant to get my 'Visiting Research Associate' contract and not be a 'Student' there! Life always works out in your favour and surprises you when you look back on it – it surprised me!
[34] On 01/09/21, publication day, and the day of the fateful HEE statement, I caved and enrolled on the BPS Level 7 course in Test Use (CCET). Future Psychometrician in Educational Testing!

when they need it most, and enabling them to accomplish their goals in any environment. I look forward to making contributions to improving the educational and socioemotional outcomes of children, young people and their families. That's why I call myself an aspiring Child Psychologist.

When Marianne first pitched the idea of this book project to me, I thought it was a brilliant idea so when she wanted to hire me for my proofreading services, I was very excited to get to work – partly because I was stuffy and hot and Covid-positive and needed an excuse to sit in one place and read something of actual interest to me, having gotten upset with Netflix for removing *Orphan Black*, instead of trying to limp about on a dodgy right knee (a story for another time but look after your knees and don't make it do any sudden movements, you need them to work to walk – yay for hypermobile joints!) and feeling sorry for myself for having to cancel a staycation AND long-awaited spa weekend over the bank holiday, but also because I was a nosey eager beaver and wanted to get involved wherever I could.

Proofreading this book has been more than just another freelance task for me (apart from keeping me sane when normal people (as in, all other people living in the UK who are not me) are asleep; midday wakings have been a thing as Covid has made me nocturnal – I do have a very low pain threshold and can be a huge whiner so it's very lucky I've not had the symptoms bad!). The contents from these stories have allowed me to take a step back and put my values into perspective. This stuff is unique, and beneficial. It works. I do admit that I was a bit nervous when Marianne asked me to write a contribution though (in fact she asked me twice so I thought maybe I should), so...

Chrissie's Review:

I hope you find something in this ramble interesting and relatable!

Hugs,

Chrissie

Pearlaine Christabel (Chrissie) Fitch BSc (Hons) MSc MBPsS; Self-Employed, London: T: @fitchychris. Please email me on chrissie@goodthinkingpsychology.co.uk if you want free copies of my research papers!

Slack Message from: Dr Marianne Trent

To: Chrissie Fitch

Oh Chrissie….the lady with the most beautiful collection of names possible! Whilst I of course wouldn't wish COVID-19 on anyone how fun has this project been though? Hannah and I are both so lucky and happy to have you on board. I hope you are soon able to rebook your spa trip. It's been lovely having you in my world since April 2021 and looks like I'll have to get myself another 'best customer' because you're now on Team Good Thinking as a freelancer too!

You've been amazing to have in my corner for the last 4 months and now you're in my camp and I know that we will go from strength to strength with you on board. Although you're always super busy so I was honoured you even wanted to help let alone to the extent where you have been so invaluable to this project!

I'm so jealous you actually got to see Loftus! I just read about it in the textbooks. I bet that was fascinating!

To anyone reading this do please know that opportunities can definitely crop up for you by interacting with the socials of people you admire and by messaging them like Chrissie did!

Thanks for everything you're doing both for me and everyone else too Chrissie. I'm so excited to see which branch of 'working with people' you end up in!

Marianne

Alternative Paths

I hope you manage to achieve your dreams whatever they are and whatever they include. I'd like a fridge full of Rachel's organic rice pudding, that would be up there on the wish list. Given that Clinical Psychologists are not the only breed of Psychologists I thought it would be really helpful to include some narratives and advice from other qualified psychologists too. I'm sorry I didn't think to recruit for this with the original recruitment drives. I only had this idea when I was in the shower 4 days before publication! This was after the deadline for other submissions and yet I still put adverts out and I was so delighted when we received 7 submissions over the next few days. I do hope that you will find them useful and they're fantastically interesting! I've certainly learned a lot!

32

Jolel's Story:

Lecturing & Health Psychology

My name Is Dr Jolel Miah, and I am Lecturer in Psychology at the University of Sunderland. I am also a Health Psychologist in Training and doing the independent Stage 2 route with the British Psychological Society Health Division.

Why did I choose Health Psychology after graduation?

After graduating with a BSc in Psychology from the University of Hertfordshire, I was at a crossroads for what to do. I had tried to make my situation clearer for myself by working during my second and third years during my undergraduate days. I had volunteered and worked in a range of settings (e.g., schools, workplaces, universities) to help me gain some experience working with people. Clinical Psychology was the only area people most talked about, so I conformed very easily and started to look only for these posts. With little luck and no one getting back to me, I started a job as a support worker for an HIV charity. I initially spent most of my time organising and helping the staff to deliver information workshops to the community. I then reflected on this experience and sat in the office thinking; *can I do anything with this because I'm really enjoying it!* The biggest question for me was: *which area of Psychology does this belong to?*

I then went to my local University and spoke to someone in Psychological Approaches to Health and Management. After listening attentively, the course director recognised this was not the area and sign posted me to the person who was teaching the MSc Health Psychology course. I spoke to the individual who allowed me to explore my interests. After a couple of weeks of talking to my support network, I enrolled on to the program.

After the MSc

After completing the MSc in Health Psychology (stage 1) at the University of Bedfordshire, I had three options for further training and development 1) Apply to do a doctorate in Health Psychology, 2) Do a research degree (PhD) or 3) Apply to do the independent route to becoming a Health Psychologist. I decided to do my PhD, but I still wanted to practice as a potential psychologist in the future. So, then I decided to do my PhD part-time and the independent route. With the help of my supervisor, I put together a training plan to cover the 5 competencies:

1. Professional Practice
2. Psychological Interventions
3. Research
4. Consultancy
5. Teaching and Training

I continue to work to this day on my portfolio and I did initially think about rushing my training. However, I decided to take time after listening to a talk by someone who advised the group not to rush this process because it is harder to learn on the job rather than in training. Helping people is a real privilege and a diverse experience so take your time to develop yourself.

To make sure my portfolio was completed here are the roles that I did

- Health Improvement Advisor in the HM Prison Service.
- Support Worker in a care home in the third sector
- Support Worker for an HIV Charity
- Senior Care Coordinator for an out of hours service at a call centre in a private company
- Outreach worker for Chlamydia screening for the NHS
- Commissioner in a Local Authority
- Visiting Lecturer in Psychology
- Research Assistant
- Editor, Publicity & Liaison Chair for the Health Psychology Public Health Network
- Time to Change Lead (Mental Health Stigma Campaign)
- Chair of the Suicide and Self Harm prevention group
- Co-Lead South Asian Psychology UK Network

There is a great a diagram by the BPS of the training route to becoming a Health Psychologist in the UK[35]

Source:
https:// www.bps.org.uk/member-microsites/division-health-psychology/careers

---

[35] Jolel pasted the image into the original document but as I don't have permission to reproduce it within these pages, yet I will ask that you click on the link or get busy on google to find it because it is lovely and worth checking out.

271

My parting advice

There is a lot of noise when you graduate, and you can be pulled in all sorts of directions. My advice is to pay attention to how you feel when you think about an area of Psychology. Are you getting excited or feeling dread? Speak to people in the field; ask to shadow them for the day. Ask people in the field about their day. Do your research and allow yourself to think that no one has the answers. All of us, are on our own journey who want to help people, and this is all that matters. Be patient and kind to yourself, do not rush this process. There is no wrong or right answer; the most important thing you can do is be you.

Find out more about Dr Jolel Miah at www.drjolel.com. You can also reach him at info@drjolel.com.

Email from: Dr Marianne Trent

To: Dr Jolel Miah

Dear Jolel,

Thank you so much for your submission and also for the speed at which you wrote it. Less than 12 hours after I put the request out on to socials your finished account was in my inbox and ready for publication.

I'm sorry that thinking to include this section was a last-minute consideration on my part because actually it's an incredibly important section. Your account so wonderfully reflects that people can end up in the clinical psychology track feeling lost and confused and not really knowing which route to take and how to get somewhere which might feel more like 'a bit of them.' It sounds like you received some wonderful careers advice by directing you to the health psychology department and I'm so pleased that was your experience and that it led you to where you are now.

Thank you again, people are going to find your account so informative, useful and of course inspiring.

With my best wishes,

Marianne

33

Claire's Story:

Striking a Balance

When I was a little girl, I told everyone that I wanted to be a nurse, because I wanted to 'save people'. By my teens and following at least two episodes of passing out at the sight of blood, it became clear that this was not a realistic ambition for me!

I can't remember exactly when or how I decided that I wanted to be a Psychologist, but I found myself taking a psychology A Level and then going off to university to do a psychology degree. At that stage, I hadn't heard much about different areas of psychology other than Clinical and so that is where I expected I would end up. It was during my course that I became aware of the competition around places on the doctorate and the need to be able to demonstrate experience in order to get on. Eager to plow ahead, I started to do voluntary work, in the hope that it would assist me in getting a place sooner rather than later. Initially this was with the university counselling service, although when I didn't find this particularly fulfilling (it was solely on an email basis with no in-person interaction), I found a voluntary position with Victim Support and the Witness Service. Here, I supported victims of crimes in the aftermath of the event and during any court proceedings. I really enjoyed this work and the variety of people I met, both the clients we worked with and my colleagues. It was very clear to me that crime surpassed all boundaries, and anyone could be a victim, increasing my awareness of the prevalence of this as a source of trauma across all ages, genders, sexual orientations, cultures and socio-economic groups.

It was during this time that there was a high-profile murder investigation in the town where I was at university. Sadly, the young victim had been dismembered and parts of him had been found in various locations. There was a huge amount of media interest and Victim Support were involved in supporting his family. The details of the victim's suffering are still, to this day, the worst that I have read. Even after more than fifteen years of working with serious offenders, I have never forgotten what that child experienced. With hindsight, I now recognise this as a turning point for me and my career pathway; I started to notice the negativity within my work supporting victims. Some individuals had been victimised repeatedly and there was a general sense that things would not change for them. Lots of witnesses didn't show up for court, believing that there was 'no point' and that it wouldn't achieve anything. I started to feel frustrated at the general acceptance of the problem, the belief that we just had to live with it, and the negativity about the Criminal Justice System. It was then that an opportunity came up with the local Youth Offending Team, for a voluntary Support Worker to work with young people who had come to the attention of police and were on their 'last chance'. Who better, I thought, to work with and effect change than the young people who are at that crossroads? I spent a year supporting a number of young people for a variety of different behaviours. I saw success and I saw those that sank deeper into a criminal lifestyle and I became more aware of the challenges facing those trying to move away from a life of crime.

One of the most influential experiences for my career choice came when one day I was invited to escort a young man to a Young Offenders prison for a day. It was a way of trying to show him what would happen to him if he continued on the path he was on. As well as being an eye-opener for him, this was a hugely impactful experience for me. We met young men convicted of serious violent offences who sat down and told us their offence accounts. In my head, I had carried the victim perspective; the knowledge of the impact of crimes and, quite often, assumptions about the 'bad people' who had committed them. That day, I came away with a greater sense of the offender perspective; the knowledge that some of these individuals had suffered tremendously in their lives before their offences and had been victims themselves. Despite committing crimes that we might consider to be 'evil'; these boys were not evil themselves and I fully saw that distinction between the act and the person. This experience inspired me. I realised I wanted to work with people, like these young men, and help them to overcome their past trauma and create more positive futures for both themselves but also for the people that might have otherwise been targeted by them.

When I left university, I already had a job lined up at the prison just outside of my hometown. I had written to the Area Psychologist for the Prison Service, with my CV, and had secured a post as Assistant Psychologist. I also registered on an MSc in Forensic Psychology as I had, by now, realised that this was where my true interest lay. I was an Assistant for nine months before I was promoted to Trainee Forensic Psychologist. I can honestly say the Prison Service was the best start my career could have had; I was privileged to be offered training in so many forensic areas and treatment interventions that I feel this gave me a brilliant grounding to start off with.

Whilst the Prison Service gave me a wealth of knowledge for which I am grateful, I found this a difficult place to complete my training and to become a Chartered Psychologist. As a Trainee, I needed to demonstrate to the British Psychological Society (BPS) that I was competent to work in a range of different areas. However, at that time, prison psychology was focussed upon the delivery of offending behaviour programmes and the opportunities for experience in the other areas (research, training, consultation etc) were scarce. I continued to progress in my prison roles, treatment managing programmes and managing teams of other trainees and assistants, but it wasn't long before I was frustrated at the lack of progress and the lack of opportunity to do more than run group work programmes. I was also increasingly challenged by the conflict between treatment integrity (running interventions in line with what research tells us is the more effective approach) and meeting prison targets. The two do not often go hand in hand and I struggled to find myself satisfied when it felt that the effectiveness of treatment was being compromised due to a target that needed to be met. I eventually moved on from the Prison Service and into a medium secure unit. Here I felt more satisfied at the ability to tailor interventions to the needs of the individual and to address a wider range of criminogenic needs within group and individual work. It was within a medium secure unit that I finally completed my training and became a Chartered Forensic Psychologist with the BPS and a Registered Psychologist with the HCPC, having also been afforded the opportunities for research, training and consultation as was necessary.

Since completing my training in 2013, I have embarked on attempting to strike a balance between being employed by an organisation and working privately. I spent some years writing reports for the Parole Board and attending parole hearings as a witness before I joined as a Specialist Member of the Parole Board myself in 2017. I continue to sit as a panel member now and I also write court reports on an independent basis. I really enjoy both of these roles; I find the opportunity to continue to meet with and assess offenders to be very fulfilling as I feel that, in those individual cases, I can continue to make a difference by recognising and acknowledging their own experiences and communicating this on their behalf to others involved in the Criminal Justice System, in order to better meet their needs. Within parole work, I have had the opportunity to meet a variety of other professionals and have learnt something from everyone I have encountered that informs my ongoing practice and decision making. I have also found that, in experiencing the process from 'the other side of the table', I have a greater appreciation for those that make decisions within this field; I cannot describe the weight of responsibility that I feel when making decisions about someone's risk and their suitability for release from prison. However, I recognise the importance of this role and the need for it to be carried out by professionals with knowledge and expertise in the area, so as to ensure the right decisions are made for the protection of the public.

In 2018 I took the step of leaving secure settings (and working therapeutically with offenders) and joined an organisation that engages with victims and survivors of child sexual abuse to make recommendations to protect children in future. As a Forensic Psychologist, it is somewhat unusual to be involved in a victim-focused organisation, however my interest lies in recognising those individuals who are both victims and offenders. I do not in any sense intend to suggest that being a victim leads to becoming an offender, however there is a grey area of people who sit in both of these groups. This is an area that I am hugely passionate about and want to draw more attention to. Many people in prison, regardless of their crimes, have been victims themselves and so often we focus on their behaviour rather than the trauma that led to it. Prisons in the UK are pretty dingy estates and, whilst we may see headlines likening them to Butlin's holiday camps, I can attest that they are far from it. There is no doubt that, whatever rehabilitative interventions are available in prison, prisoners themselves see the experience as a punishment. So rarely is there an understanding of their own victimisation or the opportunity to address this whilst in custody. Whilst in my current role, I have been able to offer a space for individuals in prison to share their experiences and feel heard, although I am painfully aware that there are a huge number of people that have not yet been heard and whose traumas may not be related to sexual abuse.

At some fifteen years into my career as a Forensic Psychologist I am not sure that I fit the profile a traditional Forensic Psychologist has, in that I no longer work within any institution and have, most recently, spent my time working more with those who are the victims of crime as opposed to those committing it. However, if there is a point to me writing this piece, it is probably just that there is a grey area between victims and offenders where there is a cohort of individuals who fulfil both groups. As a Forensic Psychologist, it is no good focusing on these as distinct presentations; I must be able to work with both parts of these individuals in order to effect change and reduce future risk. Wherever I go next in my career, I endeavour to work on increasing the opportunities to recognise and address trauma within the offending population.

In going back to my early ambition to be a nurse, I may not be in a role where I am physically saving lives. However, I certainly consider the role of a Forensic Psychologist to have a dramatic impact upon people's futures and assisting people to make these as positive as they can be.

Claire's Story:

Claire Barker is a Forensic Psychologist. You can contact her via email at claire.barker@tullyforensicpsychology.com **or via her LinkedIn profile:** https://uk.linkedin.com/in/claire-barker-4408003a

Email from: Dr Marianne Trent

To: Claire Barker

Dear Claire,

Thank you so much for your submission and also for your enthusiasm and speed for writing it for us. I found it fantastically interesting, and I know our readers will to. My specialism is developmental trauma and I absolutely hear you about the staggeringly high correlation between high ACE scores and prison stays. Our prisons are full of traumatised people, and this is something also highlighted in the book 'Justice on Trial' by Chris Daw QC, do check it out if you've not already read it as it's a great read.

I too have worked in forensic services, and I think it's also important to consider the impact of vicarious trauma on people working close to victims and offenders too. I do hope you are able to stay compassionate to yourself and have regular debriefs and a supportive supervisor and of course family around you.

With my best wishes,

Marianne

34

Tara's Story:

Creating Benchmarks!

Counselling Psychology is a branch of psychology that places emphasis on the relationship between theory and evidenced based research. It also focuses on the therapeutic process and relationship between psychologist and client. Training is formed of two parts: an accredited degree in psychology that meets the requirements for Graduate basis for Chartered Membership of the British Psychological Society, followed by a three-year postgraduate training course at Doctoral level.

Despite misgivings, Counselling Psychologists are trained in robust assessment, formulation, treatment and risk assessment. In addition, they must demonstrate core competencies in specific therapeutic models and complete 400+ hours of therapy to qualify. We are trained to provide evidenced based assessment, formulation and treatment approaches and we provide interventions to a wide range of client groups in both primary and secondary care as well as private practice and other settings including voluntary organisations. Many are also additionally trained in the use of clinical assessment tools and psychometric testing.

My Study Journey:

I started my training in Counselling Psychology in 1999. I was extremely lucky to be accepted onto the first ever training run by Professor Rob Bor, an eminent Counselling and Health Psychologist who is now world renowned for his work in Aviation Psychology. At this time in order to qualify as a Counselling psychologist, the training consisted of a Master's degree followed by a Postgraduate Practitioner diploma. The doctorate wasn't automatically included, which is commonplace in current times. I completed my training in 2003.

I later went on to complete my top-up Doctorate at The Tavistock Clinic as this was personally an important personal goal to become Dr Quinn! I was able to complete this while working full time in the NHS as a qualified Counselling Psychologist. I remember having my thesis on one side of my computer and a wedding magazine on the other side as motivation to complete and hand in my 40,000-word thesis before my wedding! Small motivators like this were so important when self-funding and working towards a goal while also working at the same time.

During my training we were required to undertake various placements and of course complete every one of those 400 hours of clinical input with clients. We were also required to undertake 40 hours of personal therapy, which provided an invaluable insight into the client experience and the therapeutic relationship. Counselling Psychology is self-funded, so I will be honest in my account when I say that it was hard at times managing the demands of study and course attendance while working in jobs to fund my training. I have an interesting working background including working as a rehabilitation assistant in a private head injury hospital, a deputy manager for a Mencap residential home and later back to the private hospital again working shifts as a support worker on a complex PTSD unit and Young Person's mental health unit. I remember working nights and then studying and attending lectures during the day. It was certainly character building and gave me a wealth of experience and memories of the people that I supported and also worked with. I also completed training placements in both learning disabilities community teams and adult mental health teams including a specialist learning disabilities service in Hounslow. I can recall physically writing that number "400" on my practice log of clinical hours and the feeling was just immense!

When I look back on my training journey, I can honestly say that it has shaped me into the resilient and determined Psychologist I am today! I think that you have to have a 'creative flair' as a Counselling Psychologist and it helps me develop my practice and also my collaborative and media work.

Work:

At the time of my training, you were allowed to work as a "Counselling Psychologist in Training" after completing your Master's degree. I applied for a job in an adult learning disability team where I worked while completing the remainder of my training. I ended up staying once qualified! I look back on this time with such fondness. I have also worked in adult mental health services.

Following the birth of my second child in 2014 I decided to set up in private practice. It has been an amazing few years and I have developed a thriving client practice and also been able to tap into my creative flair and love for community psychology and use my autonomy to develop community projects, collaborations with some really amazing and inspiring people and also dive (a little head first!!) into the world of media psychology!

My additional roles have included being a specialist advisor for the CQC, and also a clinical reviewer for NHS England. This came off the back of the Winterbourne View Scandal which identified the need for better monitoring of individuals with learning disabilities in inpatient units. I have found this role to be so rewarding. I am also a Psychological reserve Volunteer for the British Red Cross. I was in the first cohort of these practitioners as a joint venture between the Red Cross and the British Psychological Society. I was also honoured to be able to provide my help with the recent Plymouth Shootings.

As a Counselling Psychologist I pride myself on my relationships with others and being able to harness this to help those in need. During the coronavirus pandemic I set up a Facebook support group to help people emotionally during the past 18 months. This has been purely voluntary. I have also been contributing to other emotional support forums nationally and internationally. I have also set up a local voluntary project in my community to help people to manage their emotional wellbeing. The "Conversation Starter Project" includes weekly 'walk and talk' sessions that I host. The feedback I get from this work is so lovely and the feeling when seeing people take that step to come and join us is just indescribable!

I have also done extensive media work helping people cope throughout the pandemic and also speak on other psychological topics to various media outlets. I want to bring the principles of psychology to individuals and communities. I think that my counselling psychology training has helped to shape my ability to initiate and forge relationships with others including those in the media; people I collaborate with and most importantly the clients I work with in my clinic. While I appreciate that my 22 years clinical experience plays an important part in the service that I deliver, it's the feedback about the therapeutic relationship that I value the most. Being able to have the skills to establish a connection with people, especially when they are often at their most vulnerable is just the most humbling thing. Creating a safe, containing space for clients to begin to explore and work on their difficulties is essentially what Counselling Psychology is all about. I love my job; I love my role and I am excited to see where Counselling Psychology will take me next!

Best of luck with your psychology path,

Dr Tara Quinn-Cirillo (C.Psychol, AFBPsS) Owner of Horsham Psychology.

www.horshampsychology. com

Tara's Story:

Honestly Tara, I do actually think I love you a tiny bit, maybe a bit more than that even. I can't thank you enough and not just for your story which you wrote on annual leave from your sunbed! You had heard about the new non-clinical extension to this project on the Saturday lunch time and by Sunday your story was with us! But also, just generally for being you. I believe we first crossed paths on Instagram. You often like and comment on my stuff and as a small business owner that's just so appreciated and always noticed. Also, as a naturally straight-haired girl your lovely hair in your profile picture also caught my attention too! Aside from your hair, your writing and your social generosity, you're also just so thoughtful and kind. On a Monday in July 2021, England had just lost the Euro's the night before and the country was hurting. 'Compassionate disappointment' was a hot topic that day and I had already planned to do my first ever live webinar that day too. The webinar was set to start at 10am and I was actually feeling pretty nervous, it felt like kind of a big deal. Anyway, 9am rolled round and I got a phone call from a BBC radio station to book me for a live radio chat. Then I got another call to book me for another radio show. Then I got an email telling me that ITV news wanted to interview me too. Suddenly my 'pretty nervous' day went off the charts (excitement feels like nerves, too right?!) Anyway, just after this I got a message from you wishing me luck for my webinar and that you were excited to watch the replay later. It meant more to me than you could have known and was so nice to feel that you were on my team rooting for me. I am confident that your clients and your family and friends are also equally held in mind by you, and I am so pleased that you are in my world and of course, now in The Collective!

Your story is going to be so helpful to so many people. Thanks once again for taking the time to share it with us.

With my best wishes, Marianne

35

Emma's Story:

Educational Psychology

Many people already know this about me (not sure what this says about my adulting) but I was not the easiest teenager. Stubborn, opinionated and fiercely loyal - I ended up getting myself into quite a bit of trouble at the grammar school that I went to and, ultimately, was asked to leave. This worked out well for me as my sixth form did not offer a Psychology A Level course and the local college did. Once I had started my journey in Psychology at 16 that was it - I was hooked. I sucked up the fall from grace, worked hard and did well with my A Levels with minimal spoon feeding to pass the exams. Pat on the back, I was off to Uni to complete my Undergraduate in Psychology.

3 years of fun and hard work later I graduated with a BSc in Psychology but with no idea of what I could do with it in terms of an actual job. By this point I had already done a fair bit of work with children in my summer breaks, supporting and then managing at a playscheme, so I thought that this was the age group that I could see myself working with. Looking into the

287

various career paths for psychologists I came across Educational Psychology. It seemed right up my street. Perhaps I could even help some disillusioned teenagers to achieve their potential as some straight-talking adults had once helped me...

At the time, the route to Educational Psychology was still through teaching, so I decided to train as a primary school teacher and enrolled onto the Postgraduate Certificate in Education (PGCE) at the Institute of Education. A year and multiple practices / assignments later I was thrown into the world of teaching full throttle, where I remained for the next four years. At points during this time, I admittedly, did forget a little about my original dream of becoming an Ed Psych. I enjoyed teaching, particularly the relationships that developed with the children over the course of a year teaching them, and I wondered if I might stick to that. However, after a few years (and a Master's in teaching and learning), I felt that the time was right to explore the next challenge. Hats off to teachers - I found it incredibly emotionally draining and knowing that I wanted to have my own family at some point I did not feel that I could reasonably manage children at home and all day at work! So, I applied for the doctorate in Educational Psychology.

To my surprise and delight I was offered an interview on my first round of applications and after a shaky interview (literally - I had three black coffees while waiting and am usually a tea drinker - error), group and written task I was surprised to find out a few months later that I had been accepted onto the course! Hand on heart it is the BEST decision of my life, and I threw myself whole heartedly into the next three years, making friends for life and learning so much from the practice and theory of the course. I was lucky to be placed in Hackney, where I lived at the time, which was a creative, forward thinking EP service providing support to an amazing community full of challenge, reward, and some of the most incredible young people I have ever met. This is where my passion for putting children and young people at the heart of my work really developed and it is a value that I have taken through all of my work as an EP. After 7 years (and two children) I moved out of London, and I started up my own independent practice. This has helped me to be flexible around my family and pick and choose the type of work that I do. Currently I support 5 secondary schools, a group of children's residential care homes and a university. I have undertaken additional training in Autism and work as part of a multidisciplinary diagnostic team serving children and families. The diversity and breadth of work is fantastic, and I can choose all sorts of Continuing Professional Development (CPD) to continue to enhance my practice and application of psychology. I love the fact that I'm in a different place every day. Ultimately my drive is to ensure all children have equal access to education, no matter their profile of strengths and needs, and if I can play any small part in helping the school / education machine to do this a little bit more effectively then I will be a very happy girl. I do still think of myself as that 16-year-old girl who so very nearly took the wrong path in life. Still stubborn as hell - but now I'm called "tenacious" and applauded for it - instead of having my knuckles rapped. Getting the Dr title feels like a personal victory for me. And using it in a way to help other kids is even better.

Emma's Story:

Email from: Dr Marianne Trent

To: Dr Emma Sheffield

Dear Emma,

You are so ace. Thanks so much for your story and for doing so super speedily within 12 hours of first making contact! Educational Psychology is such an important part of education and I love the way you describe your role as helping every child to be able to optimally access and benefit from their education.

I am confident that the children, families, and schools you work with get tonnes of value from what you do with them. Also hats off to you for having been a teacher for 4 years. A few of my friends are teachers, and the expectations are high! I'm sure kissing goodbye to the longer stretches of holiday was tricky, although of course I also know just how much they are needed to recharge and get over the term time stresses and strains of super long workdays and holding children and families in mind around the clock too.

Shining some light on the training requirements for Ed Psychs is so useful, thanks again, with my best wishes,

Marianne

36

Priya's Story:

I let my interests guide me

Pursuing a career in Psychology can be a minefield, we see and hear this a lot. The route is often never a planned one, very dependent on what course or experience you manage to secure which guides your interest. The value of gaining meaningful work experience shaped my journey leading me to where I am today.

I thought counselling might be cool when I started my BSc Psychology & Counselling degree. It wasn't until I sat down in front of a client as a volunteer counsellor, that I realised this career was not for me. However, I was still very keen on understanding human behaviour. Not long after, I did some work experience working with children; this was the shortest experience I had. I knew there and then, working with adults was more for me.

Midway through my degree, an opportunity came up for a part time job to work with patients living in the community who had brain injuries. This was interesting as every patient's case

291

differed but also provided a real insight in how to manage long term care. This job was more akin to clinical psychology. Still, I didn't feel content, it wasn't really my area of interest, but I did enjoy working in the community. I was leaning more towards 'health' as I found the management of long-term health conditions fascinating. Right after that I got a volunteer position as a therapeutic carer across multiple wards at an NHS trust. Surprisingly, it still wasn't what I expected. I was interested in health, but I felt happier when I was doing community work as opposed to working in a hospital setting.

It was during my 2nd year of my undergraduate psychology degree that I got an internship as a health promotion assistant. I travelled across different communities to develop health interventions for long term health conditions to tackle health inequalities. This was also an opportunity to build my own network of contacts in public health as I worked collaboratively alongside the Local Authority Public Health Teams. This experience was new to me; this was the first time I was seeing how psychology can be applied in a different way beyond the more clinical. Most importantly, I saw how the barriers towards accessing health services predominantly affected marginalised groups such as ethnic minority communities. This resonated with me on a personal level as I saw first-hand how prominent type 2 diabetes and cardiovascular disease were in the South Asian community. I understood that the solution to health inequalities was complex and required better understanding of health behaviour using health behavioural models. I finally found the 'missing part' in this job role when I had the opportunity to showcase my creativity and logistical skills when designing and delivering different health initiatives for specific vulnerable groups. This allowed me to make my own unique contribution in my role by developing theory driven health interventions using government statistics on health status to build a rationale.

That internship experience was a real eye opener which later led me onto MSc Health Psychology. This is the first stage towards the independent stage 2 route to qualify as a community health psychologist. I knew that to make a real difference in the community for ethnic minority groups, further research into theory driven interventions was needed. Fast forward to today, I am halfway through my PhD which is on developing my own community health intervention for improving dietary behaviour for the South Asian community. My PhD research meets two of the five competencies (professional skills, teaching & training, psychological intervention, research & consultation) needed to complete the stage 2 route. Alongside my research, I have been involved in teaching on the undergraduate psychology programme and consultation work with small organisations to deliver training on cultural competence. All of which leads back to the contacts I developed from my internship. I have a clear direction of where I want to go with my career. I essentially let my interests guide me through different work experience and volunteering jobs to get me to where I am today.

Priya Ahmed is currently working on her PhD in Health Psychology at Teesside University. You can contact her via email on Priya.ahmed@tees.ac.uk, tweet her at PriyaAhmed94 or visit her Instagram, Priya_healthpsych.

Priya's Story:

Dear Priya,

Wow! I am just blown away by the level of relevant experience you managed to achieve within your undergraduate years. I think that when balanced with study that those years are a really great pocket of time to sneak in some extra CV time whilst applying newfound knowledge. I'm also aware that when I had 'work in the morning' I was much more likely to return from the union earlier than I was when I 'only' had to get up for my own lectures, so it was probably helpful from that perspective for me too!

Thanks so much for the speedy time you managed to turn around this account for us. Health Psychology is an incredibly important area and is so useful for all of us both individually and as a society. It sounds like you are doing incredible things and I would like to wish you all of the very best of luck and of course joy, satisfaction and achievement with it in future. Go out there, do your thing, change the world!

Marianne

37

Avni's Story:

#HealthPsychologistDiaries

My name is Dr Avni Chauhan and I have a few professional hats in the world of Health Psychology. I currently work for a CAMHS service, as well as seeing private patients and doing clinical supervision for companies in my own time. I am also module lead at the University of West London (UWL) on their Psychology undergraduate degree course as well as a lecturer on the Health Psychology Master's. It was a long road to get here, but definitely worth it.

Why Health?
After doing the standard journey of GCSEs, A Levels and then my degree in Psychology - I really didn't know what I wanted to do with it. Whilst studying, I had done lots of volunteering positions (in cancer services, pain, drugs, prisons, sexual health), and it was whilst I was volunteering for two services that I felt *this could be for me!* I was working for a pain management service (Camden and Islington NHS Trust) for a few days a week and then a drug and alcohol service (Central and North West London NHS Trust (CNWL)) for another few days. I can

hear people say – 'how are these even remotely similar?' Well, having done some meticulous research, I found that they both fell in the Division of Health Psychology. I then looked into it further and found the connection between mental health and physical health so extraordinarily interesting, especially in the two fields I was volunteering in. As you have probably encountered yourself, a Doctorate in Clinical Psychology (DClinPsy) appeared to be the only path for most aspiring psychologists, it's an established doctorate and you get paid to do it! I took a risk and went against the grain as scary as it felt.

My interest really did lie in the health-related issues people face; I knew Health Psychology was pretty new, but I found a Master's at City University so I went ahead and applied for it! This is Stage 1 of course. Even whilst doing the Master's, we were mostly encouraged to go onto do the DClinPsy and many of my colleagues on the Master's did eventually go on to be Clinical Psychologists, however not I! I looked into the Stage 2 for Health Psychology and found that actually the taught route was for me, so I applied and enrolled at Queen Margaret University (QMU) in Edinburgh (and I am from London, so this was quite a commute)!

During the Doctorate

Back then, there were limited universities that were teaching the doctorate and QMU had a good course set up that worked for me (as you don't get paid to do this doctorate) and allowed me to still work full time. By this point I was working for an organisation based at Hounslow Borough police station, people would be getting arrested and if they tested positive for Class A, I would be then called to work with them and make behaviour changes with an ultimate goal of abstinence or reduction. Great job! I really loved the nitty gritty of the role and then the more I would learn on the doctorate, the more I could apply to my work. There were five competencies I had to complete at work and the way I was able to make changes at a service-need level just by completing my competencies allowed me to be recognised and promoted. The doctorate took many, many years as I was working full time and doing this in the evenings and all weekend. By the end of the doctorate, I had changed my job, and was employed by CNWL to develop a young person's service from scratch within an adult service for Drug and Alcohol use. This was a great opportunity to not only complete some of my doctoral competencies but also make some changes to the service. I developed a Motivational Interviewing Workshop for children of drug using parents – evaluated that, and it was a success, so that was my dissertation sorted! My manager at the time was a Clinical Psychologist and she would always make me doubt my 'Health Psychology' choices and I even came to a point where I thought *What am I doing? Am I faking it to make it?!* It really wasn't easy, to then convince others of the value of what I was doing, to the point of needing to now convince myself!

Reflections

The sense of achievement I now feel for getting through those gruelling times gets me through any difficult times I currently get at work. I essentially juggle three roles, so it crops up more than you'd imagine! Sometimes I do still think *'AM I faking it??!'* but I choose to prove those *'unhelpful thinking styles'* wrong, I ventured into private work, petrified of what I was doing. This could all go wrong, and I would do it in my own time so when would I do anything else... like find a husband (I'm an Indian woman, it's a thing, trust me!) When I look back, I do wish I had someone who had 'been there and done that' so I could feel more confident in the choices I had made. I was lucky I had the proudest and most supportive parents you could want for, but it took a long time to get my head around what I was doing and why I was doing it! I am now 21 years on, and I think I sort of know what and why I am doing it.

It can be scary, but I assure you, you are the expert of your field and the best part of being a Health Psychologist is that no-one really knows what we are! Every time I have started a new role, the intrigue is great, I have been able to mould all my roles to include everything I love so much about psychology. I now know I love working with children and young people and being the only Health Psychologist in my CAMHS team (and in fact the only one in my Trust that is in CAMHS), means I can show everyone else the value of having one in the team. One thing I would really like to say to anyone considering this path,

'Please never feel like it limits or hinders you.'

I have been able to train in so many techniques (CFT, ACT, SFT, trauma informed care) and am currently in the process of qualifying in EMDR. There is nothing you cannot do as a Health Psychologist so please do it – whatever you want to do in whatever service, go for it. We may all want the same; to help, to support, to give tools to allow people to thrive but it is only with our mixed bag of knowledge and passion do we give the best standard of care, whichever one of my three roles I am doing in that particular moment!

'No one is you, and that is your power'

-Dave Grohl

Dr Avni Chauhan is a chartered member of the BPS and registered with the HCPC. She is working in the NHS, private practice and as a lecturer. Find out more at MyHealthPsychologist.com. If you would like to contact her, you can via Instagram @Health.Psychologist.Diaries or email her on avni.chauhan@NHS.net

Email from: Dr Marianne Trent

To: Dr Avni Chauhan

Dear Avni,

Oh, you are just splendid, and your happiness and work satisfaction just beam out of your story. It really is the most incredible feeling to feel so content in your work!

Thank you also for being one of my speedy turnaround contributors. Working on a bank holiday weekend really does go above and beyond and thanks also for your perseverance when our email accounts just wouldn't communicate with each other!

I genuinely believe that if Psychology access routes other than Clinical were also funded, that it would lead to people making different career choices, because, as you'll know, health can have such an impact on all of the areas and clinical specialities where Clinical Psychologists work. I love the idea of you working in CAMHS and I can definitely appreciate how incredibly useful you'd have been as an asset when I was working in there. Heck, who am I kidding? We needed you in CMHT too! I never once in almost 6 years managed to achieve the health psychology department picking up a referral I had sent through. As a result, I was often left holding the clinical and therapeutic reins when actually, I firmly believed that the client would be best served with someone with specific health and pain frameworks and expertise. That said, the health psychologist was always super helpful at offering email advice to me, but I do still think I wasn't the best choice at that time for those clients! I feel like I could discuss this overlap with you all day, perhaps we should do a live stream chat on socials one day soon?

Hope you had a lovely rest of bank holiday weekend and wishing you all of the best for the future, including the husband finding, I find that they seem to hang out in the most unlikely of places!

Take care of you, Marianne

38

Michele's Story:

"I got an Ology!"

*R*everse back to 1987 and the launch of the famous BT Advert starring Maureen Lipman (as Gran Beattie). She is seen on the phone being told by her grandson Anthony that he has just failed all of his exams. Just as she is carefully putting the final decorations on the precisely iced cake. He laments that he has only passed pottery and sociology, and his Gran Beattie says: "He gets an -ology and he says he's failed... you get an -ology you're a scientist...!"

I loved that Advert; it still has me in stitches today. I loved the persistence of his gran but also the idea that my interest in sociology and psychology could have some credibility somewhere! Truth be told at the time I had just successfully passed my Sociology exam but had never really had much thought about Psychology.

I am of African Caribbean heritage and grew up in a vibrant part of Northwest London. I was the youngest of 6 siblings and the first to attend university. So, in many ways that in itself was a great accomplishment, this may be why, once I completed my degree, I actually had no idea what I was going to do. In fact, I recalled achieving my Degree in Social Studies and feeling such a great sense of anti-climax because I just could not think of what I wanted to do. v

Whilst having a conversation with my great Oracle, otherwise known as 'My Mum ', she informed me that I actually came from a strong line of teachers. My oldest cousin, who I held in high esteem, was a teacher, so I thought why not? All fees paid PGCE here I come! My thoughts were further confirmed that Summer when I took a life changing trip to Ghana with a dear friend. It was an incredible four-week holiday, where I was able to go off the beaten tourist track because we were hosted by her extended family. The trip meant so much to me because it was my first trip to Africa, (the land where my ancestors come from). It had always been a great dream of mine to go there voluntarily, because history had told me that my ancestors had been forced to leave enslaved. The journey was amazing and one of my many engraved memories was that of seeing people who looked like me in a range of positions in a place where I did not hear or see skin colour being a barrier to achievement.

I came back with a newfound drive and enthusiasm for my teaching career, I keenly completed all the initial assignments successfully achieving my PGCE. I then began my first work placement teaching History in a secondary school. In my very first term of teaching, I came across a conundrum. A keen and enthusiastic form pupil who, despite all his efforts could not seem to put his many ideas on paper. He was referred to an Educational Psychologist and I was asked to meet with her to discuss his difficulties. There I was listening to this woman explain why he could not read or access learning and I was fascinated when she said he was dyslexic (a term I had not yet heard of), and she went on to explain what it meant and how she would offer advice to the school for us to optimally to support him.

And there it was - Eureka!!!! This was it, she was an Educational Psychologist, and that was exactly what I wanted to do! I recalled leaving school and going straight to the Library to investigate how I would go about becoming an educational psychologist! I was a woman possessed!

- I attended every single university introductory session

- Set up camp at the Institute of Education to read as many journals as I could

- I promptly realised that I needed a minimum of two years teaching experience which was fine, I was almost halfway there!! but it would also be better if I specialised in SEN

- I applied for a job as a specialist SEN Teacher and got my first application!!!!

But it was not plain sailing at all I did not have a full psychology degree so attended part time University to complete an MA in Education and Psychology and additional course in order to achieve a Psychology degree equivalent. Once I had achieved that, I had to apply for the MSc In Educational Psychology (every single introductory talk I went to told me how highly sought after the courses were, and there were over 100 applicants for each place!) Well, I said to myself I just need one place and *I will just not be* one of the other 99!!

I was obsessed. I spent every weekend at the Institute of Education reading and scouring current research in educational psychology. I contacted every single Educational Psychology Service in the London area to request shadowing opportunities (of course this was in term time, so I had to make a special request for non-paid days).

I then applied. It was so tough because I had to put all those months of reading and years of experience and summarise it to fit within a word count. I had a trusted group of friends who proofread for me and then it was off!!!! I remember the stomach churning wait from posting off to hearing from the Association of Educational Psychologists like it was yesterday!

But it didn't stop there, I then took all the notes that I had gathered along the way and began to orchestrate possible interview questions. I methodically went through each question practicing again and again. When it got closer to the decision date, I asked a dear friend to support me with interview practice - it felt like I did over 100 run throughs (not really, I am sure it was probably 2!!) but I felt confident and ready and then the day came I received all four interviews!!!!!!!!)

I was elated, so, so happy, it was incredible to have a dream, pursue it and finally it was paying off! Along the journey I met some great friends who had the same dream, and it was such wonderful camaraderie. The interview weeks were a blur I was sooo focused on the end goal, before I even knew what they were I was using affirmations and visualising this end goal - I wanted it so much!!!

And finally, the day came I received four offers!!! And off I went to the Tavistock and Portman Clinic to pursue my dream job; 'I had an -ology!!!!'

And the END!!!

Mmmmmmmh no. Not Really!!!! I got my first post and was gob smacked with the difference in the role to the actual training; much more paperwork, much less creativity - but there were ways around it and as I became more experienced, I found great opportunities and I worked with multi- agency teams. I began to work independently and began to find a variety of ways to pursue Psychology including working as an expert for court. So, it felt like a natural next step to pursue the professional doctorate when the course began in 2006. I wanted to pursue research in areas of interest and knew that my career would continue to evolve, so a doctorate would only enhance my journey. As per my history, it was not a straight road:

- I became fully independent

- Bought a franchise

- Pursued expert witness work

- And finally graduated with a 2-week-old baby

In summary, I would say:

"If you want an 'Ology' then: Pursue, Persist, Persevere, and believe in yourself!!"

Dr Michele McDowell is an Educational Psychologist, and you can contact her via LinkedIn.

Email from: Dr Marianne Trent

To: Dr Michele McDowell

Dear Michele,

Thank you so much for your story and also for your humour and enthusiasm for your role which jumped out at me from your words. I smiled from ear to ear at times as I read your account. I too vaguely recalled that series of adverts advert so I gave it a google and then lost 10 minutes to YouTube, but it made me smile: "Anthony! People will always need plates!"

It sounded like an incredibly powerful experience when you went to Africa for the first time, and I was moved by your choosing and wanting to go back yourself voluntarily.

You are clearly incredibly determined and once you have something in your sights there's no stopping you. It's an admirable quality for sure.

Thank you for helping showcase other brilliant 'ologies' other than the 'clinical one' and for being so super speedy and also amusing in your writing. I'll let my proof-readers know to leave the exclamation marks because I adore the spirit behind them.

Thanks again,

Marianne

Acronym Busting

One thing we do well in psychology is to abbreviate terms and use the acronyms regularly.

Whilst we have used the full terms and added brackets in this book, we thought it might be helpful to have a handy reference guide for them too.

ABA	Applied Behavioural Analysis
ABI	Acquired Brain Injury
ACT	Acceptance & Commitment Therapy
ADHD	Attention-Deficit Hyperactivity Disorder
A Level	Advanced Level (Stage 2)
ANOVA	Analysis of Variance (statistical test, SPSS)
AS Level	Advanced Subsidiary Level (Stage 1)
AP	Assistant Psychologist
BABCP	British Association for Behavioural and Cognitive Psychotherapies
BAME	Black Asian and Minority Ethnic
BLB	Better Lives Booster Programme
BPS	British Psychological Society
BSc (Hons)	Bachelor of Science with Honours
CAMHS	Child and Adolescent Mental Health Services
CBT	Cognitive-Behavioural Therapy

CFT	Compassion-Focused Therapy
CMHT	Community Mental Health Team
CNWL	Central and North West London NHS Trust
CPD	Continuous Professional Development
CV	Curriculum Vitae
CWP	Children's Wellbeing Practitioner
CYP	Children and Young People
DCP	Division of Clinical Psychology
DClin	Doctorate of Clinical Psychology
DClinPsy	Doctorate of Clinical Psychology
DCounsPsy	Doctorate of Counselling Psychology
EMHP	Education Mental Health Practitioner
EP	Educational Psychologist
(D)EdPsych	Doctorate of Educational Psychology
EMDR	Eye Movement Desensitisation & Reprocessing
ESRC	Economic & Social Research Council
GBC	Graduate Basis for Chartership (was GBR, graduate basis for registration).
GP	General Practitioner (Doctor's office)
GCSE	General Certificate of Secondary Education
GTiCP	Group of Trainers in Clinical Psychology
GRACES	Gender, Geography, Race, Religion, Age, Ability, Appearance, Class, Culture, Ethnicity,

	Education, Employment, Sexuality, Sexual Orientation & Spirituality.
HCA	Healthcare Assistant
HCPs	Healthcare Professionals
HCPC	Health & Care Professions Council
HEE	Health Education England
IAPT	Improving Access to Psychological Therapies
IBM	International Business Machines Cooperation
LD	Learning Disabilities
MDT	Multi-disciplinary Team(s)
MA	Master of Arts
MRes	Master of Research
MSc	Master of Science
NHS	National Health Service
NICE	National Institute for Health & Care Excellence
NIHR	National Institute for Health Research
OSCEs	Observed Structured Clinical Examinations
PGCE	Postgraduate Certificate of Education
PhD	Doctor of Philosophy
PR	Public Relations
PsychD	Psychology Doctorate
PTSD	Post-Traumatic Stress Disorder

PWP   Psychological Wellbeing Practitioner

PQG   Pre-Qualification Group

QCoP   BPS Qualification in Counselling Psychology

RA   Research Assistant

SALT   Speech and Language Therapy

SENCo   Special Educational Needs Coordinator

SOTP   Sex Offender Treatment Programme

SPSS   Statistical Package for the Social Sciences

Recommended Resources

Many contributors have recommended resources within their stories. We have tried to collate them so you can check them out if you would like to.

Books

- Daw, Chris (2020). Justice on Trial: Radical Solutions for a System at Breaking Point. *Bloomsbury.*
- Duffield-Thomas, Denise (2011). Lucky Bitch. *Hay House UK Ltd.*
- Duffield-Thomas, Denise (2013). Get Rich, Lucky Bitch. *Hay House UK Ltd.*
- Duffield-Thomas, Denise (2019). 'Chillpreneur'. *Hay House UK Ltd.*
- Gilbert, Paul (2009). The Compassionate Mind. *Robinson.*
- Harris, Russ (2019). ACT made simple: An easy-to-read primer on acceptance and commitment therapy. *New Harbinger Publications.*
- Pallant, Julie (2001). SPSS Survival Manual. A Step-by-Step Guide to Data Analysis Using IBM SPSS (7th edition). *Routledge, London: Taylor & Francis Group.*
- The British Psychological Society (2021). The Alternative Handbook 2021: Postgraduate Training Courses in Clinical Psychology (2nd Edition). *The British Psychological Society, Leicester: BPS Shop.*
- Trent, Marianne (2020). The Grief Collective: Stories of Life, Loss & Learning to Heal. *KDP.*

Podcast series and Youtube channels

- Berry-Khan, Shabnam (2020). 'Case Management: A creative and flexible way to work for psychologists' with Dr Shabnam Berry-Khan, Spotify.
- Duffield-Thomas, Denise (2021). 'Chill & Prosper' with Denise Duffield-Thomas, Spotify.
- McDermott, Noel (2019). The Well-Being Show, YouTube.

- Telford, Linnie (2020). 'We need to Talk: Candid Conversations on Mental Health' with Dr Linnie Telford, Spotify.

Acknowledgements

First and foremost, I would like to thank all of the contributors within this book who believed in this project and so freely gave their time. What sings out to me from the pages is the memory, the fire and striving for Clinical Training and of people being passionate about wanting to support the next generation of Clinical Psychologists. We recall well that a helping hand with relevant advice is oh so welcomed!

Thanks also to Dr Tim Mahy, a health psychologist in my network who, in 2020, challenged me to write a book in a month. Without him, *The Grief Collective* would not have been born when it was, and this book therefore would have been unlikely to ever come to fruition.

I'd like to thank everyone along my professional path who has believed in me and championed my originality and spark. From Mrs Radcliffe my English teacher, Mrs Handyside my GCSE drama teacher and 6th form tutor and Mr Miller for letting us hang out in your office and use your phone more than was wise. I have also been incredibly fortunate to be surrounded and encouraged by so many wonderful supervisors and managers whom I will name check from their first names in case they don't want to be shouted about publicly. Patricia, thanks for showing me how to be a wonderfully thoughtful human and helping me to slow down and reflect, and also plan and manage risk. Sammy, thanks for taking a chance on me and giving me *the phone call*, which set all of this in motion and also for rocking those ugg boots with such panache! Emma for inducting me so wonderfully into the role of a trainee and treating me with such compassion, empowerment and friendship too, which lasted throughout my training and beyond. Joy and Kate, for being the

313

most perfectly dynamic duo and for all the cackling we did in your offices but also the wonderful ways you helped shape my thinking and develop my approach. Tom, who was with me throughout one of the grimmest moments of my life, my thesis viva. Katy, for showing me that it's entirely possible to swear loads and yet still be wicked at your job. I remember when I first started in your team you enabled me by *not* treating me with newly qualified 'kid gloves' that actually I thought I wanted. Instead you said that I was a band 7 now and I could absolutely do it. Lisa, oh! I recall our supervision so fondly; it was more important than you know and took me through such important milestones in my personal and professional life. Lastly, Claire, for liking what you saw at interview and helping me to grow into my 8a role and beyond. I would not be the psychologist I am without your nurture, guidance and humour.

I have also been so incredibly fortunate to be surrounded by such inspiring clinicians who have become wonderfully important friends, 'Mrs Nicholls', Dr Murphy, Kara and Flavelle-y, my life would not be the same without you in it. You have taught me so much about being human, not needing to be perfect, and also having lots of fun whilst being great at your jobs! Honestly, I could list so many people who have been instrumental in making me the psychologist you see before me. My Mum was of course also super keen to see me as 'Dr Durran' which indeed I did become for a year until I then got married! My brother Oli too, who most certainly won't read this book but would give me a 'well done Bunions' all the same.

More recently I have also had some pretty fantastic cheerleaders in my world whose enthusiasm has been just wonderful. My accountant Amanda (do check out Axe Valley Accountancy), is just wonderful. I'm so pleased we crossed paths during Phil's challenge and then added each other on LinkedIn. Since getting you on board as my accountant my business and my confidence has gone from strength to strength. Always on hand, and so kind: you've quickly become a friend.

My journey has also been supported and encouraged by my mentors Phil Harrison and Helen Pritchard. They told me I could. I believed I could. So I did. Thanks.

Michelle and Christian Ewen, my media cheerleaders, thank you. You are beyond lovely and support and celebrate everything I do. It means more than you can know and I'm so lucky to be in your world. Thanks for your advice on the book blurb, you were totally right!

Thanks once again to my husband, Damien Trent and my children for giving me the freedom and the necessary games of Ludo and Uno to get through this project. When I was planning it out, due to the anticipated publication date of 01/09/2021 I didn't really consider that it would mean doing the bulk of the editing within the summer holidays. So, I should probably thank YouTube, Minecraft and Roblox for helping me out a fair bit so I could crack on when I needed to. My mother-in-law was also superb at swooping round to take the kids for treasure hunts and walks too. Boys, if you ever choose to read this book, you'll see why I was such a stickler for you being in your beds by 7pm each night! To my youngest, my fellow early morning riser, who, when I told him this project was almost finished said "Oh, but I like you being on the sofa under the blanket with me in the mornings!" To my eldest who said: "Oh good, now we can play Harry Potter Trivial Pursuit again!" Thanks also to my husband for helping me out with the book cover again too. It's another beauty and I'd be lost without you, your technical skills and your newly diagnosed peculiar shoulder blades. If anyone wants to check out more of his work, or book him for a project please do at: https://damientrent.wixsite.com/photography

Thanks to Hannah, my wonderful virtual assistant who has now been with me for over a year, we are indeed the dream team, and you make every aspect of my professional and personal life better. How you manage to do everything you do for me whilst also Mummying 4 kids I have no clue! You're an inspiration. You are so brilliant at what you do and also have the biggest heart and a wicked sense of humour. I'm sorry we didn't get to do 'Index Bingo' this time as I know you loved it last time! Also, sorry that you developed COVID-19 as a family in the very late stages of this project. Thanks also to Chrissie who is newly onboard as of this project as my editorial assistant! I just love how thorough and able you are and also how bizarrely excited you are to do stuff, which is wonderful, especially for me who is only recently putting down the belief that I must 'do it all!'

I'd also like to thank *you* dear reader for sticking with us right to the final pages. Reading the acknowledgements, that's dedication that is! Wishing you all the best in your journeys. I do hope that you have found this a helpful resource. If you have, please do tell others about us, and do consider leaving us a review on Amazon and Good Reads. and do take photos of you holding or reading your copy of the book and tag me in! I would also love to know whether the advice and guidance in this book is *actually helpful* for you in shaping your future direction so do please keep me posted by connecting with me on socials.

The End

Website: www.goodthinkingpsychology.co.uk
Instagram: @GoodThinkingPsychological
Facebook: Good Thinking Psychological Services
Facebook: The Grief Collective Book
YouTube: Good Thinking Psychological Services
LinkedIn: Dr Marianne Trent
TikTok: Dr Marianne Trent
Twitter: GoodThinkingPS1

Index

Also by the same author:

The Grief Collective: Stories of Life, Loss & Learning to Heal

I hope you enjoy this snippet of The Grief Collective. It will give you a good idea of what the book is like and of how helpful it will be for you or someone you care about. It's also a fascinating insight into real human stories and an excellent way of developing empathy for grief if you have not yet experienced its impact within your life.

Whatever the reason for you seeking The Grief Collective, we are confident that the answer is waiting for you within its pages.

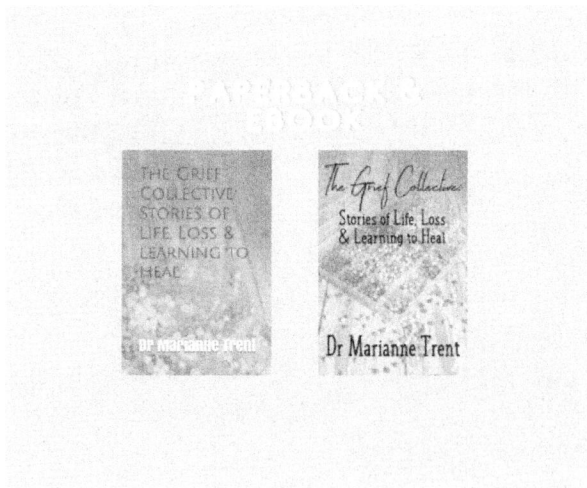

About The Book

In August 2020, Tim, a fellow Psychologist posted in one of my favourite Facebook groups to ask if anyone fancied taking part in a book writing challenge. More specifically, 'Does anyone fancy writing and publishing an entire book in a month?' Now, for anyone who knows me, you'll know that I love a challenge, and for a number of reasons this was one I just couldn't resist!

I've known my dear friend Kara, who'll you'll read about later, since 2007. It's fair to say that these days our lives are pretty different to the seemingly carefree and hedonistic lives we were leading when we met as Assistant Psychologists at St Andrew's Healthcare. Back then, in between the dancing and the curry clubs and the superb psychology work, we would use work emails to discuss the intricacies of our lives. Even then, she would say to me: 'Marianne, you have to write a book one day!' Whilst this wasn't the first time I had thought about writing, I loved knowing that I'd always got this little cheerleader in my corner who supported my creativity and spurred it on. Every now and then she would say: "when are you writing that book?!" It was in fact her who alerted me to the book writing challenge and as soon she'd tagged me, I knew that I was jumping aboard! With hindsight, maybe all those years ago she knew she wouldn't be able to resist a book writing challenge herself one day too and knew that my love of words and grammar would come in handy for my proof reading of her own beautiful book!

I knew immediately which book it was I would 'write' in a month. This very book you hold in your hands was an idea I'd had soon after my dad died. Initially, I wanted to call it 'The Dead Dad Club'. I know the title is potentially quite shocking, but there is a reason. When my dad was palliatively ill, and in the time after he passed, I used to speak to a number of people

323

about how I was feeling. I affectionately called these people my 'Dead Dad Club!' It felt like a club because I tended to get much better containment and support and discussion from these people who were already 'in the club' and understood grief. However, I knew that the book would hopefully go on to feature a wide variety of different loss stories from parents, children, siblings, colleagues, friends, even much-loved pets. I knew it was never going to be a book 'just' about 'Dead Dads,' although of course there are a fair sprinkling of those within these pages too. In terms of Acceptance and Commitment Therapy (often known as ACT), it can be useful to be frank about topics because there's less ambiguity and less room to hide. Loss doesn't get any easier by packaging it in fancy words. However, I know that we're all at a different stage on our 'grief club' journeys and some prefer 'passed' to died.' A friend and contributor, Kara actually, although I promise I do speak to other people too! Anyway, she suggested she wouldn't want to read a book called 'The Dead Dad Club' because her Dad is alive and well and she wouldn't want to tempt fate. I can appreciate that. A fellow story writer said that if they were struggling with the loss of a Mum, they would never think to pick up a book called 'The Dead Dad Club!' Another excellent point! Another contributor also said that whilst she was okay with it and appreciated its frankness, that it might potentially upset other loved ones who were now having to fathom a way through their lives without their much-loved people who are depicted within these very pages. So it was that 'The Grief Collective: Stories of Life, Loss and Learning to Heal', was born. It does what it says on the tin. It still suggests the 'club' element but also encompasses different types of grief; not all of the grief you read about within these pages will feature death.

Whilst my ideas for the book were already formed, it is only this challenge which gave me the impetus to actually 'put pen to paper.' Well, that bit about a pen is of course a creative lie –

the whole thing has been edited, written and collated on my laptop. My handwriting is dreadful and if I'd had to personally scribe it with my trusty ballpoint I'd have needed about 3 years even just to decode what I'd said on the first page let alone get it published in a month! An Assistant Psychologist friend once proudly presented me with a handwriting pen. I was excited for a moment, but nope, it didn't help! I'm thankful for computers which make book creation and calls to action a much simpler process.

So it was, that in September 2020 I started asking for grief case studies on my Good Thinking Psychological Services social media channels. I created a 'grief brief' which explained the project and gave details about what I was hoping might be achieved with the book. However, the description was deliberately non-specific. The emphasis was very much on how important it was to hear each individual's own unique experience of grief. When someone expressed an interest in contributing to the project, I sent them 'the grief brief' and asked them to put something together if they would like to. The only caveat being that it had to be ready before the end of the month!

The case studies, or 'stories' as they're referred to in this book, started to come in. When I began to read them, I was so humbled and honoured that people had put them together because I asked them to and that they were so willing to share them with me, to share them with you! It's honestly one of my greatest privileges in life so far. I also think that it demonstrates my point that once you're in 'the club' that you just know how to talk to others about grief and that it's in fact okay to talk about and important that we do. I began to get even more excited about what a potentially useful resource it was for people on their own unique grief journeys.

Each story is wonderful and they're all their own. I edited them and changed some of the order and the flow and tidied up the odd typo here or there and asked for clarification in some areas. But I hope you will find that you can hear each person's individual voice and writing style. By the way, for anyone who doesn't know, the word 'cwtch' is Welsh for cuddle or hug! You would have heard Bristolian in one story but I'm sorry to say that I did change all of the 'cant' to 'can't' in that story so now it may just be me who reads that particular one in Bristolian! With that in mind, some of the stories I can read in the accents of those people who have written them because I know them personally. Others, I don't know at all and yet all of these people have been so kind and generous in sharing their stories with us. See what other voices and accents you can 'hear' too!

 The stories vary in length and style. I purposefully haven't grouped them in terms of loss or length. I think there is so much to learn and to gain by reading about another's life without necessarily knowing in advance which 'genre' it falls into. That said, if you did want to read about particular types of losses then there's an index at the back of this book which will give you a helping hand on which page to start.

In terms of our free chapter...the story on the next few pages is the first story in the book and is wonderful. We at 'The Collective' hope that you enjoy it.

Also by the same author:

The Grief Collective Book Review

You have created
something special!
Well done!

Grief Collective Reader Dr Marianne Trent

The Grief Collective Book Review

I'm really enjoying this book. I find I'm really
connecting to a lot of the ideas within the
stories. I'm also really enjoying the process of
reading it and just taking myself off to immerse
myself in it. So thank you!

Grief Collective Reader Dr Marianne Trent

The Grief Collective Book Review

I found this book very moving. I had suffered
with my mental health for many years. After
reading other people's grief stories it gave me a
great feel of calmness. I also bought a copy for a
friend who is struggling with the loss of her
family member as I feel it will also help her get
through. Would highly recommend this book.

Grief Collective Reader Dr Marianne Trent

The Grief Collective Book Review

I really recommend this book to anyone who has
ever lost anyone they've ever loved.
It sounds like it might be depressing but I honestly
found it uplifting to hear people's stories of love and
of their strength.
It gave me alternative insights into my own
experiences of loss and it felt like good therapy.

Grief Collective Reader Dr Marianne Trent

1

Holly's Story

It is twenty years since I 'lost' my Mum. All these years later I find myself working as a clinical psychologist in specialist palliative care. You'd think I'd have steered clear of this area as it was all so painful and intense. But, if anything, death is our connecting, universal, human experience. It is unquestionably profound. In Buddhism there is a phrase along the lines of: 'it is only at the moment that we understand the certainty of our own death that we truly begin to live. Perhaps the ability to hold our own personal fragility close is what gives life greater meaning? I certainly see the emotional impact of the work on myself and my colleagues, but I also see the vicarious resilience. When I've asked what motivates staff to do this work, I've heard the expression 'them today, us tomorrow.' I never lose sight of that. Keeping this in mind is levelling. It keeps things real and gives perspective to the day to day. It's deeply compassionate and really very beautiful.

What's interesting though is that I'm frequently mindful of the language used in relation to grief, death and dying in my work. It's striking to me that I often avoid using the word 'lost' (after all, our loved ones aren't 'lost'; we know exactly where they are) yet it's the first word that came as I began to write this. Because

328

really and truly; my Mum is lost to me. And I was lost without her. I didn't know my way. She was my navigational point. I am still lost at times. One of the things said frequently in palliative care is that there's 'one chance to get it right'. And whilst there were a lot of things that weren't right about my own Mum's death, the thing that stands out (the humdinger of the whole experience for me) was the nurse who sang to her as she died. That is something unforgettable.

I had taken some convincing to go home to shower after days of sitting next to my Mum's bed, helping with self-care, massaging her feet, singing to her. I didn't want to leave. But the nurse assured me that she would sing to my Mum in my absence (Mum always sang to us when we were ill, anxious, upset. I can still hear her beautiful, deep, rhythmic voice in my mind). It seemed the most natural thing in the world to sit and sing (and for the record; I am no singer). But it brought a certain energy to the room. It was comforting. This small act of deep compassion by a nurse (who for the record also couldn't sing) is something that I will never forget and will always be grateful for. And how do I know she didn't just tell me that she sang to my Mum? Because the first thing she said when I returned was "she didn't like the Beatles did she? So, I switched to Elvis and she settled again." I cannot tell you how many times the memory of this has given me comfort.

My Mum died of a subarachnoid haemorrhage. She was doing some Christmas food shopping for a friend. She hadn't felt well but the person that she was (evacuated in the war as a child and so part of that unstoppable generation of 'get on with it'), meant that she wouldn't let a grim headache, of 2 days duration, stop her from helping out a friend. I thought about that for a very, very long time. The fact that she sat in the middle of the shopping centre, clutching her friend's shopping, bleeding from the brain, totally alone. Our brains are brilliant at torturing us

329

like this. I had intrusive images and auditory intrusions of the ambulance siren that took her to hospital for the longest time; for a good six months hearing a siren would make my stomach turn. And, of course, these were completely fictitious; I had generated them to build the story and connect with what that life shattering moment had been like for her. This precious, gentle woman, who meant the world to me, was now facing the end of her life. She collapsed two days before Christmas and died on New Year's Eve. The last words she said to me as we sat listening to the chimes of Christmas Day on the radio from the nurse's station, were "Is it Christmas? Oh, Merry Christmas darling". She slipped into a coma a few hours later and never regained consciousness. There was nothing remotely merry about that Christmas.

I tell myself how blessed I was to have had those last words. To have had moments when she was first in hospital when we could talk, and I could tell her how much I loved her. She re-told my sister and I stories from her childhood. In the past we'd have rolled our eyes and said "yes, you've told us this story before!" But knowing those moments would never happen again made every fibre of my being come into sharp focus. I remembered her telling me that she had a horrible moment after her own Mum died when she couldn't visualise her hands. She went hunting through boxes of photographs to try to bring back the memory of them. I remembered this and spent so much time looking at my Mum and her hands, committing them to memory. I needn't have bothered. I have her hands. My sister has her hands. I look down at my hands and I see that she is part of me.

I spend a lot of time in my job talking about death and dying and am often struck by how many families just don't talk about it. It's taboo. It's 'dark.'. It's 'depressing'. But that wasn't the way things were in our family. My Dad died when I was two years old. My Mum talked of him often and in doing so kept him 'alive' for me; I had a Dad, he loved me dearly, but he wasn't able to be there. This is 'continuing bonds' in action. So, we spoke about his death, my grandparent's death and at times about the future and my Mum's death. She was a very spiritual person and when her brother died (at 33 years old; the same age as my Dad and Grandad strangely) she told us that she "felt him there, giving me comfort". So, the joke would start about "well don't think about coming back and giving me comfort!" We would laugh and I remember saying "you can come and give me comfort in a dream. But not in real life." That was our deal. And for about 6 months after my Mum died, I had the same dream over and over and over. It was me sitting with my head on her knee, sobbing, telling her I couldn't cope without her, telling her I missed her. She would stroke my hair; tell me it would be OK, and I would wake up (usually in tears) but feeling close to her. The dream was in some ways such a perfectly ordinary interaction. But the ordinariness of it made it all the more real. Then one night I had the dream, but the conversation was different. She said to me "I can't keep coming to you like this anymore. I have to go away now. But you don't need me. You can do this on your own." I protested, but she assured me it would be OK. I have never dreamt that dream again since. I find it quite mind-blowing to think either we have an absolute innate ability to access that bond and receive comfort when we need it; or, there is an alternate dimension out there that we know nothing about that perhaps I need to keep an open mind to! Either way, my mind (or my Mum) called it right. It was at that time that things began to feel more bearable. And in some ways, there was a changing from the pain and distress to a desire for things to be more meaningful and different in some way.

I tormented myself about the fact that I turned down an invitation to see my Mum just a few days before she collapsed because I had a pile of Christmas presents to wrap and no other time to do it. *How pathetic does that sound now?* I say to people that I work with all the time; we make so many decisions every day with the information we have to hand. I didn't know my Mum was about to die. I didn't know she was unwell. So, in my head I can tell myself I made a choice with the frivolity of assuming I would see her over Christmas, and we would be spending time together then. But that thought process doesn't cut it when it comes to the knot in the pit of your stomach and the self-loathing that you picked a pile of rubbish presents over precious time. Again, our brains are masters at making us feel bad. I was working full time, studying a few evenings a week, scuba diving twice a week, trying to get to the gym; I had friends and a fiancé that I also wanted to spend time with. I felt I had no time (or I thought at the time that I had no time. Truth is we can always make time). Of course, hindsight is a beautiful science. Had I known, I would have spent every moment with her. But I didn't know. We never know. That is something that I absolutely take away and remind myself of regularly. I have never since cancelled a person over a task. It's a simple life rule and it helps me. This is the best advice I can offer to people in this situation: we can't undo things; we don't have a time machine. All we can do is to choose to view things differently and choose to commit to a different path in the future. If not, those layers of guilt can be corrosive.

The first Christmas after Mum died, I found the thought of presents so distasteful that they sickened me. I talked about it with my sister who, luckily, was on the same page. We agreed on a book with meaning (a 'chicken soup for the soul' kind of book; or for me, the veggie version). Instead of gifts, we would ask what people wanted in the way of a 'doing' task or activity (this was my sister's idea). So, I could offer to wash her windows or help out with some decorating (or go with her to 'Go Ape' which was what she actually requested). As the years have gone on, the joy of Christmas has returned. I've since had a child of my own (which incidentally, no one tells you how painful that experience is without your Mum). It brings back all those loss feelings quite acutely for a time. Who is there to remind you how heavy you were when you were born? The story of your weaning? Crawling? Sleeping? These are all aspects of your life story that have new meaning as you face those things with your own child. I felt simultaneously closer to her and yet further away than ever. Becoming a parent gave me more understanding of her. It was painful.

I think if I had a pound for the times people say that being around children really helps, I'd be a very wealthy person. It's probably why our caveman ancestors lived in kin groups with the whole generation. Being around young people and their joy and enthusiasm is very healing. So, despite the newfound pain of missed connections with my Mum, I had the joy of new life and seeing the world through the eyes of this new little person.

Another important part of keeping the bond alive, for me anyway, is the whole 'what would Mum say?' thing. It's the metaphorical t-shirt that we wear, and this is powerful for me. I know Mum loved Christmas and got so excited about it. So, the traditions that were meaningful to her (like drinking a sherry whilst making the family Christmas cake) became the traditions I carry forward; along with the story. So, every year as I do this I talk about 'Nanny Fox' and we get out the sherry glass and have a toast. We smile, we laugh, we remember.

Loss is brutal. It's a sucker punch to the gut. It gets easier, but it doesn't go away. And sometimes new life experiences make the loss reappear in full glory (the night before my wedding was another corker; a deep wave of sadness hit, and I lay crying cuddled up to my wonderful bridesmaid). But, what does change is the fact that we can carry it much more lightly when we remember, when we smile, when we take parts of that special person forward. I'd like to send a huge, huge hug (from the written word if that's even such a thing) for all of you going through this experience right now. It will get a lighter load to carry. I can promise you that. But whilst it's heavy; share it. Because we in the club understand.

The Grief Collective Book Review

Real people with real stories about their own grief.
Heartfelt stories which captures the raw emotions felt by
real people. True stories of the effects of death, during
&the aftermath.
I found it very helpful as could relate to a few of the
stories.
You won't want to put the book down- plus I'm a little
nosey too!

Grief Collective Reader

Reading More

The Grief Collective and I hope you have enjoyed this free trial chapter.

The whole book contains 54 stories in total and it is a wonderfully helpful and inspiring read. For more information or to buy a copy for you or for someone you care about, search for 'The Grief Collective' on Amazon or head to:

www.goodthinkingpsychology.co.uk/thegriefcollective

If you do go on to buy the book and you enjoy it, we would be ever so grateful if you could stop back at

Amazon and / or Good Reads and leave a review. Reviews help Amazon know that people like products and they are then shown higher up in search results for topics. This helps us to be able to bring *The Grief Collective* to a wider audience to be able to support more people to cope with grief and to support those who are experiencing grief.

Thank you so much for your interest in *The Grief Collective*. We are also on Facebook as The Grief Collective Book and on Instagram as Grief Collective Book. We share useful and inspiring articles and quotes about grief which might well help you or someone you care about so please do stop by and like and follow our pages.

Thank you.

Good Thinking
Psychological Services
HELPING YOU THRIVE, NOT JUST SURVIVE.

The Our Tricky Brain Kit

Using compassion-focused therapy theory to aid understanding and ease distress in a wonderfully engaging, memorable and effective way. Discover this simple solution for helping clients understand why they feel the way they do whilst reducing shame and improving self-compassion.

Who is this for?

This is for any professional who works with people who experience symptoms of trauma and / or depression.
Full training is given in the course and the kit is ideal for use by a variety of professions including:

Psychologists, Counsellors & Therapists, Community Mental Health Staff, Social Workers and Social Care, Staff Educational & Pastoral Professionals, Physical Health & Medical Professionals Justice and Custodial Workers

The 'Our Tricky Brain' Kit is available exclusively from the Good Thinking Psychological Service Website at:
https://www.goodthinkingpsychology.co.uk/tricky-brain

Good Thinking
Psychological Services
HELPING YOU THRIVE, NOT JUST SURVIVE.

The Words to Books Course

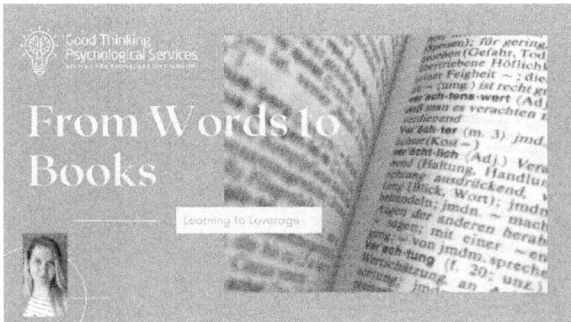

If this book has inspired you to silence the self-critic and give yourself permission to finally write that book you've always dreamed of then let Marianne show you how with the From Words to Books Mini-course!

- Includes step by step guidance to edit your word document to create and functional and aesthetically pleasing 6" x 9" paperback or eBook.
- Includes simple guidance to navigate kindle direct publishing (KDP) with ease.
- Helpful, reassuring and simple presentation style makes the process of becoming a published author less daunting and more enjoyable!

The From Words to Books Mini-course is available now for a really affordable price exclusively from the Good Thinking Psychological Service Website at:

https://www.goodthinkingpsychology.co.uk/words-to-books

Good Thinking
Psychological Services
HELPING YOU THRIVE, NOT JUST SURVIVE.

The 4 minute Clinic
#4minuteclinic

The 4 minute clinics are *'your daily prescription for better mental health',* and cover topics such as: trauma, grief, compassion, anxiety, depression and parenting.

Since March 2021 Dr Marianne Trent has been creating inspiring and helpful daily content 5 days a week. It streams live on her business socials, and you can also catch daily replays or watch the playlist on YouTube too.

It's a great way to see how a qualified clinical psychologist makes mental health an accessible, jargon free daily conversation. Do tune in.

**Good Thinking
Psychological Services**
HELPING YOU THRIVE, NOT JUST SURVIVE.

Passive Income Streams Coaching

Plan and create your passive income stream asset such as an online course, book or product.

- **Get Your Passive Journey Off to A Flying Start with Bespoke 1:1 Support & Guidance**
- **Let Marianne Support and Guide You, 1:1, to Navigate the Often Daunting and Confusing Aspects of Leveraging Passive Income**
- **Convenient Zoom sessions with 6 months to use them.**

For more information head to:
https://gtps.kartra.com/page/passive-coaching or contact Marianne via
www.goodthinkingpsychology.co.uk

- Pg 18-22 – HEE funded roles? Clarify. Does it mean need to do 2 years PWP before being funded on doc?
   Pg 238 – yes   28L - counselling psych self-funded?
- Do need experience in academia
   - Salisbury?
   - write article for BPS?
- Pg 57 - uni of York/Hull
   - undergraduate post. doc?

· Assistant pysch does not mean = onto doc. course – still have to apply to get on doc course & may not get on.

· The Compassionate Mind by Paul Gilbert.

· Pg 95 answer these q's!

· pg 111 'Apostate' research - look into it.

· Opposite ~~Morgrove~~

· Zarse et al., 2009

· Chase BPS for magazine

· EDMR and schema training.

· Wellcome Trust research bursary?

ts of advice pg 137-138

Julie Pallant's SPSS survival guide

NHS funded doc programs pg 164.

100K into research into dementia & therapy.

see who 's closer $ reach out
- Clive B in Poole 206.

Reflect - what are your strengths $
weaknesses? review reg.

do Belbin's self perception test.

to get on doc course need to understand
how NHS works?!

need to work on statistics & formulation

need to set up Linkedin

Maslow's hierachy of needs.

pg 262 post graduate cerif. in conselling
psych? what if it?

ch 34 Tara - counselling

psychological reserve volunteer for British Red
cross. experience idea?

Printed in Great Britain
by Amazon